T0300906

COMMUNICATIONS
Methods and applications for financial managers

James Carberry

Chartered Global Management Accountant®

Powered by

12743-359

Notice to Readers

Communications: Methods and Applications for Financial Managers does not represent an official position of the American Institute of Certified Public Accountants, and it is distributed with the understanding that the author and the publisher are not rendering legal, accounting, or other professional services in this publication. If legal advice or other expert assistance is required, the services of a competent professional should be sought.

© 2013 AICPA. All rights reserved.
American Institute of Certified Public Accountants, Inc.
New York, NY 10036-8775

Distribution of this material via the Internet does not constitute consent to the redistribution of it in any form. No part of this material may be otherwise reproduced, stored in third party platforms and databases, or transmitted in any form or by any printed, electronic, mechanical, digital or other means without the written permission of the owner of the copyright as set forth above. For information about the procedure for requesting permission to reuse this content, please email copyright@CGMA.org.

The information, and any opinions expressed in this material, do not represent official pronouncements of or on behalf of AICPA, CIMA, the CGMA designation or the Association of International Certified Professional Accountants. This material is offered with the understanding that it does not constitute legal, accounting, or other professional services or advice. If legal advice or other expert assistance is required, the services of a competent professional should be sought. The information contained herein is provided to assist the reader in developing a general understanding of the topics discussed, but no attempt has been made to cover the subjects or issues exhaustively. While every attempt to verify the timeliness and accuracy of the information herein as of the date of issuance has been made, no guarantee is or can be given regarding the applicability of the information found within to any given set of facts and circumstances.

1 2 3 4 5 6 7 8 9 0 PIP 1 9 8 7 6 5 4 3

ISBN: 978-1-93735-196-0

Publisher: Linda Prentice Cohen
Acquisitions Editor: Robert Fox
Developmental Editor: Suzanne Morgen
Project Manager: Amy Sykes
Composition Specialist: Belinda Blakley

ACKNOWLEDGMENTS

Many people helped in many ways to make this book possible. To all of you, thank you for your insights, guidance and assistance.

At the AICPA, I would like to thank Robert Fox, acquisitions editor, practice and industry publications, and the book development team who managed the production of this book from concept to editing of the manuscript to publication. Slade Chelbian, CPA, CGMA, MBA, CPE development manager for management accounting and CGMA, was a resource for the section on cross-cultural communication. Paul Parks, CPA, CGMA, senior technical manager, business and industry group, assisted with some of the research.

Jim Morrison, CPA, CGMA, chair of the AICPA's Business and Industry Executive Committee and CFO of Teknor Apex Co., discussed trends in management accounting, the importance of communication skills and other topics in an interview for this book; he also suggested others to interview.

Andrew Harding, FCMA, CGMA, managing director of the Chartered Institute of Management Accountants, discussed the strategic role of CFOs in corporations, why CFOs and management accountants must have strong communication skills, and other subjects in an interview.

I also interviewed CFOs, management accountants, educators, consultants and others who commented on emerging trends in management accounting, the growing career opportunities for management accountants in organisations, how management accountants can develop their communication skills and other topics. I would especially like to acknowledge the following people, whose interviews appear in appendix A of this book:

James J. Benjamin, Deloitte Foundation Leadership Professor and head of the accounting department, Mays Business School, Texas A&M University;

David Duncan, president, Denihan Hospitality Group;

Greg Conderacci, president and founder of Good Ground Consulting;

Thomas D. Foard, CPA, executive vice president and CFO, Publishers Fulfillment Inc.;

Kenneth Kelly, senior vice president & controller of McCormick & Company;

Anoop N. Mehta, CPA, vice president and CFO of Science Systems and Applications Inc.;

Christopher J. Papa, executive vice president and CFO of Post Properties, Inc.;

Chris Rogers, vice president, finance and administration, Infragistics Inc.;

Sarah Vaudrain, business analyst (financial analyst), Teknor Apex;

Donna Viens, assistant professor and chair of the department of accountancy and finance, Johnson & Wales University; and

Amy Weinreich, CPA, vice president, finance and administration, Publishers Circulation Fulfillment Inc.

Tom Hood, CPA, CITP, CEO of the Maryland Association of CPAs and The Business Learning Institute, offered suggestions on the content of the book and recommended people to interview.

Finally, special thanks to Gail Carberry, wife of author James Carberry, for her patience and support during the many hours spent on this project.

CONTENTS

INTRODUCTION

Today, the ability of management accountants to communicate effectively is being tested as never before. From entry level accountants to senior financial executives, management accountants must be able to communicate not only with their peers but also with managers and employees across the corporation, as well as with investors, shareholders, regulators, the media and others about complex audit, tax, business, financial, regulatory, strategic and other issues. Communicating effectively is one of the most important—and challenging—issues that management accountants face.

Study after study has confirmed that business communication skills are essential, regardless of accounting specialty. The Vision Project of the AICPA groups communication and leadership skills together as one of the five core competencies of accountants. The project defines these skills as 'Able to give and exchange information within meaningful context and with appropriate delivery and interpersonal skills. Able to influence, inspire and motivate others to achieve results.'[1] That statement mirrors this book's conviction that communication and leadership skills go hand in hand. Whether you have just entered an accounting programme or are at the pinnacle of your career, improving your communications skills can help you to become a better leader and more valuable employee.

How, then, can management accountants use communication to inform, influence and persuade others? How do they know if they are effective at communicating? This book explores these and other communication issues of vital concern to management accountants. It looks at how management accountants communicate within and outside of their organisations, identifies best practices in the use of communication, and offers guidance about how management accountants can improve their communication skills. In short, this book is intended to help management accountants become better communicators.

The book begins with an examination of the changing role of CFOs over the past two decades. Future CFOs can learn from the challenges facing today's CFOs and prepare themselves to take on more responsibilities. As the first two chapters explain, excellent communications skills are essential for the next generation of management accountants.

The third chapter delves into what good communication skills are and how they apply to a business setting. Listening, speaking and writing skills are the three core communication skills, along with an awareness of nonverbal communication. Some cross-cultural communication considerations are also discussed.

Chapter 4 applies the information about communication presented in the previous chapter to specific business scenarios, such as hosting meetings or writing e-mails. Chapters 5 and 6 focus specifically on writing business reports, while chapters 7 and 8 focus exclusively on presentations. Throughout the text, the importance of good listening, speaking and writing skills is emphasised.

Finally, the last chapter explores a new frontier in business communication: social media. Social media platforms, such as LinkedIn and Facebook, are still fairly new, but their benefits for communicating with clients, customers and investors are enormous. The benefits and risks of social media are discussed, along with some considerations of specific social media platforms.

If you want more information on any specific area, the bibliography compiles the sources cited in footnote references with other relevant articles and books organised by topic. Also, throughout the book, references are made to interviews that can be found compiled in appendix A. These interviews give first-hand accounts of the importance of communication to people at various stages of their accounting careers. From accounting professors to analysts to CFOs and vice presidents, each interviewee offers insights on the role of communication in his or her career. The appendixes also provide other helpful material, such as a resource list and checklists to help you write documents and compose presentations.

Endnotes

1 'CPA Vision Project: The Vision in the CPA
  Vision Process,' AICPA www.aicpa.org/about/
  missionandhistory/CPAvisionproject/Pages/
  CPAVisionProject.aspx

1

BUSINESS COMMUNICATION: ISSUES FOR MANAGEMENT ACCOUNTANTS

The role of accountants within companies has been changing rapidly in recent decades. Once employed to simply report numbers, management accountants are now called upon to interpret those numbers and provide recommendations and guidance to other executives. In this expanded role, successful management accountants need excellent communication skills to be able to serve as business advisers. As future CFOs, current management accountants need to be prepared for the highest level of responsibility. This chapter will discuss the evolving nature of current and future CFO roles and responsibilities as well as barriers to effectively communicating complex data.

THE CHANGING ROLE OF THE CFO

Jim Morrison, now the CFO of Teknor Apex Co., a diversified material science company headquartered in Pawtucket, Rhode Island, remembers a time earlier in his career when he worked in the accounting department of Monsanto. A financial analyst, he was in a different location than the business manager he was supporting. It was not an efficient work arrangement, and after he was promoted to manager of financial analysis, he asked for and received approval to move from accounting to business operations. (See interview 1 in appendix A for Morrison's thoughts on how to communicate effectively.)

Morrison's original inefficient work arrangement was not an uncommon one. At many companies, management accountants were separate from line managers, and corporate accounting was largely a history lesson. Accountants provided a detailed look at an organisation's past performance based on revenues, profits or losses, operating expenses, capital expenditures and many other metrics. Those numbers were useful mainly in telling management where a company had been but not where it was going. This was somewhat analogous to the management of a baseball team looking at a player's statistics (his performance history) and trying to decide whether he would continue to perform at the same level. Past performance was no guarantee of future results.

In any case, corporate managers often had difficulty trying to understand the information accountants provided. Accountants seemed to speak a different language, one understood by their peers but not necessarily by others. Nor were accountants always adept at providing clear explanations. As a result, management accountants were largely confined to the periphery of companies, providing support but not deeply engaged in the management of the enterprise.

Over the past decade, the role of the CFO and other finance professionals has begun to transform. An article in the *Harvard Business Review* notes how much the CFO's function has changed: 'Prior to the early 2000s, the typical CFO was a bean counter, responsible mainly for reporting the numbers, measuring performance with integrity and accuracy, and managing the company's checks-and-balances processes.'[1] The purview of CFOs was narrow and largely confined to their own departments.

No more.

Now, the top finance job has a wide scope and demands skills beyond the fundamental skills in finance, investment and capital management. The new job of CFO demands a far broader background, including experience with capital markets, mergers and information technologies, as well as operations and other corporate functional areas. CFOs and other senior finance executives are now strategic business partners, providing critical analysis and strategic insights that inform executive decision making. The role of CFO in the organisation has become more prominent and their influence and authority far greater than in the past. 'Few jobs today can rival the CFO's role in terms of breadth, influence and profile,' Ernst & Young said in a report.[2] The report goes on to argue that the CFO position has become the most influential role in the organisation, especially in times of economic uncertainty, and as financial leadership is needed to cope with issues like cash flow and unpredictable demand.

Because the CFO as adviser is a relatively new role, some management accountants may not be prepared for the increased breadth of experience required. 'Finance professionals have moved beyond simply reporting and record keeping to serving as strategic advisors to management,' said Kenneth Kelly, senior vice president and controller at McCormick & Company, a global company that markets and distributes spices, seasoning mixes, condiments and other flavourful products. 'Today the key question for finance professionals is how to work with management to grow the business.' (See interview 2 in appendix A, where Kelly discusses how McCormick helps managers and employees develop communication and other skills.) Although CFOs may have more influence, their rapidly changing jobs may require new skills for which they were not prepared. According to a CGMA report, 'For many, finance leadership roles, and the CFO role in particular, are more diverse and complex than ever before.'[3] Based on interviews and roundtables with senior professionals globally, the report found that two-thirds of CFOs thought the CFO title did not adequately describe the scope and complexity of their responsibilities.

With the evolution of roles and responsibilities, new skill sets for CFOs are essential to achieve and maintain success at the highest levels. In particular, strong communication skills are now a necessary part of the CFO role. In a report based on interviews with international CFOs, Ernst and Young said one of its key findings was that CFOs must be highly skilled communicators. 'Communications skills are an imperative, as CFOs must convey complex financial results and business performance to external stakeholders while championing specific initiatives internally,' the report said.[4]

CFO RESPONSIBILITIES

To provide a framework for discussing how a robust set of communication skills fits in with a changing paradigm for CFOs, it is important to outline the primary duties CFOs share. Although the duties and responsibilities of CFOs vary depending on the company and other variables, CFOs generally focus on areas that require interactions with many facets of the company, including

- ensuring business decisions are grounded in solid financial criteria.
- providing insight and analysis to support the CEO and other senior managers.
- leading key initiatives in finance that support overall strategic goals.
- funding, enabling and executing the strategy set by the CEO.
- developing and defining the overall strategy for the organisation.
- representing the organisation's progress on external goals to strategic stakeholders.[5]

Being able to communicate information and strategy to internal and external stakeholders is a vital skill that underpins many of these responsibilities. The sections that follow represent examples of major roles in which CFOs are expected to provide leadership. These roles exist for each of the responsibilities previously listed (and extend to additional CFO responsibilities) but will certainly be applied differently.

Finding Insights in Data

Turning the information and data generated by organisations into meaningful insights that the business can use to plan and make decisions can be particularly challenging. A CGMA report based on interviews with senior professionals worldwide confirms that 'participants are quite clear that organisations need better information and analysis, but the crucial skills required are the insight and capability to act on it.'[6] That is where CFOs come in. CFOs—with the support of management accountants and others in the organisation—can provide the insights to help companies make informed decisions about managing data.

Budgeting

The restructuring of the budget process is an example of CFOs leading key initiatives. Some companies have abandoned the traditional budget as an archaic tool that does not meet the needs of modern corporations in today's fast-changing business environment. Preparing an annual budget can be a time-consuming and expensive process, and in some cases, by the time management finally approves it, it is out of date. Dissatisfaction with traditional budgeting is part of a larger concern with traditional planning processes. In a survey of 273 companies worldwide, Accenture found that only 11% of companies surveyed are fully satisfied with their planning capabilities.[7]

As alternatives to traditional budgeting, some companies are adopting rolling forecasts, flexible budgets and event-driven planning. Thus, a company might use a six-month or eight-month rolling forecast and revise it based on events such as stronger-than-anticipated demand for its products or services or higher-than-expected materials costs. Other companies are retaining the traditional budget but using it in combination with flexible rolling forecasts. Whatever approach they take to budgeting, companies are looking to their CFOs to provide leadership in the budgeting process.

Measuring Value

The value that people bring to companies is of paramount concern to corporate leaders, according to a CGMA report. 'CEOs consider that the first challenge is to understand **value**—where it comes from and how much there is of it. They see people's ideas, skills, knowledge and relationships representing the unique value of their companies.'[8]

The question is—how can value be measured? The CGMA report notes that although it is difficult to measure and manage the value of human resources, companies who want to achieve long-term success need to overcome the challenge. To do so, CEOs need people equipped for the task who can develop tools and lead initiatives to measure and manage value. Often, CFOs are the ones called upon to tackle assignments such as measuring value.

Managing Risk

Even as the role and responsibilities of the CFO expand, the global recession and the financial crises of recent years have increased the importance of the CFO's traditional role of financial leader. Increasingly, company boards and management are looking to their CFOs for risk management leadership not only within finance but also across the corporation. CFOs are working more closely with audit committees, as well as with directors of tax, information technology and others in the organisation to better identify, manage and mitigate risks.

With such broad responsibilities and accountability to different constituencies, CFOs find themselves in a balancing act. 'The best CFOs balance accountability to the board and shareholders for maintaining the integrity of the financials and appropriate risk management with loyalty to the CEO,' *Bloomberg BusinessWeek* commented.[9]

SPECIFIC COMMUNICATION CHALLENGES CFOS FACE

The previous section explained the variety of roles and responsibilities CFOs are expected to perform. As the scope of responsibilities for CFOs increases, they face the challenge of communicating complex issues to internal and external stakeholders. As appetite for all facets of business data increases, accountants must be prepared not only to provide appropriate data, but also to identify how to effectively communicate information to a diverse set of stakeholders. The following two sections discuss specific communication challenges that management accountants face: explaining complex issues and communicating with investors.

Explaining Complex Issues

Finding insights in data, budgeting, measuring value and managing risk all require the ability to provide simple, but not simplistic, explanations of complex issues. Communicating these complex issues to a variety of audiences is one of the biggest challenges that financial professionals face. Audiences including investors, financial analysts, customers, partners and employees rely on the information communicated by financial professionals to make important decisions. With information available 24 hours a day, 7 days a week in myriad formats, stakeholders demand accuracy and transparency. More than ever before, CFOs are expected to be world-class communicators.

Box 1-1 provides an overview of the goals and responsibilities of company boards and management. It shows how management accountants generally, and certified global management accountants (CGMAs) specifically, can help boards and management achieve their goals.

The left column lists the aims, roles, skills, behaviours and influences of company boards and management. For example, a role might be to develop short- and long-term strategies for achieving the aims of their companies. Skills include the ability to assess and mitigate risk or allocate capital and resources. A behaviour is articulating a clear vision for the company. It could also be considered a communication skill.

The right column shows how management accountants, specifically CGMAs, assist boards and management. The aim of boards and management is the company's long-term success. Management accountants link this aim with the business. The link enables the right decisions to be made, appropriately funded and correctly implemented throughout the organisation.

Box 1-1: Board/management requirements and CGMA capabilities

	What the board or management needs	How a CGMA delivers
Aims	Responsible for leading long-term, sustainable success of the company or organisation	Links the board objectives and the business, enabling the right decisions to be made, be appropriately funded and correctly implemented throughout the organisation—short- and long-term
Roles	**Determine/approve/oversee** • Short- and long-term strategy • Business model • Risk appetite	• Manage performance, support and drive decision making • Be the 'financially grounded business navigator' • Understand both the business and its finances • Creating, reporting and preserving value
Skills	**Quality decision making:** • Strategic development • Risk mitigation and assessment **Oversight of** • Capital and source allocation • Strategy implementation • Enterprise risk management • Business control • Talent identification, assessment and development **Setting incentives:** • Executive pay • Bonuses • Results related pay	**Management Accounting** • Map journey—strategy to planning to execution • Align key performance indicators to outcomes • Business support, eg, scenario planning, pricing • Quality information, analysis and evaluation—decisions and sources allocation • Cost leadership and improved productivity • Project and investment appraisal • Tax risk management and planning • Treasury and cash management • Enterprise risk management • Business control • Oversight—control and performance management • Effective management information (financial and non-financial) • External reporting
		Managerial • Communication—translate complexity • Strategic change, project, relationship and operational management

Continued on p. 10

Continued from p. 9

	What the board or management needs	How a CGMA delivers
		Data and Process • Transparency • Quality internal/external data (knowledge/data-warehouse) • Accounting operations
Behaviours	• Sets appropriate tone • Articulates clear vision • Inspires and empowers • Looks forward and outward	• Acts with integrity • Offers constructive challenges and objective view • Is the ethical conscience of the organisation
Influence	• Customers • The business • Business partners • Community and environmental stakeholders • Regulators • Shareholders	• The board • Senior management • Colleagues in all departments • Peers in finance function • Business partners

Source: 'How Management Accounting Drives Sustainable Success,' Chartered Institute of Management Accountants. www.cimaglobal.com/Global/CGMA/Role_Of_Management_Accounting.pdf

Among their many roles, management accountants help navigate the business, as well as support and drive decision making. In addition to their many management accounting skills, they provide quality information upon which business decisions are based; provide oversight, including control and performance management; and align key performance indicators and outcomes. In other words, they help ensure the business is performing as expected. As noted in the previous managerial section, management accountants play a key role as communicators, helping to translate complexity into information that senior executives can understand and act on.

Communicating With Investors

CFOs are increasing their efforts to communicate more frequently with investors about their companies' investment activities, especially regarding emerging trends like rapid-growth markets. Investors say that they would like to see more narrative reporting that explains how the business intends to create value and provide greater clarity on key risks. Yet, more than two-thirds of CFOs surveyed in an Ernst & Young report said they find it difficult to convey an over-arching narrative when balancing investments across these markets.[10]

Other challenges for CFOs in communicating with investors and other stakeholders were examined in the Ernst & Young report. Based on interviews with CFOs, the report noted that more business leaders are looking to the world's rapid-growth markets to sustain growth. Traditional reporting frameworks and communication strategies need to be re-evaluated when managing this type of investment. CFOs need to be able to communicate their investment strategies to investors despite inadequate data and poor transparency. They may also need to explain their rationale to investors who question their interpretation of the market.

CORE SKILLS FOR MANAGEMENT ACCOUNTANTS

So far, this chapter has focused on the responsibilities and challenges facing management accountants who already occupy leadership positions. However, accountants who aspire to climb higher on the career ladder can use this information to better prepare themselves to become effective CFOs. The challenge for aspiring leaders currently working at the staff level or in middle management is to find opportunities in their organisations to develop the broad skills required of CFOs. Among these skills are

- leadership skills, beginning with helping the CEO unite people behind a shared vision for the organisation and inspiring them to achieve that vision.
- facilitation skills, or taking the initiative to help line managers and others in the organisation to achieve objectives or find solutions.
- breadth of finance experience in all facets of the function, including financial reporting and tax.
- broad commercial skills developed from experience in a company's operating businesses.
- building relationships with senior management and the board, as well as outside stakeholders, including shareholders, lenders, rating agencies and the media.
- international experience, including working in emerging or developing markets.[11,12]

Management accountants who start their careers with strong communication skills will be better prepared to face the challenges they will encounter wherever their career path leads. Listening, speaking and writing skills can benefit management accountants working at every level in today's global marketplace. A CFO can lead only by helping to articulate the company's vision. A management accountant can learn the operating business only by listening to and talking with business managers. An American management accountant working in Asia for a global company must learn to communicate with people of different cultures, social norms and worldviews.

The rest of this section focuses on the six core skills that CFOs should possess and that the next generation of CFOs can begin to hone now: communication, building relationships, participation in training programmes, taking the initiative to learn, meeting expectations and managing change.

Communication

The core skill underlying all the CFO skills outlined in the preceding list is the ability to communicate effectively. Leaders must have strong communication skills. A management accountant must be able to communicate with people across the organisation in order to acquire broad commercial skills. Communication skills allow management accountants to cultivate and maintain relationships with senior management, clients and stakeholders. Those relationships are the focus of the next skill.

Building Relationships

The skills, expertise and experience required of CFOs are so broad that it would be particularly difficult for a CFO to master everything. CFOs must be adept at building relationships with those who can complement their skills, for example, by naming individuals or forming teams to advise them on areas such as information technology or mergers and acquisitions.

Those who can master the broad and complex skills required of the modern CFO will be in strong demand. In a global survey of executives, the Economist Intelligence Unit asked them which skills are most difficult to find in candidates for senior executive positions. The large percentage—or more than half the executives—said candidates with 'strategic vision' skills would be hardest to find. About a third said 'analytical skills' and 'ability to handle complexity' would be the most difficult to find.[13]

Participation in Training Programmes

More companies are instituting programmes for the training and development of the next generation of CFOs and other leaders, including the development of strong communication skills. In some companies, training is informal or loosely coordinated with other divisions. In others, formal training extends all the way up to the CFO level. These companies are preparing CFOs to become CEOs by rotating them through division operations roles to give them more commercial experience.[14]

At yet other companies, it may be difficult for management accountants to get the necessary training and experience for future leadership roles, among other reasons because companies may not have a plan for rotating them through business lines and operating groups to give them broad exposure to the business. The failure of companies to prepare management accountants to move up in the organisation—the organisations' lack of bench strength—could cause them problems. Despite the current recession, global demand for accountants is strong. Some management accountants could leave organisations that do not provide the necessary training and opportunities. When their CFOs retire or move on to other organisations, these companies may not have qualified internal candidates to replace them, and they may have to recruit outside the organisation, usually at greater cost, and with the risk that the outside hire might not work out.[15]

Taking the Initiative to Learn

Regardless of whether management accountants work for companies that provide training, they should take the initiative to learn about their organisation, its business lines and its operations. They could do this by volunteering to lead projects or by asking to work in different parts of the organisation. They could also work to improve their communication skills through reading, learning on the job, training through the company or other sources, such as courses offered by local universities and professional organisations.

Meeting Expectations

Finance professionals are well aware of their changing role within companies. They recognise that they are expected to spend more time providing support to business managers. A CGMA report examining this trend further noted that finance professionals 'recognise that they need to develop the ability to contribute commercial insight and influencing or managerial skills. These enhanced skills are necessary to help them to succeed in their careers as management accountants and for them to help their employers' businesses to succeed.'[16]

Although finance professionals are expected to contribute more, they often face constraints in trying to support business managers beyond the scope of their traditional duties. Difficulties they face in meeting expanded expectations include lack of time to take on extra duties or learn new skills, no feeling of internal obligation to acquire new responsibilities, or they may be slow to acquire new capabilities. Above all, financial professionals must have basic communication skills to meet the broad expectations of their internal and external stakeholders. Without these skills, they could struggle as they move up the corporate ladder. The good news is that the CGMA report also found that finance professionals already have core technical skills and professional credibility. Through continuing professional development, they can earn a mandate for a broader role by delivering the insight and support that organisations need to sustain their success.

Managing Change

Companies need finance professionals who are skilled in managing change. Half of the senior executives responding to a survey conducted by the CGMA programme said the top skill they are looking for in their staff is experience with or knowledge of change management.[17] The executives also sought staff with experience in different business sectors and with emerging markets and fast-growth economies. Few of the executives felt they already had the finance staff with these key skills.

Throughout this chapter, you have been exposed to a number of issues facing management accountants today. The role of finance professionals is rapidly changing, as are the expectations of business leaders and stakeholders. In addition, the next generation entering the workforce demands greater guidance and development opportunities. Now, more than ever, management accountants need excellent communication skills to be able to overcome the challenges facing them. The rest of this book will help you to develop those skills and guide you to sources to address your specific needs.

CHAPTER SUMMARY

- Finance professionals have moved beyond simply reporting and record keeping to serving as strategic advisers to management.

- Today, CFOs and other senior finance executives are strategic business partners to senior management, providing critical analysis and strategic insights that inform executive decision making.

- One of the biggest challenges facing CFOs is to communicate complex issues in ways that a variety of audiences can understand.

- Companies need to provide management accountants with experience in the commercial side of the organisation and help them to develop the communication, leadership and other skills to advance to leadership positions.

- Management accountants themselves must take the initiative in developing their communication and other skills. This will open the door to career opportunities across the organisation.

Endnotes

1 Boris Groysberg, L. Kevin Kelly and Bryan MacDonald, 'The New Path to the C-Suite,' *Harvard Business Review*, Mar. 2011 http://hbr.org/2011/03/the-new-path-to-the-c-suite/ar/1

2 'Finance forte: the future of finance leadership,' Ernst & Young [website], Mar. 2011. www.ey.com/GL/en/Services/Assurance/Finance-forte--the-future-of-finance-leadership

3 CGMA stands for chartered global management accountant. For a description of the CGMA designation, its purpose and its value, visit CGMA. org. CGMA Report: 'The Fast Track-Track to Leadership: The challenges, opportunities and action plan,' AICPA and CIMA www.cgma.org/Resources/Reports/DownloadableDocuments/CGMA_Fast_Track_to_leadership.PDF

4 'Views. Visions. Insights. The Evolving Role of Today's CFO,' Ernst & Young [website]. Jun. 2012 www.ey.com/GL/en/Issues/Managing-finance/The-DNA-of-the-CFO---perspectives-on-the-evolving-role

5 'Views. Vision. Insights. The evolving role of today's CFO,' Ernst & Young [website] www.ey.com/Publication/vwLUAssets/Americas_CFO_Views VisionInsights_062012/$FILE/Americas_CFO_ViewsVisionInsights_062012.pdf

6 CGMA Report, 'Fast Track to Leadership: The Challenges, Opportunities and Action Plan,' AICPA and CIMA www.cgma.org/Resources/Reports/DownloadableDocuments/CGMA_Fast_Track_to_leadership.PDF

7 Robert Bergstrom, Sarah Batchelor and George Marcotte, 'The Future Used to be Easier: Planning for Success in a Dynamic Environment,' Accenture [website] www.accenture.com/SiteCollectionDocuments/PDF/Accenture_The_Future_Used_To_Be_Easier_Palnning_Success_Dynamic_Environments.pdf

8 CGMA Report, 'Rebooting Business: Valuing the Human Dimension,' AICPA and CIMA www.cncima.com/uploads/docs/CGMA_launch_report_-_REBOOTING_BUSINESS__VALUING_THE_HUMAN_DIMENSION.pdf

9 Karen D. Quint and T. Christopher Butler, 'Boards and the Expanding Role of the CFO,' *Bloomberg BusinessWeek*, Sept. 2009 www.businessweek.com/managing/content/sep2009/ca20090922_634820.htm

10 'A tale of two markets: Telling the story of investment across developed and rapid-growth markets,' Ernst & Young [website] www.ey.com/Publication/vwLUAssets/CFO_A_tale_of_two_markets/$FILE/CFO_A_tale_of_two_markets.pdf

11 'Preparing tomorrow's leaders: nine steps that CFOs can take now to prepare for the future,' Ernst & Young [website] www.ey.com/GL/en/Services/Assurance/Finance-forte--the-future-of-finance-leadership---Nine-steps-for-CFOs-to-prepare-for-the-future

12 Matthew G. Lamoreaux. 'CFO 101: Five Prerequisites,' *Journal of Accountancy*, Sept. 2009 www.journalofaccountancy.com/Issues/2009/Sep/20091501.htm

13 'Plugging the skills gap: Shortages among plenty,' *The Economist*, Economist Intelligence Unit, 2012 www.managementthinking.eiu.com/sites/default/files/downloads/EIU_SuccessFactor.pdf

14 David McCann, 'For CFOs, There's No Place Like Home,' CFO [website], 9 Mar. 2012 www3.cfo.com/article/2012/3/job-hunting_heidrick-struggles-cfo-turnover

15 Maxwell Murphy, 'The Inside/Outside Pay Gap,' *CFO Journal*, Sept. 2012 http://blogs.wsj.com/cfo/2012/09/11/the-insideoutside-pay-gap/

16 CGMA Report, 'New Skills, Existing Talents: The new mandate for finance professionals in supporting long-term business success,' www.cgma.org/Resources/Reports/DownloadableDocuments/CGMA_new_skills_existing_talents.pdf

17 Emily Chasan, 'Economic Volatility Heats Up War for Finance Talent,' *The Wall Street Journal*, 17 Sept. 2012 http://blogs.wsj.com/cfo/2012/09/17/economic-volatility-heats-up-war-for-finance-talent/?mod=wsj_valetleft_email

2

DEVELOPING COMMUNICATION COMPETENCE: FROM SCHOOL TO CFO

It's never too late to acquire or improve your communication skills, but accountants who enter the job market with strong skills have an advantage. Whether you are looking to advance your own career, are responsible for training junior accountants, or are generally invested in the next generation of management accountants, this chapter will help you understand the importance of having and promoting excellent listening, speaking and writing skills. To understand the extent to which communication is a required skill set in management accounting today, you need only look at the online job listings for accounting positions at every level. The following is a sampling of recent listings and job requirements that can be found online on any given day:

- Staff accountant for a leading communications company: 'Strong written, verbal and interpersonal skills; must be able to communicate ideas and issues effectively and concisely to all levels of management, internal and external auditors and outside contacts.'

- Senior corporate accountant, large multinational, publicly traded company: 'Candidates must have excellent communication skills (oral and written), the ability to interact with all levels of management through the organisation, and the initiative to get the job done.'

- Finance manager, international textbook distributer and retailer: 'Excellent communication and persuasion skills.'

- Corporate treasurer, builder and developer: '...solid organisational, interpersonal and communication skills.'

From the day they start their first job with a corporation or small business, management accountants put their communication skills to use. As they advance in an organisation to positions with greater responsibility, they will have to develop the communication skills required at each level of the corporate ladder. Communication becomes increasingly complex at higher levels, but it is based on elementary communication principles: attentive listening and clear speech and writing. These skills will be discussed in depth in the next chapter.

COMMUNICATION COMPETENCIES

Wherever you are on your career path, honing your communication skills can help you advance to where you want to go next. Take advantage of any resources your school or company offers to improve communication skills. Box 2-1 is a sampling of the communication competencies or skills required of management accountants and others in an organisation. The chart is intended simply to provide a general idea of such competencies. Some companies or education programmes may have more comprehensive and detailed skills standards.

Box 2-1: A Sampling of Required Communication Competencies at Different Levels in an Organisation

	LISTENING	SPEAKING	WRITING
ENTRY LEVEL	What is your purpose in listening?	What is your purpose in speaking?	What is your purpose in writing?
	Know the speaker: background, views, career history, other information.	Know your audience: Who are they? Why should they listen to you? How receptive will they be to what you have to say?	Know your audience: Who are they? Why should they read what you write?
	Know yourself: your assumptions, biases or misconceptions that might distort what you're hearing.		
	Show respect for the speaker.		
	Appreciate the speaker's perspective.		
	Empathise: be attuned to the speaker.		
	Ensure you understand what speaker intended to say, eg, by summarising or paraphrasing.	Planning: What will you say?	Is your writing clear and concise?
		How will you say it? Organisation, structure, key points.	Is it consistent—does it stay on message?
			Did you use correct grammar?
	Ask questions to help speaker clarify a point, add new insights, etc.	Concise: Be clear about what you want to say.	Is your writing coherent?
		Say only what is necessary to make your point—no more, no less.	Is it well organised? Does it have a logical structure?
		Economise on words. Can you say something in fewer words?	
	Be patient: hear the speaker out; listen for key points.	Avoid jargon.	Is the timing right for delivering your message? Are the circumstances such that readers will be receptive?
		Explain technical subjects in plain English.	
			For example, proposing an acquisition could be appropriate if the company is in a strong financial position.
	Watch for nonverbal cues to the speaker's feelings; note tone, pitch, volume of voice.	Be authentic, open, transparent.	Is the language and tone appropriate for your readers?
		Show confidence.	
		Use nonverbal communication to amplify, enhance and reinforce your message.	

	LISTENING	SPEAKING	WRITING
TEAM LEADER	Engages team and individual members in conversations, meetings, presentations.	Understands the big picture: team vision, purpose, goals, and work product. Clearly communicates vision and goals to team members.	Collaborates with team in developing written material that influences target audience.
	Actively listens to team members—their ideas, comments, and suggestions.	Simplifies complex information to ensure understanding.	Assigns team members responsibility for contributing to writing of material.
	Promptly responds to team's questions and concerns.	Anticipates needs and questions of team and prepares to respond accordingly. Shares information openly.	Leads team in reviewing, commenting on and revising material as necessary.

	LISTENING	SPEAKING	WRITING
MANAGER	Attentively listens to speaker.	Facilitates group discussion to ensure understanding and effective decision making.	Simplifies complex information.
	Listens empathetically to understand speaker's real motivations.	Delivers presentations to senior management with confidence. Able to say 'I don't know' to a question. Followed by assurances to try and get an answer.	Adapts style and substance of communication to audience.
	Attuned to non-verbal cues of speaker. Picks up on information that others may miss.	Shares information as appropriate.	
	Encourages others to speak their minds.	Encourages sharing of ideas and best practises.	

Continued on p. 18

Continued from p. 17

	LISTENING	SPEAKING	WRITING
EXECUTIVE		Provides critical analysis and strategic insights that inform executive decision making.	
		Able to communicate complex issues in ways that a variety of audiences can understand.	
	Leads company forums to obtain wide perspective of ideas.	Able to give and exchange information within meaningful context and with appropriate delivery and interpersonal skills.[*]	Leads development of written information for highly visible or complex situations.
	Creates forums and procedures to actively source and hear diverse perspective to enhance understanding.	Able to influence, inspire, and motivate others to achieve results.[†]	Creates forums, systems, and processes that result in information sharing.
		Confidently presents controversial or complex information to all levels of the organisation.	

[*] 'Core Competencies from CPA Vision Project Final Report,' AICPA www.aicpa.org/research/cpahorizons2025/cpavisionproject/pages/cpavisionproject.aspx
[†] Ibid.

Companies expect management accountants to have strong listening, speaking and writing skills because they will be working with people across the company and at different levels in the organisation. Look back at the job listing for a communications company staff accountant at the beginning of this chapter. It states 'strong written, verbal and interpersonal skills; must be able to communicate ideas and issues effectively and concisely to all levels of management.' Sarah Vaudrain, a business analyst with Teknor Apex in Pawtucket, Rhode Island, echoes that listing when outlining her job responsibilities in interview 3 in appendix A: 'I am part of the business team, working with different departments and managers, talking to people all over the company...' The ability to communicate with different audiences is especially critical for senior executives. Developing and practising that skill early can only help you on your career path.

How, then, do management accountants progress from the entry level communication skills listed in box 2-1 to the higher level skills of an executive? Most management accountants already have some level of skill when they start with a company as the result of studying communication in school, whether as part of accounting classes or in business communication classes, and from working in public accounting, as many management accountants do before joining a corporation or business. Additionally, more companies are instituting programmes to help management accountants learn a company's businesses and develop communication and other skills. Management accountants should also take the initiative to learn on their own, especially if the company does not provide specific training in communications.

Some ways you can learn new communication skills independently include

- reading the business and financial press, online news sites and other sources to increase your knowledge of business generally.

- learning about the industries in which your company and its clients and customers operate and seeing what's being written about your company.

- observing how business publications and online news sites write about complex subjects and issues in clear, concise language that their diverse audiences can understand.

- learning from people in your company who are considered excellent speakers and writers and your peers, by asking them to provide feedback about your speaking and writing and doing the same for them.

- practising your listening skills every time you are engaged in a conversation or listening to a presentation.

- writing a plan for improving your communication skills, perhaps using a class you have taken or books or articles you have read as guides. With a plan, you are an active learner with specific goals and benchmarks to measure your progress.

The next section examines how management accountants develop their communication skills in school and continue to improve them in the corporate world. Most graduates go into public accounting, and some later switch to corporate accounting. In the process, they learn to adapt the communication skills developed in public accounting to a corporation or small business setting. Communication skills are portable. If management accountants have a foundation of strong listening, speaking and writing, they can apply those skills to any type of job anywhere.

COMMUNICATION IN UNIVERSITY ACCOUNTING PROGRAMMES

The process of developing the communication skills to work as a management accountant begins in school. In many universities and colleges that have accounting programmes, business communication is interwoven with accounting instruction. For example, at the National University of Singapore, business communication is one of fifteen core classes students are required to take. At some schools, such as Johnson & Wales University in Providence, Rhode Island, students take a communication class offered by the English department. (See interview 4 in appendix A with Donna Viens, an assistant professor and chair of the university's Accountancy and Finance department.)

Some of the business schools and accounting programmes at large universities, such as Texas A&M University, have faculty members who teach business communication. (See interview 5 in appendix A with James J. Benjamin, head of the Accounting department at the Mays Business School of Texas A&M University.) Box 2-2 outlines a sample accounting programme from Seneca College in Toronto, Ontario, that emphasises communication in the curriculum.

Box 2-2: Sample Accounting Curriculum

Semester 1	Hrs/Wk
Introduction to Canadian Business	3
Financial Mathematics	4
Computer Applications for Business I	3
Introduction to Financial Accounting	4
Writing Strategies	3
Semester 2	**Hrs/Wk**
Business Statistics	4
Computer Applications for Business II	3
Introduction to Business Law	3
Introduction to Marketing	3
Management Accounting	4
Applied Communication for Business and Industry	4
Semester 3	**Hrs/Wk**
Intermediate Financial Accounting I	4
Finance	4
Business Information Systems	3
Microeconomics—Theory and Practice	3
Presentation Skills	3
Liberal Studies Elective	3
Semester 4	**Hrs/Wk**
Organisational Behaviour	3
Intermediate Financial Accounting II	4
Management Accounting— Intermediate	4
Macroeconomics—Theory and Practice	3
Liberal Studies Elective	3

Semester 5	Hrs/Wk
Income Tax I	4
Auditing	4
Database Management	4
Quantitative Methods for Decision Making	2
Ethics and Social Responsibility	3
Co-op Professional Practice	2
Semester 6	**Hrs/Wk**
Income Tax II	4
Computerised Auditing	4
Financial Management	3
Business Cases I	3
Liberal Studies Elective	3
Co-op Integration and Career Planning	1
Semester 7	**Hrs/Wk**
Project Management	3
Accounting Theory	4
Advanced Financial Accounting	4
Operations Management	3
Applied Research Methodology	3
Semester 8	**Hrs/Wk**
Critical Thinking, Analysis, and Decision	3
Advanced Auditing	3
International Strategic Management	3
Management Accounting - Advanced	3
Applied Research Project	4

Source: www.senecac.on.ca/fulltime/IAF.html

CAREER PATHS IN ACCOUNTING

After graduation, an accountant's career can head in many directions. Figure 2-1 outlines the general career path of an accountant in a company. In individual companies, the career path may include additional steps or otherwise differ from the ones shown in the figure and discussed in the sections that follow.

Figure 2-1: Corporate Accounting Career Paths

Chief Financial Officer	
Treasurer	Chief Accountant/Controller
Assistant Treasurer	Assistant Controller
Finance Manager	Manager
Supervising Financial Analyst	Accounting Supervisor
↖ ↗	
Senior Accountant	
↑	
Staff Accountant	

(See appendix B for a description of each position in the chart.)

Appendix B examines further the career tracks in figure 2-1. Figure 2-1 assumes the end goal of your career is to become CFO of an organisation. Your career goals may be different. Perhaps you eventually want to own an accounting firm or work in government. For most management accountants, however, their career path leads to the CFO position. After graduation, the majority of management accountants begin working in one of three areas: public accounting, management accounting, or financial accounting. These specialties are discussed in more detail in the sections that follow.

Public Accounting

A large percentage of accounting graduates join public accounting firms. On the job, they learn about business development and marketing and selling through training, learning from experienced professionals, working on teams, and assisting with client engagements. The 'Big Four' international accounting firms have structured leadership development programmes and online training courses. Some training programmes include instruction on improving writing, speaking, and presentation skills. To be eligible for promotion to senior levels in a firm, employees must demonstrate an ability to develop and bring in business, and they must have strong communication skills.

One example of a company that has a programme to help employees develop communication and other skills is Teknor Apex Company, a diversified material science company. This company has a finance academy, whose mission is to facilitate the sharing of ideas, skills and knowledge amongst employees across areas of specialty. (See interview 1 in appendix A with Teknor CFO Jim Morrison.)

At some point in their careers, accountants may leave public accounting to work for corporations and businesses. Although they have not previously worked for a company, the corporate world is not entirely new to them. In public accounting, they helped to provide services to corporate clients. They are knowledgeable about business and industry from their work for clients. Lastly, they have practical experience in communicating with clients.

Chris Papa, executive vice president and CFO of Post Properties, a leading developer and operator of upscale multifamily communities, made the transition in 2003, when he joined the company as CFO. Before that, he was an audit partner at BDO Seidman, LLP, CFO of Plast-O-Matic Valves, Inc., and an audit partner at Arthur Andersen, LLP, where he spent ten years.

To ease his transition from public accountant to CFO of Post, Papa focused on creating and strengthening relationships. He met one-on-one with key executives and met others in the company at meetings. He also began building relationships with representatives of the company's key lenders and bankers, ratings agencies, and other key constituencies. 'It helped that I already knew some of these people from my prior experience in public accounting,' Papa said. 'It also helped that I had a broad background in business from having worked closely with executive management and boards of my public accounting clients, firms, investment bankers and other organisations.' (See interview 6 in appendix A with Papa.)

Management Accounting

Although most accounting graduates join public accounting firms, some go directly into management accounting, usually by joining corporations (although some work for small businesses). Management accountants do not have the same early exposure to business development and marketing and sales as their peers in public accounting. However, they do have the opportunity to start learning about the company or business from the day they first walk through the door. And they can learn about the company's industry, as well as its customers or clients.

As discussed in chapter 1, management accounting has historically been a reporting function: Accountants compiled, reviewed, analysed and reported historical financial information about a company. Although management accountants still carry out these traditional tasks, advanced key responsibilities include cost accounting, a company's general accounting and assisting the company with budgeting, including operating, capital and cash budgets. However, the scope of work and responsibilities of management accountants have expanded well beyond financial reporting to meet the needs of the modern corporation. Management accountants are serving as business partners in organisations, providing senior executives and company managers with the information and guidance to develop strategic plans, set business goals, and consult on value-creating activities.

More companies are giving management accountants exposure to the commercial side of the business by having them work with and assist business line leaders and employees in different departments or operations of a company. Exposure to the business beyond numbers on paper helps accountants expand their knowledge of the business and build relationships within the organisation.

McCormick & Co., a manufacturer, marketer and distributor of seasoning mixes, condiments and other flavourful products, has a global competency model. It defines competencies such as leadership, business sense, handling complexity and communication that are common across the organisation. (See interview 2 with McCormick Senior Vice President Kenneth Kelly in appendix A.) Sarah Vaudrain started as a cost analyst at Teknor Apex Company. She was promoted to business analyst (financial analyst), her current position. She supports the company's nylon division, which manufactures nylon compounds that have broad industrial and commercial applications. 'I am part of the business team, working with different industries and managers, talking to people all over the company, and helping to investigate problems,' she said. 'I participate in monthly meetings with senior executives and others where we review the numbers and discuss how we can improve the business.' (See interview 3 with Vaudrain in appendix A.)

Financial Accounting

While management accountants and internal auditors work mainly with company executives and managers, and provide information primarily for internal use, financial accountants deal mostly with stakeholders outside a company. They prepare the company's balance sheet, income statement, statement of retained earnings, statement of cash flows, and other information for use by investors, creditors, stock analysts, government agencies, labour unions, consumers groups, the media and others. As shown in figure 2-1, the career path of a financial accountant is staff accountant, senior accountant, supervising financial analyst, finance manager, assistant treasurer, treasurer and CFO.

Of course, not every management accountant will become a CFO, and, for that matter, not every accountant may want to. But management accountants can find other opportunities in companies, for example, in specialised areas such as tax, internal audit or IT, and, as noted in the previous section, management accountants are starting to work all over companies and are advancing to senior positions in operations, human resources, IT and marketing.

RETAINING THE NEXT GENERATION OF MANAGEMENT ACCOUNTANTS

Instituting training programmes within your organisation to teach or refresh employees on skills like communication may serve two purposes. A huge challenge facing the accounting profession today is the preparation of the next generation of management accountants. If companies expect to recruit and retain talented management accountants and other employees, they will have to take the initiative in recognising, valuing and capturing the creative energies of employees, especially those of Generation Y (born 1981–2000) employees, who are now in the workforce. As baby boomers (born 1946–1964) continue to retire, more workers will be needed to replace them. Generation X (born 1965–1980) is too small to fill the gap, so the difference will have to be made up by the much larger Generation Y, also known as Millennials. Generation Y workers have a different employment philosophy than previous generations. Instead of fighting the challenges Gen Y workers introduce, companies may find that simple changes will accommodate the needs of this newest generation.

In a study of Generation Y, Deloitte said, 'In the context of the workplace, they've been described as overly ambitious dreamers who don't want to pay their dues and are only concerned about higher pay and more time off.'[1] Contrary to this perception, a Deloitte snapshot study found that while Gen Yers are fundamentally different from previous generations, they are future-oriented, opportunity-driven, and ready to contribute to the workforce. However, they are restless, preferring opportunities for advancement over job security. To tap into the potential of this generation of workers, employers may need to re-think some of their practises. Amongst other steps, employers must redesign performance management and rewards systems to encourage the rapid development of Gen Y talent and create new incentives for seasoned workers to act as mentors to young professionals.

Most important, companies must develop programmes to prepare Gen Y employees for future leadership positions. Career development and mentoring programmes will help to attract and retain Gen Y employees and guide them into leadership roles.[2] A Boston College report on Millenials in the workplace includes a variety of examples of how companies are successfully implementing programmes for the new generation of workers. These include providing opportunities to meet and work with company leaders, using social networks to foster local and global connections, and helping them develop and implement philanthropic and other projects that showcase their talents, engage their passion for meaningful work, and expand their networks. Mentoring and training programmes like these will help all workers develop the necessary competencies for advancement and create a strong generation of management accountants.

Many opportunities are available to improve your communication skills, and it is up to you to make the most of them. By reading this book, you have already taken the first step. The next chapter will discuss the fundamentals of listening, speaking and writing skills. The later chapters of this book will discuss how to specifically improve business communications, such as writing reports and making presentations. See the bibliography for more sources.

CHAPTER SUMMARY

- More schools are including business communication in their accounting programmes, and some have separate classes in communication.

- More companies are requiring job candidates to have excellent communication skills as a condition of employment.

- To advance in an organisation as a management accountant, you must have not only the requisite technical skills but also the necessary communication skills.

- More companies are training management accountants in the business side of their organisations and helping them to develop communication and other skills.

- You have many opportunities to develop your communication skills through schooling, company training programmes and other resources, as well as through learning on your own.

Endnotes

1 'Generation Y: Powerhouse of the Global
   Economy,' Deloitte [website] www.deloitte.
   com/view/en_US/us/Services/consulting/
   human-capital/organization-and-talent/
   a90f49642dff0210VgnVCM100000ba42f00aRCRD.
   htm

2 Lauren Stiller Rikleen, 'Creating Tomorrow's
   Leaders: the Expanding Roles of Millennials in
   the Workplace,' Boston College Center for Work
   & Family [website] www.bc.edu/content/dam/files/
   centers/cwf/pdf/BCCWF%20EBS-Millennials%20
   FINAL.pdf

3

COMMUNICATION SKILLS

Chapters 1 and 2 highlighted the importance of strong communications skills at every level of management accounting. This chapter addresses listening, speaking, and writing skills as the basis for strong communication skills. As you read this chapter, ask yourself, 'Am I an effective communicator?' It's an important question. Your communication skills will determine, to a considerable degree, whether you get a job, advance in your organisation, and find the career opportunities you want.

Do you agree with the following statements?

- 'In the end, the most successful [accountants] are usually the ones who manage to combine a solid technical knowledge base with top-notch communication skills.'[1]

- 'It is no longer sufficient to simply present figures and comments in a report. Finance experts need to be able to explain their meaning and relevance to an audience that could be based in Birmingham or Beijing.'[2]

- 'There is a lack of creativity, adaptability, and developed interpersonal communication skills among job seekers today.'[3]

- 'In today's highly competitive environment, 'soft skills,' such as written and oral communications, interpersonal skills, and leadership ability have become so important that companies hiring accounting students often place more importance on these skills than they do on technical accounting skills.'[4]

These statements underscore the importance of developing communication skills as soon as possible. Communication skills give accountants an advantage in the workplace, sometimes more than technical skills. Even prospective management accountants can set themselves apart from other candidates by demonstrating exceptional speaking, listening and writing skills during the hiring process.

How you are viewed in a company is partly determined by how well you speak and write.[5] If you make mistakes in grammar, spelling, and word choice, your colleagues may view you as careless, indifferent and not serious about your job. Sending misspelled e-mails or submitting a disorganised resume may keep you from being hired in the first place.

In an article in the *Harvard Business Review*, Kyle Wiens, CEO of iFixit and founder of Dozuki, says people who apply to either of his companies must take a grammar test. He won't hire people who use poor grammar. 'If you think a semicolon is a regular colon with an identity crisis, I will not hire you. ...[I]f job hopefuls can't distinguish between "to" and "too," their applications go into the bin,' Wiens writes.[6] Wiens is not alone in his concerns about grammar. *The Wall Street Journal* observed that many managers feel there is an epidemic of poor grammar in the workplace. Managers attribute this trend to the informality of e-mail, texting, and Twitter, where slang and shortcuts are common. Poor grammar is worrisome to managers because looseness with language can make a bad impression on clients, ruin marketing materials and other documents, and even cause errors through miscommunication.[7]

Management accountants themselves are well aware of the importance of communication skills. In a CGMA report, finance professionals were asked to rate the importance of specific business and technical competencies to the overall success of an organisation. The results of the survey are summarised in box 3-1. Interestingly, communication skills were ranked first in importance, far above technical accounting and risk management.[8]

Box 3-1: Importance of Skills to the Finance Professional (ranked in order)

Skill	Description
1. Communication	Written, oral and presentation skills and communicating effectively with nonfinance people
2. Problem solving	Taking a critical and methodical approach when problem solving
3. Business	Good understanding of the organisation's objectives, operations, market environment, and ethical issues
4. Interpersonal	Team-working, conflict management, and influencing and negotiating
5. Strategic	Flexibility and 'thinking on your feet'
6. Leadership	Leading others, managing resources and delegating effectively
7. Change management	Assessing and facilitating change
8. Risk management	Understanding the sources of risk and evaluating risks and methods for their control and mitigation
9. Technical accounting	Broad understanding of the technical issues and ability to keep up with new accounting rules and regulations
10. IT	Ability to keep up with new concepts, techniques, tools and technologies

The rest of this chapter examines the purpose of communication and how it is used in business. It examines the core communication skills: listening, speaking and writing, as well as nonverbal communication. It also offers some suggestions about how you can improve your communication skills. Additional suggestions on applying these skills to writing reports and giving presentations are provided in subsequent chapters and the bibliography lists articles and books on business communication, managerial communication, communicating effectively, effective writing and related topics.

PURPOSE OF COMMUNICATION

The word 'communication' derives from *communis*, a Latin word meaning 'to share' or 'to make known.' It is the process of sending and receiving messages. In its basic form, communication seems simple enough. The communicator—a person or persons or an organisation—sends a message to another person or organisation. The receiver interprets the message and may provide feedback by sending a return message.

In today's world, a message may be sent through various channels. A person may speak face-to-face with another person or group of people. A person may speak by telephone or video conference to another person or a group of people located across the globe. Written communications can take multiple forms. They may be printed communications, such as letters, reports and memorandums. They could also be sent electronically through e-mail, text message or fax, posted on the Internet or relayed by other electronic means. A complete list of forms of communications is included in the following section.

With so many different channels of communication, the risks of miscommunication are many. 'The infinite number of breakdowns possible at each stage of the communication process makes us marvel that mutually satisfying communication ever occurs,' write Carol M. Lehman and Debbie DuFrene.[9] How can communication go wrong? Here are just a few of the many ways:

- The sender uses vague language, jargon, poor grammar or otherwise impedes communication.
- The receiver doesn't understand the message because of the sender's choice of words, body language or other reasons.
- The receiver thinks he or she understands the message when, in fact, the sender intended something different.
- The receiver chooses to ignore the message, assuming that it is too difficult to understand, uninteresting or disagreeable.
- The sender did not think about how to phrase the message, so the receiver accepts and understands it. The receiver may still block out the message, but the sender has made the effort to communicate.
- The sender has used a channel inappropriately, such as a manager using e-mail to communicate an important announcement to his or her employees. The manager could have spoken to employees directly. This would have emphasised the importance of the announcement and shown that the manager appreciated its impact. It would also have given employees the opportunity to question the manager.

The consequences of miscommunication could be relatively minor, such as a colleague saying he or she didn't understand your e-mail. Or the consequences could be quite serious, such as a loss of a client, failure to get a promotion or a disastrous job interview. Communicating poorly has genuine risks, which reinforces the importance of proper communication.

FORMS OF COMMUNICATION

Because of advances in technology, people in business today have more choices than ever before in communicating. They include the following, arranged in the order they will be discussed throughout the rest of the book:

- *Face-to-face communication:* In the 2009 film *Surrogates*, American actor Bruce Willis plays an FBI agent investigating a murder in a future world in which people stayed home and connected with society through remotely-controlled androids. In the end, the androids were shut down forever, and people began venturing out of their homes to resume life in the real world. If nothing else, the film showed the importance of person-to-person communication. In today's world, technology is evolving into a substitute for personal communication. People are e-mailing colleagues down the hall rather than speaking to them. Personal communication builds the relationships that are the foundation for all other forms of communication. It also can reduce the risks of miscommunication. People can meet, discuss issues, resolve differences, plan a new project and move on. Bottom line: When communicating, start with people, not technology.

Writing emails, letters and memos, and talking on the telephone are activities you will likely do daily as a management accountant. While one method may seem faster or easier than another, consider the actual advantages and disadvantages of each.

- *E-mail.* E-mail is a quick, easy, and informal way to send messages and files inside and outside your company. Although e-mail has the advantages of speed, efficiency and convenience, it also has its risks.

  Miscommunication between you and the receivers of your e-mail can result if

  - you are not sensitive to how receivers will perceive your e-mail, for example, you use language they consider rude or offensive.

  - you write hastily and send an e-mail without insuring that it is complete, accurate, and free of spelling and grammatical errors.

  - you write in a moment of anger or frustration (only to later regret your action).

- *Instant messaging and text messaging.* These are fast and convenient ways to carry on conversations on computers, tablets and mobile devices. Like e-mail, they carry risks of miscommunication. E-mail and instant messaging are discussed further in chapter 4.

- *Memos.* People in companies and businesses routinely use memos (memorandums) to communicate internally for a variety of reasons. Memos use a standard header format of To, From, Subject and Date. They may be one or two paragraphs or several pages. They may be transmitted electronically, either separately or as e-mail attachments. They may be printed and distributed by hand, internal mail or other means. As with e-mails, you must give careful thought when composing and sending memos. Memos are discussed further in chapter 4.

- *Letters.* Companies use letters as a formal means of communication with clients and customers, vendors and suppliers, public agencies, regulators, professional organisations, and others. Like memos, they have a standard format, and they can be sent electronically or printed and delivered by mail or other means. As with everything you write, letters require careful consideration. Letters are discussed further in chapter 4.

- *Faxes.* Memos, letters and documents can easily be transmitted electronically, but sometimes faxes may be the preferred means of communication. A client or customer may want to receive certain communications by fax. When a document scanner is not available, documents may be sent by fax.

- *Telephone.* The telephone provides more of a human connection than e-mails, letters or memos. People can speak with one another and be attuned to the feelings expressed in speakers' voices. The telephone is especially useful for discussing questions, issues and problems at length; exchanging ideas; resolving issues and making decisions. If a record of the call is desired, it may be recorded, or someone may be responsible for taking notes.

- *Voicemail*. Compared with the telephone, voicemail provides more flexibility. People can call from office or home phones (or computers) or from mobile devices and leave messages at any time. To ensure their messages are understood, they should follow a protocol: Speak slowly and clearly, leave a detailed but brief message, and give their name and phone number at the start and the end of the voicemail. Like e-mails, voicemails can become part of the permanent record of the receivers and be available for retrieval for future use. And, like e-mails, they are subject to legal disclosure.

Reports and presentations may be a more infrequent but no less important part of your job as a management accountant. Knowing how to create, design and present these formal communications can set you apart and give you an advantage over your peers.

- *Reports*. A report is a document that provides objective, factual information. It usually is written for a specific audience, such as investors or shareholders; the CEO, CFO and other senior executives; a business line manager; or an account supervisor or others. Reports are discussed further in chapters 5 and 6.

  There are many different kinds of reports, including the following:

  - *Formal report*. A formal report is thoroughly researched, well organised, objective and detailed. It provides strategic, business, financial, economic, demographic or other information a company's leaders and managers use in managing the business, addressing risks and identifying market opportunities.

  - *Informal report*. An informal report usually is a short document that focuses on a specific topic, such as the cost of buying a specific piece of equipment or contracting for a service.

  - *Progress report*. A progress report informs those overseeing or managing the project about whether it is on schedule and on budget. Project reports are issued regularly over the course of a project and help managers to manage projects efficiently.

  - *Investigative report*. Management may ask accountants or others in an organisation to investigate a problem or issue, such as certain costs that are over budget, and report their findings. The investigator may also make recommendations about how to address the problem.

  - *Feasibility report*. A feasibility report examines whether a proposed project, such as development of a new manufacturing plant, is necessary, practical and achievable and whether the benefits justify the cost. It also recommends whether management should approve the project.

- *Presentations*. A presentation is speaking to an audience and using visual aides to illustrate your points. Presentations can take many forms, but they generally are used to inform, analyse or persuade. A CFO might make a presentation to the CEO and other senior executives about plans to consolidate business operations to increase efficiency and reduce costs. An accounting manager might make a presentation to a business manager that analyses the business line's production costs. A business manager might make a presentation to the CFO and other senior executives that argues for the company's expanding into a new market. Presentations are discussed further in chapters 7 and 8.

- *Videoconferencing*. A main benefit of videoconferencing is that it reduces or eliminates the travel required to attend a conference. Also, videoconferencing today is cheaper, of better quality and easier to use. More people may be able to participate in a conference through videoconferencing than if a company paid for only a limited number to attend a meeting. With more participants, more ideas may be shared, and more people may feel vested in company decision making.

Online forms of communication are evolving rapidly. Connecting with clients, colleagues and investors through social media may require specialised tools and skills.

- *Blogs*. More companies are discontinuing public blogs and concentrating their social media strategies on Twitter and Facebook.[10] A survey released early in 2012 by the University of Massachusetts Dartmouth found that the percentage of companies that maintain blogs fell to 37% in 2011 from 50% in 2010. Blogging requires a commitment of time and resources to provide a stream of fresh content, and companies must address liability and other issues. However, blogging enables a company to promote its brand, connect with clients and customers, and reach a broad audience, including prospective customers. Companies that do blog have policies saying who may blog, rules for blogging, and so on. Some companies also have private or internal blogs for sharing information, announcements and ideas.

- *Social media*. More companies are establishing robust presences on Facebook, Twitter and other social media outlets in order to build stronger relationships with clients and customers, broaden exposure to their products and services, increase their market visibility, and develop new sources of revenue. Many tools and resources are available to companies to develop, manage and realise the maximum value from their investment in social media. But other companies have yet to embrace social media, among other reasons because top management does not see the benefits, planning and budgeting for social media adoption is in its early stages, or management wants better information on the financial return to companies from investing in social media. Companies also have developed internal websites to facilitate communication amongst senior executives, managers and employees. Communicating through the web and social media is discussed further in chapter 9.

- *Web content*. As with blogs, more companies are shifting their focus from developing web content to building a social media presence, whereas other companies continue to invest in content development. Market demand for fresh, original, thoughtful content is increasing, and strong content attracts viewers to company websites, enables a company to build relationships with viewers, learn what kinds of content most interests viewers, and build relationships with current or prospective customers or clients.

- *Webinars*. Companies use webinars for conferences, meetings, training sessions, thought leadership discussions and other purposes. Some webinars are interactive, allowing participants can see and hear presenters and a moderator, ask questions and answer polls. Others are one-way communications, meaning that viewers can see and hear the presenters but cannot participate in discussions with them.

USING COMMUNICATION IN BUSINESS

Now that you have refreshed your memory of all the various forms of communication, let's consider their uses in business:

1. *Reporting*. Presentation of facts. Providing of information. Everyone in an organisation, from a worker on a shop floor to an entry level management accountant, to the CFO or CEO, is continually providing information about a company's operations, products or services, finances, accounting, human resources and more.

2. *Marketing and selling*. A company's ability to sell its products and services depends on the communication skills of those directly engaged in marketing and selling. However, others in the organisation can help promote the company's brand, and the company might create a training programme for this purpose.

3. *Persuading.* Employees, middle managers and top executives of a company at one time or another may try to win over someone. An employee may try to convince his or her boss to give him or her more time off, a manager may try to negotiate a bigger salary increase, or a CFO may try to convince the CEO of the merits of an acquisition.

4. *Influencing.* Having an effect on the perceptions or decisions of others. For example, the executive of a company that manufactures solar panels might write an editorial column for a national newspaper that argues for continuation of a tax credit for solar energy. The purpose is to convince lawmakers to extend the credit.

5. *Motivating.* From the CEO to the team leader of a project, leaders try to motivate others in ways large and small. An example of this would be a company celebration for managers and employees on the company's meeting its sales goals for the year and inspiring them to meet next year's target or a manager stopping an employee in a hallway to tell her she's doing a great job.

6. *Directing.* Most everyone in a company is directing or being directed. The CEO might direct the CFO to have a plan ready by tomorrow on reducing overhead costs 10%. The CFO directs his or her finance department to prepare a plan. A finance manager creates a team to stay up all night developing the plan. A member of the team calls a local pizzeria just before midnight and directs its manager to send over six pizzas right away.

7. *Recruiting.* Companies recruit prospective employees directly through recruiting programmes and other initiatives and indirectly through marketing, advertising, social media and other communication channels.

8. *Education and training.* Communication is at the heart of the training of a company's management and employees. Companies train and educate people on the job; in company meetings, workshops and seminars; through professional education courses and many other ways.

9. *Evaluating.* Most people in a company go through an evaluation process, either conducting or receiving evaluations or engaging in both activities. Many communication tools are used in evaluations, such as conversations, meetings, performance reviews, examinations and more.

10. *Negotiating.* Negotiations go on at every level of a company over everything from the CFO's pay and benefits package to a purchasing manager's negotiations with a supplier over office supplies.

11. *Innovating.* Whether over coffee or in a meeting or as members of a task force, people often discuss ideas for a new product or service or a new line of business. Ideas can, and do, come from anywhere in the organisation.

12. *Consulting.* A person asks the advice of another person or a group of persons. The director of marketing might ask senior management's opinions about a proposed marketing campaign. The CFO might ask the director of human resources about improving an organisation's career development programme.

13. *Collaborating.* People in a company work with others in achieving a goal, solving a problem, or evaluating an opportunity. The director of marketing might collaborate with a division head on developing a campaign around a new product launch. A line manager might form a team to collaborate on developing an idea for improving the manufacturing process.

14. *Entertaining.* Depending on your corporate culture, this might also be on the list of business uses for communication. It should always be used as a means to help accomplish a purpose, such as training employees or selling a product and not as an end in itself. Some examples of techniques that both entertain and inform include using dancers to illustrate the message of PowerPoint slides or presenting your business card using a magic trick.

What do these many uses for communication in business mean to you as a management accountant? Over time, while working for a company, you will communicate in many of the previous ways, and you will have to develop the necessary skills to report to, consult or collaborate with, train, direct, persuade or motivate others.

MEASURING RESULTS

Regardless of how communication is used in business, the intent is to produce results. 'Managerial communication is different from other kinds of communication,' writes Mary Munter. 'Why? Because in a business or management setting, the most brilliant message in the world will do you no good unless you achieve the desired outcome.'[11]

Thus, to measure the effectiveness of its recruiting programmes, a company might survey job candidates as to how they first heard about the company and the career opportunities it offers, or ask recently hired employees what convinced them to work for the company. To measure how well its training programmes are working (or not), a company might design a system for evaluating the overall effectiveness of its training or specific training such as a class or workshop. To evaluate its marketing programmes, the company might hire an outside marketing consultant. As a management accountant, you might be asked to help the company to design programmes, for example, to quantify the company's investment in training and the benefits.

Of course, not all communication fits into neat categories and distinct, measurable goals. Communication goes on all the time, in all corners of the company, concerning just about anything. And there is the far larger universe of communication occurring outside the company, some of it about the company. There are company-related conversations in the media, on social networks, in the offices of outside directors or shareholders, in the offices of a company's competitors, and many other places, on many different topics, often with consequences for the company, such as the shaping of its public image in the media and on social networks.

CORE SKILLS

The core communication skills are listening, speaking and writing, as well as nonverbal communication skills. The core communication skills are the foundation for the development of specific skills, such as the essential business communication skills discussed in the rest of this section.

Expressing ideas is a fundamental part of any business communication. As a management accountant, you must be able to communicate your ideas, starting with the day you start your first job at a company. At an entry-level position, you may, at first, be speaking mainly with other accountants about technical questions and issues. But as you work more and more with people outside of accounting, such as in operating divisions or units to support division managers, you increasingly will be required to express your ideas to people who are not accountants. As you advance in the organisation, you must have the ability to discuss increasingly complex ideas, and a wide range of ideas, with the senior people in the company. If you work for a small business, you could find yourself advising management much more quickly and much earlier in your career than in a large corporation. In any event, you need to know how to express yourself.

Asking the right questions is another important type of communication. 'We are trained from grammar school that what is important is the right answer—we didn't get any credit for asking questions,' said Greg Conderacci, a marketing consultant and instructor. 'But the right answer starts with the right question.' (In interview 7 in appendix A, Conderacci discusses the communication issues that management accountants face.)

By asking thoughtful questions—the right questions—you help management to clarify its thinking on issues, identify unexpected risks in a business strategy, spot a new business opportunity, or see ways to more efficiently manage the business. Through the questions you ask, you show that you give issues serious thought, have thoroughly researched issues, considered the pros and cons, and are helping management to achieve its strategic goals.

Finally, without being able to influence others, you will not be able to make an impact in your organisation or turn your ideas into action. You must have the ability to make informed, passionate, persuasive arguments to support an idea, discuss not only the opportunities but the risks in implementing the idea, back your arguments with thorough research, and be prepared to answer questions—and more questions from management.

'There is an argument that you either have communication skills or you don't, but these are skills that can be developed, improved and refined,' said Thomas D. Foard, Executive Vice President and CFO of Publishers Fulfillment Inc. (In interview 8 in appendix A, he offers some suggestions about how management accountants can improve their communication skills.)

Listening

Do you sometimes find yourself pretending to be listening to someone, but your mind is elsewhere? Because you're not listening attentively, you don't grasp what the speaker is trying to communicate, or you misinterpret what the speaker is saying. You come away with only fragments of the conversation in your mind. You have a listening deficit, and you are not alone.

Hearing and listening are not the same thing, even though many people think because they can hear, they automatically know how to listen. '[H]earing is passive, whereas listening is active.'[12] We hear throughout our waking hours, regardless of where we are, people chattering away, dogs barking, phones ringing, horns honking, and much more. It is the background noise of daily life, and we do not always pay attention to it.

The Swedish writer Henning Mankell spent part of his life in Africa learning to listen. An African parable muses about why human beings have two ears and only one tongue. Probably because we are meant to listen twice as much as we speak.[13] In Western culture, the reverse seems true. Talking is celebrated. In business settings, people are often praised for being terrific speakers or giving great talks. It is much rarer to hear someone being complimented as a great listener. People are not going to fill an auditorium for a great listener.

You may have great speaking skills, but if your listening skills don't measure up as well, you could find yourself at a disadvantage as you advance further in your career. Ram Charan writes that American company General Electric redefined its most desirable traits in leaders and considers listening to be among the top four in the list. Charan contends that 'listening opens the door to truly connecting and is the gateway to building relationships and capability.'[14]

Through frequent, personal communication with employees, leaders come across as more transparent, authentic and concerned than if they stayed behind their desks, remote from the everyday work of their organisations. For senior management, building stronger relationships with employees has taken on added importance as more companies adopt a flat organisational structure with an emphasis on collaboration and teamwork. Communication flows more freely up, down and across the organisation than in the traditional hierarchical structure.

So what does it mean to be an active listener? There are several things you can do before, during and after a conversation, meeting or presentation to be a considerate listener.

Before a meeting, prepare as much as possible so that you are focused and ready to consider the speaker's words. Some ways that you can prepare before a meeting include:

- *Have a clear purpose.* Is your purpose to obtain information, acquire knowledge, get the speaker's opinion on an issue, respond to the speaker's request for a meeting, discuss a problem, find a solution or other purpose? If you're clear about why you listen, you are more likely to want to listen.

- *Know the speaker.* What is the speaker's background? Views on business or other issues? Career history? Position in a company or other organisation? Even if you know the speaker well—your boss or a colleague, for example—you should think about these questions. Like you, the speaker brings to the conversation a set of assumptions, beliefs, hopes, fears, and values.

- *Know the context.* What is the context of the conversation? Context includes background information, assumptions by speaker and listener, the professional relationship of the speaker and listener, and more. For example, an employee might suggest an idea for a product improvement to a manager, who knows from experience that this is an idea that has not been proposed before and is worth pursuing.

- *Know yourself.* Be aware of how your assumptions, biases or misconceptions might colour what you are hearing. Learn to keep these from distorting the speaker's message. Observe how the speaker is responding to you. Is there something in what you've said and how you've said it that is making the speaker show annoyance, confusion, relief, happiness? Watch for nonverbal signals.

- *Remove distractions.* Examples of this include noise coming through an open window, blinding sunlight pouring into a room or someone talking loudly in the next room. These and other annoying distractions interfere with communicating. Eliminate them, if possible, and try not to add any with your own behaviour.

Once the meeting or presentation begins, be attentive and focused. Take notes if appropriate. Other ways to demonstrate active listening include:

- *Be attuned to the unspoken message.* Does the speaker appear to be angry, sad, pensive, bewildered? You can tell the speaker, 'You seem upset about this.' Suppose the speaker is an employee who has just been told she is being promoted. Maybe she's happy about the promotion, but apprehensive about taking on the responsibility of the new position. What does the speaker's tone, speed, volume or pitch tell you? Be patient. It takes time to truly listen to, and empathise with, a speaker. This is not easy in today's fast-paced business world, where communication sometimes seems to be at lightning speed, with not enough time for a thoughtful exchange of information and ideas. Just be patient, and you will receive messages correctly.

- *Show respect for the speaker.* Maybe you disagree with the speaker about certain issues, or you don't like the speaker. Never rudely interrupt or cut the conversation short. Wait for the speaker to finish a thought, and then make a brief comment or ask a question.

- *Make a deliberate effort to focus on the speaker.* Let the speaker know that he or she has your full attention through your expression, posture, language and eye contact. Imagine she's telling you that you've just won $5 million in a lottery. If that doesn't get your attention, nothing will.

- *Appreciate the speaker's perspective.* What is the speaker's goal in the conversation?

- *Empathise.* An original Star Trek episode[15] featured a powerful 'empath,' a being who could absorb not only the emotions but also the physical pain of others. You don't have to go that far, but try to empathise with the speaker. Can you relate to the speaker, their point of view, their passion?

At the end of the meeting or presentation, you should be able to demonstrate that you have been an attentive listener in the following ways:

- *Summarise the speaker's message.* Show the speaker that you are trying to understand. One way is to paraphrase or summarise the key points in the speaker's message. You show the speaker that you were paying attention and you grasped the substance of his communication. The speaker can then validate or correct your summation.

- *Ask thoughtful questions.* Ask questions that help the speaker to clarify a point, provide more details, strengthen an argument, offer new insights or otherwise improve upon what they are saying. Learning to ask discerning questions will serve you well as you advance in the organisation. Your peers and superiors will value your ability to use questions to crystallise an issue, look at a problem in a new way or offer a new solution.

Now that you understand the importance of being an active listener, box 3-2 offers some specific activities you can do to improve your active listening skills.

Box 3-2: Learning to Listen

The following are ways to improve your listening skills:

- Start by asking others to evaluate you as a listener. Are you attentive or distracted? Engaged or pretending to listen? Did you remember what the speaker said, or did you forget?

- Record a conversation or presentation on the radio, TV, Internet, or at a conference. After you finish listening, write a summary, and play back the recording to see if you captured the important points.

- While speaking with someone, or with a group of people, tell them what you heard them say, and see if this matches with what they intended to say. Meet with some business colleagues or personal friends to practice listening. One person talks, and others in the group summarise what they heard.

- Take a class in business communication that includes listening skills. You may find a class at a local college, through a professional society, or online Or, your company may offer classes taught by a business communication consultant or other communication expert.

- In your daily activities, make a concerted effort to listen. Can you capture the key points of what was said? Why are some people better speakers than others? How well do they listen to you?

Speaking

Like listening, speaking is a skill that you can develop if you weren't born with a silver tongue. As part of your job, you will have to speak in many different situations. In this section, I will briefly discuss some considerations for verbal communications. Presentations are discussed further in chapters 7 and 8.

- *Purpose*. What's your reason for speaking? To propose an idea? To suggest some course of action? To argue for or against something? To learn something? Some other purpose?

  Suppose you're a management accountant who has been moved out of the finance department to one of your company's operating units. You're meeting your supervisor for the first time. Your immediate goal is to learn generally about the unit's operations and the specifics of your job. Your long-term goal is to perform well in your job.

- *Audience*. Whether you are speaking to another person, a group of people, or hundreds of people, think about your audience.

  Let's say you're the leader of a newly formed team that's meeting for the first time. The purpose is to decide on project assignments. What do you want to know about team members that will help you make assignments and help them complete their assignments? What does the team want to know about you? You need to know this information so you can make well-informed decisions in matching up team members and assignments. Then, the team is more likely to perform well during the project.

- *Planning*. Like listening, speaking requires planning. You know your purpose in conversing or presenting, so what do you want to say?

  Planning can be as simple as taking a second to think about what you are going to say before speaking to a colleague. It can be as complex as taking hours to prepare a 20-minute presentation for the senior management of your company.

  Of course, you won't have a plan every time you speak. You may encounter a colleague in a hallway and engage in a spontaneous conversation about improving a company product. It is out of such spontaneous conversations that ideas can come for new or improved products, new services, ways to reduce costs or other ideas. But take every opportunity to plan. Then, you will get in the habit of planning and not regret failing to plan.

- *Be concise*. If there is one speaking skill that management accountants—and accountants in general—should develop, it is conciseness. Conciseness comes from planning. If you plan, you will be clear in your own mind about what you want to accomplish with a simple conversation or a formal presentation. If you plan, you will say only what is necessary to make your point, convey information, ask a question, and nothing more.

  To economise on words, imagine that you have to pay a dollar for every word you speak. You might start with 100 words, which, if you said them all, would cost you $100. By eliminating 60 words, you cut the number of words to 40, for a $60 savings. And people can still understand you.

- *Avoid jargon*. Like every profession, accounting has its jargon. Within the profession, it may be acceptable to use terms without explanation. However, if you lapse into jargon in speaking to people outside the accounting field, you will most likely be met with blank stares.

- *Be respectful*. Do not come across as arrogant, superior or condescending. 'A good communicator never makes their listener feel like they just left the principal's office,' says Sarah Stevens, a human resources consultant.[16]

- *Be attuned to your choice of words*. After you've explained something to someone, do you ask, 'Do you see my point?' or 'Got it?' What these questions imply is that your listener should understand you. They put your listener on the defensive, ready to disagree, argue or debate. The burden is on you to be understood. So, a better choice of words would be, 'Please tell me whether I'm being clear about this,' or, 'I had trouble understanding this myself, so if I'm not being clear, please let me know.'

- *Use concrete words*. 'I need this delivered in ten days' is not as precise as 'I need this delivered to my office at 8am on January 9.' Use strong words. 'We can do better than our biggest competitor' is not as strong as 'We will sell twice as many units as our biggest competitor.'

- *Be authentic.* Be open, transparent and authentic. You will win the confidence and respect of your peers, supervisors and others. They will trust your judgment, respect your opinions and hear what you have to say. Conversely, if you are seen as pretentious or deceitful, people will mistrust you, lose confidence in you, and be circumspect in communicating with you.

- *Be confident.* Regardless of your level of skill as a speaker, show confidence when you are speaking. Your audience, whether just one other person or a room of people, is more likely to trust what you say than if you come across as uncertain and insecure. This does not mean that you should pretend to have a higher level of skill than you do but that you have confidence in your ability to communicate, develop your skill, and become a better speaker.

Writing

There is no shortage of advice on how to write more effectively. In 1998, the US Securities and Exchange Commission (SEC) Office of Investor Education and Assistance issued 'A Plain English Handbook: How to Create Clear Disclosure Documents.'[17] Although the handbook was intended for the investment community— investors, securities dealers, etc—its guidance could equally apply to documents and other writings of management accountants and financial executives.

First, what is 'plain English'? The SEC handbook explains it this way:

> We'll start by dispelling a common misconception about plain English writing. It does not mean deleting complex information to make the document easier to understand. For investors to make informed decisions, disclosure documents must impart complex information. Using plain English assures the orderly and clear presentation of complex information so that investors have the best possible chance of understanding it.

In that last sentence, instead of *investors*, you could fill in any audience: the CEO, CFO, the board, shareholders, employees and others. The handbook goes on to explain plain English in further detail:

> Plain English means analyzing and deciding what information investors need to make informed decisions, before words, sentences, or paragraphs are considered. A plain English document uses words economically and at a level the audience can understand. Its sentence structure is tight. Its tone is welcoming and direct.

As discussed in chapter 1, CFOs must have the skill to explain complex information in language that others can understand. That's true not only of the CFO but every management accountant. Yet, when they start with a company, management accountants don't necessarily have this skill.

'Companies expect management accountants to support management decision making by making sense of complex data,' said Andrew Harding, managing director of the Chartered Institute of Management Accountants (CIMA). 'Very often this is a challenge for the management accountant, who is trained as an expert. The language of the expert doesn't always make for effective communication.'

Harding said large companies are addressing this issue by having management accountants work alongside line managers to learn a company's businesses. Some also have training programmes to help management accountants learn about a company's businesses. In the process, they are learning how to communicate with managers and employees across the organisation. (See interview 9 with Harding in appendix A.)

See chapters 4, 'Communicating in the Workplace,' and 5, 'Writing the Report,' for a more detailed discussion on writing business communications.

NONVERBAL COMMUNICATION

Listening, speaking and writing may be the core skills of communication, but sometimes, what isn't said can be heard loud and clear. Nonverbal communication had been a subject of study since the naturalist Charles Darwin wrote *The Expression of the Emotions in Man and Animals* in 1872. Psychologists and other professionals have been researching and writing about the subject ever since, and it's no wonder. Long before humans developed language, they used—and still use—nonverbal communication. It is as important to communicating as verbal communication. Why? Because it's not just what you say, but how you say it. The *how* is expressed in your body language, tone of voice, volume, rate of speaking and other nonverbal signals.

Despite its importance, people give about as much attention to nonverbal communication as they do to listening. Joe Navarro, an ex-FBI agent and expert in nonverbal communication, writes that '...when it comes to the silent language of nonverbal behavior, many viewers might as well be wearing blindfolds, as oblivious as they are to the body signals around them.' [18] They don't know what they're missing. Navarro says that careful observation of body language gives you critical insight in the same way that mindful listening is vital to truly understanding speech.

Management accountants need to develop skills in kinesics, or body language interpretation, which includes the skill to interpret how people communicate through facial expressions, as well as nonverbal communication using the movement of the hands, arms, legs, feet and torso. In fact, Navarro describes the feet as the most honest part of the body.

Understanding your own body language is just as important as knowing another's. You can use your body language to help make an effective presentation, or, in a negotiation or team meeting, to help communicate your position or keep your intentions hidden. Showing your enthusiasm for your proposal could help to win over your audience. Remaining impassive in negotiations over the price and other terms of an acquisition could keep the other party guessing about what terms you will accept and, perhaps, help you to negotiate the best possible terms. Showing your disappointment at a team's poor performance on a project could incentivise them to do better on the next project.

METACOMMUNICATION

Accountants also need to develop skill in metacommunication, or detecting the hidden message in a spoken message. Together, a person's body language and metacommunication can reveal much about how they truly feel, and this can be useful in a variety of situations, for example, in everyday conversations, phone calls, meetings, presentations, evaluations and negotiations.

Thus, if a boss praises an employee's work, but the boss' arms are crossed, his or her tone is flat, voice soft, and face expressionless, the boss is signaling that he or she is not at all enthusiastic about the employee's work. The boss might not be aware that there's a disconnect between his or her words and actions, but the employee certainly is. The employee may not show it, but he or she is annoyed, angry or hurt by the boss's actual indifference.

Then again, there are times when a person's words and body language are in alignment. A team leader says she's excited to tell members of her team that they will receive a 10% bonus for exceeding their goals, and the team can see that she's excited.

CROSS-CULTURAL COMMUNICATION

As a management accountant, you may work in your home country with people who have relocated from other countries. In addition, you may communicate with people in your company who are located abroad. On the other hand, maybe you are working, or have worked, at one of your company's offices in another country. In an increasingly global business environment, you will communicate more and more with people from other cultures and to communicate effectively, you need to understand and appreciate their cultures. This section offers some general considerations to keep in mind when communicating across cultures.

In every culture, first impressions matter, and being able to properly greet and introduce people of other cultures can make a favourable impression on them. For example, 'How are you?' is a perfunctory greeting in the United States. In other cultures, it is taken seriously. In Mexico, if someone asks, 'How are you?' they really want to know.[19] In the United States, people usually exchange business cards only if they expect to communicate later. In Japan, business cards are exchanged at every opportunity, and the exchange follows a formal protocol. For example, Japanese treat business cards with respect, and writing on a card is not acceptable.

One fundamental cultural difference that can greatly affect communication is whether a person comes from an individualist or collectivist culture. People who identify with the cultures of the United States, Canada, and the United Kingdom see themselves mainly as individuals who pursue their own goals. If you need help, a person from an individualist culture may decide whether to assist you based on what you've done for them in the past. People in the cultures of China, Japan, Korea and Mexico tend to see themselves as part of wide social groups that pursue collective goals. If you need help in these collectivist cultures, having a relationship with others in a social group, especially someone in authority, may make a difference.[20]

When working with colleagues from different cultures, be aware that your differences in experience may lead to unintentional misinterpretations of each other's actions. Young Americans who have gone to China to work in recent years come from a society where directness and openness is part of the culture. But that directness can be seen by Chinese workers as rude and overbearing.[21] Young Chinese workers were brought up in a society where deference to authority and indirect ways of expressing opinions are the norm. But to Americans, they can be seen as indecisive. The differences can lead to misunderstandings in the workplace, but these can be resolved through mutual efforts at understanding cultural differences. In some societies such as the United States, people are encouraged to deal directly with conflict through face-to-face meetings and other ways to resolve differences. By contrast, open conflict is considered embarrassing or demeaning in many Eastern countries, and differences are resolved quietly.[22]

Multicultural teams are common in global business. Remember to be sensitive to cultural differences when working in teams, as well as one-on-one. On teams consisting mainly of Western managers or employees, team members from non-Western cultures can have difficulty participating. Team members from China are used to discussions in which the boss speaks and others politely wait their turn, and they may be reluctant to jump into the free-for-all discussions of Western colleagues. While they may see this as the mark of a team player, others on the team may see them as unwilling to contribute.[23]

One of the largest and most obvious barriers to cross-cultural communication is language. English is the language of global business, and more people are learning English as a second language. Proficiencies vary, and you have to be sensitive to this when speaking or listening to non-native speakers. Pay close attention when listening. Speak slowly and in short sentences. Enunciate clearly. Chris Rogers, vice president, Finance and Administration, of Infragistics Inc., a global software company, says that while travelling in other countries, 'Above all, you must listen. It shows respect and a willingness to learn. And you will learn from listening and observing.' (See interview 10 with Rogers in appendix A.)

In many cultures, it takes time to build relationships and trust and get things done—more time than you may be accustomed to. But patience can be rewarded with new connections, deeper relationships, and new insights into other cultures.[24] This section covered only a fraction of what you need to know when interacting with other cultures in a business setting. There is much more to learn. Andrew Harding, FCMA, CGMA, managing director of the Chartered Institute of Management Accountants (CIMA), says, 'To work globally, you must always be open to learning. It requires focus and hard work, and you will never stop learning.' (See interview 9 with Harding in appendix A.)

CHAPTER SUMMARY

- Your skill in communicating will determine, to a considerable degree, whether you get a job, advance in your organisation, and find the career opportunities you want.

- You will have to develop the ability to communicate in a variety of ways: reporting, persuading, directing, training, motivating and much more.

- Don't fail to work on your listening skills. They are as important to communicating as your writing and speaking skills.

- If you demonstrate an ability to explain complex topics in simple terms, you will be highly valued in your company.

- Acquiring strong communication skills requires focus, discipline and hard work, but these skills are essential to your career success.

- In an increasingly global business environment, you need to learn how to communicate with people of different cultures and have the dedication to keep on learning. It's a life-long process.

Endnotes

1 Louis Grumet, 'Quantity Over Quality: How to Improve Accounting Education,' *The CPA Journal*, Jan. 2007 www.nysscpa.org/cpajournal/2007/107/perspectives/p7.htm

2 Neil Wolstenholme and Simon Bennett, 'Sharpening an FD's soft skills,' *Financial Director*, Jan. 2012 www.financialdirector.co.uk/financial-director/feature/2142534/sharpening-fds-soft-skills

3 David Bolchover, 'Plugging the skills gap: Shortages among plenty,' *The Economist*, Economist Intelligence Unit, 2012 www.managementthinking.eiu.com/sites/default/files/downloads/EIU_SuccessFactor.pdf

4 Claire B. May and Gordon S. May, *Effective Writing: A Handbook for Accountants*, Ninth edition (Upper Saddle River, New Jersey: Prentice Hall, 2012).

5 Kristyn Schiavone, 'Hone Your Business Communication Skills,' *Chicago Tribune*, 4 Aug. 2012 www.chicagotribune.com/classified/jobs/chi-business-communication-skills-20120804,0,5670679.story

6 Kyle Wiens, 'I Won't Hire People Who Use Poor Grammar. Here's Why,' *Harvard Business Review*, Jul. 2012 http://blogs.hbr.org/cs/2012/07/i_wont_hire_people_who_use_poo.html

7 Sue Shellenbarger, 'This Embarrasses You and I,' *The Wall Street Journal*, 19 Jun. 2012 http://online.wsj.com/article/SB10001424052702303410404577466662919275448.html

8 'From ledgers to leadership: A journey through the finance function,' Chapter two: the competencies required of finance professionals, CGMA.org www.cgma.org/Resources/Reports/Pages/ledgers-to-leadership.aspx

9 Carol M. Lehman and Debbie D. DuFrene, *Business Communication*, 15th edition, (Mason, OH: Thomson South-Western, 2008).

10 Roger Yu, 'More Companies Quit Blogging, Focus on Facebook Instead,' *USA Today*, 20 Apr. 2012 http://usatoday30.usatoday.com/tech/news/story/2012-04-19/corporate-blogging/54419982/1

11 Mary Munter, *Guide to Managerial Communication: Effective Business Writing and Speaking*, Ninth edition (Upper Saddle River, NJ: Prentice Hall, 2012).

12 Gerald J. Alfred, Charles T. Brusaw and Walter E. Oliu, *The Business Writer's Handbook*, Tenth edition, (New York: Bedford/St. Martin's, 2011).

13 Henning Mankell, 'The Art of Listening,' *The New York Times*, 10 Dec. 2011 www.nytimes.com/2011/12/11/opinion/sunday/in-africa-the-art-of-listening.html

14 Ram Charan, 'The Discipline of Listening,' *Harvard Business Review*, Jun. 2012 http://blogs.hbr.org/cs/2012/06/the_discipline_of_listening.html

15 'Empath, The; Star Trek: the Original Series,' 6 Dec. 1968 www.startrek.com/database_article/empath-the

16 Sarah Stevens, 'Doing Business Better—Critical Communication Skills,' Oregon Society of CPAs [website]. Stevens is Human Resources Consultant, AmeriBen/IEC Group. https://secure.orcpa.org/about/doing_business_better/3/1229-critical_communication_skills.

17 'A Plain English Handbook, How to create clear SEC disclosure documents,' U.S. Securities and Exchange Commission, Office of Investor Education and Assistance [website], Aug. 1998 www.sec.gov/pdf/handbook.pdf

18 Joe Navarro with Marvin Karlins, Ph.D., *What Every Body is Saying*, (New York: HarperCollins Publishers, 2008).

19 Jeanette S. Martin, Lillian H. Cheney, 'Communication Skills Needed for Successful Integration With America's Largest Trading Partners,' Association for Business Communication [website] http://businesscommunication.org/wp-content/uploads/2011/04/PABC-2009-03-MartinandChaney.pdf

20 Steve Martin, 'Being Persuasive Across Cultural Divides,' *Harvard Business Review*, 7 Dec. 2010 http://blogs.hbr.org/cs/2010/12/being_persuasive_across_cultur.html

21 Hannah Seligson, 'For American Workers in China, A Culture Clash,' *The New York Times*, 23 Dec. 2009 www.nytimes.com/2009/12/24/business/global/24chinawork.html?_r=0

Endnotes Continued

22 Marcelle E. DuPraw and Marya Axner, 'AMPU Guide: Working on Common Cross-cultural Communication Challenges,' PBS.org [website] www.pbs.org/ampu/crosscult.html

23 Andy Molinsky, 'Leveling the Playing Field on Cross-Cultural Teams,' HBR Blog Network [website], Apr. 2012 http://blogs.hbr.org/cs/2012/04/leveling_the_playing_field_on.html

24 David Livermore, 'How impatience undermines cross cultural effectiveness,' management-issues. com [website], Jun. 2012 www.management-issues.com/2012/6/19/opinion/how-impatience-undermines-cross-cultural-effectiveness.asp

4

COMMUNICATING IN THE WORKPLACE

Communication is such a large part of your workday as a management accountant that you may not notice the many ways and how many times during the day you communicate. You stop a colleague in the hall to ask about the status of a project. You e-mail the draft of a report to a company manager in another city to review. The CFO asks you to join a meeting on developing a social media policy for the company. Throughout the day, you communicate with people inside and sometimes outside of your organisation. But that is just the beginning.

This chapter expands upon the list of the different forms of communication in chapter 3 and offers suggestions about how management accountants can communicate more effectively in the workplace.

FACE-TO-FACE COMMUNICATION

In today's world, people are increasingly using technology as a substitute for personal communication. More time is spent on e-mails, texting, web postings and social networks and less on conversing in person. 'We live in a technological universe in which we are always communicating,' says a *New York Times* article. 'And yet we have sacrificed conversation for mere connection.'[1]

As methods of communication proliferate, more people are gravitating towards impersonal methods of contact. According to the Pew Research Center's Internet & American Life Project, some 83% of American adults own cell phones, and almost three-quarters of them (73%) send and receive text messages.[2] The Center asked those text users in a survey how they prefer to be contacted on their cell phone. The response: 31% said they preferred texts to talking on the phone, while 53% said they preferred a phone call to a text message. Heavy text users are much more likely to prefer texting to talking. Perhaps not surprisingly, the survey found that young adults are the most avid text users by a wide margin.

The rise of texting concerns some communication experts. They believe people should have the ability to text and talk—and to know when to use each skill. Face-to-face communication and the ability to engage in direct conversations are essential to success in personal relationships and the workplace.[3] Furthermore, conversational skills are crucial in meeting people at networking events and other venues, developing relationships and building a network of colleagues, friends, advisers and mentors.

Don't neglect the development of your conversational skills. It may seem more convenient to send an e-mail or leave a voicemail for someone, but don't forget the benefit of face-to-face conversations. You may recall from the previous chapter that nonverbal and metacommunication can reveal a person's true feelings behind their words. You will miss these clues unless you have a face-to-face conversation. When communicating face-to-face in a business setting, try to remember the tips presented in the following list:

- *Be clear in expressing yourself.* If your conversation is muddled or confusing, your listeners will stop paying attention, and they may question whether you have the ability to think clearly and communicate effectively.

- *Be concise.* In conversing, as in writing, use the fewest amount of words necessary to communicate. Your listeners will appreciate your ability to get to the point.

- *Listen.* Don't dominate the conversation, as some people tend to do. Listen to the other person, and make an effort to understand them. (See the discussion of listening in chapter 3.)

- *Show confidence.* Show self-confidence through your body language, eye contact and tone of voice.

- *Engage people.* People will warm to you if you are engaging, friendly and attentive.

- *Be sincere.* Build trust with your listeners. Show that you are sincere, genuine, and caring.

- *Think first.* Don't blurt out something you wish you could take back later. Pause for a moment to think before you respond.

- *Know how to network.* If you are attending a networking event, think about whom you want to meet, how to get introduced (such as through a mutual friend attending the event), what to say when meeting someone for the first time, and how to arrange for future conversations with people you want to follow up with.

- *Speak up.* If you have an issue with your boss, a problem with a co-worker or a concern about a colleague, say what's on your mind, and listen to what they have to say. The conversation could be difficult, and perhaps awkward, but you can clear the air, prevent misunderstandings and maintain good relationships.

TEAM COMMUNICATION

Communicating with and leading a team are common challenges in business. From your school days to your current stage in your career, you probably have worked previously on a team, with varying degrees of success. You may have joined a team that worked on a specific project and then disbanded and other teams that worked on multiple projects together. Perhaps you have already been the leader of a team. What your experience may have taught you is that a team's success depends on strong communication amongst team members and between the team and others in the organisation. The better the communication, the better the team.

Two factors that will help drive improved team communication are a shared vision and shared sense of responsibility. First, the team should share a vision and know how to achieve that vision. For example, a team may be asked to suggest ideas for research projects to develop new product lines. This fits into the company's larger purpose of investing in research and development that will result in product innovations, generate new sales and increase market share. The vision is product innovation; research projects are a means to realise that vision. Team members should agree on how they will contribute and help one another. If team members feel that responsibility is equally shared and everyone is contributing, they will be able to work together towards a common goal.

Here are some other suggestions for maintaining communication amongst team members:

- *Be transparent.* Team members must be open and honest in their communications with one another. Transparency is built on trust. The leader should take the initiative in developing strong relationships with each member of the team and encourage team members to do likewise. When team members understand one another and appreciate what each member of the team has to offer, they will feel more comfortable working together.

- *Show appreciation.* The team leader should show appreciation for the accomplishments of individual members. But the leader should know when praise is truly deserved—routine praise might not mean much. Conversely, withholding praise may make team members feel they are not appreciated or even not deserving of praise. Judicious use of praise can do much to inspire and motivate people.

- *Provide criticism privately.* By providing constructive criticism, a team leader can help a team member to realise their mistakes and how to correct them. But this criticism should be given in private, not in front of other members of the team. Every member of the team, including the leader, should be prepared to listen to, and act upon, constructive criticism.

- *Have a process to resolve conflicts.* The team should agree on a process for resolving the conflicts that inevitably will arise. This includes acknowledging the conflict (rather than allowing it to fester), discussing how it is hindering the team from achieving its goal, and having team members give their point of view about the issue that is causing the conflict, as well as their reasoning to support their viewpoint. Once the views of individual members are clear, the team can decide how to resolve the conflict. Not everyone may be happy with the solution, and the leader may need to talk to them and let them air their differences. Then, the leader can try to persuade them to set their differences aside in the interests of the team. This may not be easy, but the team must move on.

- *Share praise.* If management praises the leader for the team's progress towards achieving a goal, the leader should share that praise with team members. The leader may have been praised, but success would not have been possible without the efforts of the entire team.

- *Recognise that good ideas can come from anyone.* Anyone, from the most junior to the most senior member of the team, can come up with ideas to help the team accomplish its goal. And that means the team leader and members must be receptive to ideas regardless of who suggests them. Otherwise, important ideas could be ignored.

You may find that as a team, you are called upon to make a presentation or write a report upon completion of a project. The specifics of writing a report and making a presentation will be discussed in chapters 5–8. However, if you will be completing these tasks as a team, you may want to keep in mind these few additional considerations:

- *Prepare as a team, not as individuals.* The team should agree on the content, structure and organisation of the presentation. It should decide which team members will create and present the sections of the presentation within the overall framework. This process will help to ensure a structured, organised and seamless presentation. Otherwise, if team members worked on their presentations independently, the result could be a patchwork of individual presentations that do not fit well together.

- *Plan delivery of the presentation.* The team should agree on who will introduce the presentation and preview the speakers and their topics, the sequence of speakers, what speakers will say in transitioning to the next speaker, and how the final speaker will conclude the presentation.

- *Rehearse.* As with any presentation, the team will need to practise several times until it is comfortable delivering the presentation. It may ask observers to evaluate the presentation.

MEETINGS

As a management accountant, you will attend and host many meetings throughout your career. Meetings can be time consuming. But if they produce results, the time was well spent. So if you're organising a meeting, how can you ensure that you and the other participants will get the most value from it? The following list offers some tips on what to do before, during and after hosting a successful meeting:

- *Have a purpose.* Do you want advice or a decision from meeting participants? Help in framing a problem and defining a solution? Be clear in your own mind about your purpose, and then you can decide whether a meeting is the best way to accomplish your goal.

- *Consider alternatives.* Do you have to meet? Maybe you could accomplish your goal more easily and efficiently by communicating with others by phone, e-mail, a memo or letter, or speaking to them individually. If you simply want to provide information, a meeting may not be necessary. Instead, you could send a memo or report to those who would have attended. If you need a consensus on a course of action, then a meeting may be necessary.

- *Choose appropriate attendees.* Who really needs to attend the meeting? How can they contribute? Some participants may have special expertise in the topic under discussion. Others may be enablers, such as senior managers who have the power to move ideas forward. Some with excellent analytical skills may help to crystallise thinking about a question or issue.

- *Preview.* A day or two before the meeting, inform the participants of its purpose, the agenda, who is responsible for presenting items on the agenda, the time allotted for discussion of each agenda item, and the expected outcome. To encourage participation, consider giving every participant an assignment, for example, several participants might collaborate on addressing a topic, and select someone to do the presentation. Ask the participants to prepare for the meeting, for example, by reading background material you provide or offering topical suggestions.

- *Pick the venue.* Check the meeting room to make sure it is clean, comfortable and conducive to a meeting. Arrange for food and refreshments as appropriate, eg, if the meeting is expected to run several hours or during lunch.

- *Keep a record.* Arrange for someone to take notes at the meeting. Have them prepare a summary of key points discussed and follow-up responsibilities. Use this information to prepare a meeting report for participants and other interested parties.

- *Start on time.* Start on time regardless of whether everyone is present. If someone arrives late, you can tell them what they missed after the meeting is over. If someone cannot attend but should, let them know that decisions may be made without them. Then, they can decide whether it's more important to them to attend the meeting or attend to something else. Incidentally, if you consistently start on time, participants will know that they won't waste time waiting for the meeting to start, and they are more likely to show up on time.

- *Stay focused.* At the start of the meeting, briefly review the agenda, who will speak on a topic, and the expected results of the meeting. Concentrate on getting through the agenda on schedule. You might ask someone to be a timekeeper. If someone wants to discuss something that wasn't on the agenda, thank them for the suggestion, but note that there isn't time for a discussion. Ask the group if the topic can be discussed at another meeting or later by e-mail or phone.

- *Be clear and succinct.* Speak succinctly and to the point. Be clear in your statements. If someone starts to ramble or is confusing, try to help them focus by asking questions or politely restating what they said.

- *Encourage participation.* Encourage open, constructive discussion and debate. Try to get everyone involved. If someone is holding back, ask them questions to draw out their thoughts. If someone asks you a question, paraphrase and repeat the question before answering. This shows you want to be sure you understand the question. Thank people for their comments, ideas and insights.

- *Engage everyone.* While speaking, look around the room or conference table, maintain eye contact, and engage everyone. If someone asks you a question, don't stay focused on them. Address everyone else.

- *Listen.* Use your listening skills. Listen to other people, and try to understand their point of view. Be attuned to their expectations and concerns. Don't dismiss their ideas outright. Hear them out, even if you disagree with them. If everyone feels like they've been heard, you are more likely to reach a consensus on a course of action.

- *Pay attention to your body language.* Your facial expression, posture and other body language communicate your feelings more powerfully than what you're saying (refer to the discussion of body language and metacommunication in chapter 3). If you're angry, participants will realise this even if you're speaking in an even tone. If you're happy, they'll know. Pay attention to your body language and the non-verbal signals you're communicating.

- *Finish on time.* If you are disciplined about keeping the meeting on schedule, and participants are cooperating, the meeting will finish on time. Participants will appreciate this, and they will be more comfortable knowing that your meetings will run on time and not waste their time.

- *Follow up.* At the close of the meeting, summarise what was discussed. Get the agreement of the participants on follow-up actions to be taken, the deadlines, and who is responsible. Ask the participants for feedback on the meeting itself. Was it run efficiently? Did they feel like they were actively participating? Did they have the chance to express their opinions?

WRITTEN COMMUNICATIONS

Many of the techniques used for writing reports that are discussed in chapters 5 and 6 can be applied to writing any kind of document. In this section, we will discuss some of the most common types of written communications that are used in business on a daily basis: e-mails, instant messaging, texting, memos and letters. During your career, you may also be called upon to write longer communications.

E-mails

Before you finish reading this sentence, another e-mail could hit your inbox. Soon to be followed by another. And another. Receiving, reading, sending, responding to and organising a constant stream of e-mails can consume valuable minutes or hours of your day.

So, how can you efficiently manage your e-mail?

Receiving E-mails

Making a schedule can help you manage your time spent reading e-mails so that it does not take over your workday. E-mail can be addictive. People fall into the habit of constantly checking their e-mails. They divert their attention from a conversation, a meeting, a conference, an afternoon in the park, or walking across the street in rush hour traffic to see what's in their inbox. 'When we don't control our e-mail, we are controlled by it,' writes Peter Bergman.[4] He suggests scheduling specific times to check e-mail. For example, check your inbox three times a day: first thing in the morning, at midday, and just before finishing work. Otherwise, leave your e-mail alone. That may be hard to do at first, but by practising e-mail discipline, you'll manage your e-mail more efficiently, be less distracted by it, and focus on productive work. And, after work, you can focus on your personal life. Use an autoreply function to let people know when you'll next be checking your e-mail. If someone needs to reach you immediately, he or she can call or text.

Acting on e-mails decisively can also help save you time when checking e-mail. Decide immediately whether to delete, reply to, act upon or file an e-mail in a folder for later action. Don't procrastinate, otherwise, the next time you open your e-mail file, the same e-mail will be there, and, you still have to decide what to do with it. If a sender asks you to take some action, such as completing a report by a certain date, let the sender know whether you can or whether you may need more time.

Composing E-mails

When composing an e-mail, you will want to prepare and plan just as you would for any other type of business communication. Knowing your purpose and audience will help you to write an appropriate, suitable communication that reflects good business practice.

Before you write an e-mail, think about why you want to send it. What is your purpose? It may be to inform, for example, by sharing a document with your team. Or, it may be to ask a question, for example, asking to meet with a line manager to discuss an accounting issue. Or, it may be to ask the receiver(s) to take action, such as asking your team to complete a project by a certain deadline. Always be clear about your reasons for sending an e-mail.

Along with your purpose, you should have a clear understanding of who should receive your e-mail. Primary recipients might be members of your team, a business line manager, a management accountant in your department, or others inside or outside of your organisation. You may copy others who you think would like to be informed or have asked to be kept informed. For example, you could copy your supervisor on messages to your team—perhaps not every routine message—but those that might interest your supervisor, such as a progress report on a project. Send e-mails to groups of people only if they will find the information useful. People will be annoyed by e-mails that don't concern them.

Salutation

Begin your e-mail with the name of the recipient or 'Dear' and the person's name ('Dear Mr Smith,' or 'Dear Miss Johnson'). Once you have established a relationship, you could use the informal 'Hello' or 'Hi.' But do what your recipient does. If your recipient stays with the formal 'Dear,' do likewise. If your recipient finds an informal 'Hello' acceptable, then you can use it.

Subject Line

Recipients are hurriedly skimming through what could be a large number of e-mails. Write a subject line that will catch their attention. Succinctly state your purpose, and be specific. 'Project deadline' is too general. 'Project deadline Oct. 20 at 9am' is specific. 'Request meeting' is too general. 'Request meeting re: how to improve accounting for inventory' is specific. If you have multiple subjects to discuss, create a separate e-mail for each subject. Don't try to cover more than one subject in an e-mail.

E-mail Body (Message)

Recipients do not have the time or patience to read a long e-mail. E-mails should be short, and no more than a few paragraphs. Explain why you are sending the e-mail and what you want from the recipients. For example, you write an e-mail proposing a project to your supervisor or others in your organisation. You briefly explain the project, the reasons for the project, and its value to the company. You conclude by requesting a meeting with the recipients to discuss your proposal in more detail.

To be sure, there may be times when you need to write a long e-mail. In that case, write a summary and then go into the details. Use paragraph headings, bullet points, boldface, italics, and other tools to facilitate reading and emphasise important points. Alternatively, you could write a summary in the e-mail and provide the details in an attached memo.

Signature

Conclude with standard sign-offs, such as 'Regards' or 'Best Wishes' but not 'Cheers' because receivers may view it as inappropriate. In addition to your name, include your mailing address, phone numbers and web address in your signature.

Sending E-mails

Because of the informality of e-mails and the speed (sometimes the haste) with which they are written, it is easy to fall into the habit of careless writing. Use correct grammar, punctuation and spelling. Use sentence case: capitalise only the first letter of the first word in a sentence. Don't use devices such as coloured text, emoticons or special formatting that some recipients may consider unprofessional. Your e-mail should be clear, concise, direct and easily understood by the recipient(s). E-mails that are wordy, ambiguous and confusing could be ignored or misunderstood.

Assume your e-mails are not private. Your company may have a policy that company e-mail accounts are company property, which can be monitored, retrieved and examined at any time. You or a recipient could hit the 'reply all' button by mistake, forward your e-mail to the wrong person, or accidently include someone in the 'cc' or 'bcc' line. See box 4-1 for a discussion of how to use the 'bcc' feature. Because you can't avoid or predict these situations, never write something in an e-mail that you would be embarrassed to have read by an unintended recipient. Demonstrate your professionalism and ability to communicate effectively by the quality of your e-mails.

Box 4-1: About Bcc:

Bcc: (blind carbon copy): You can use 'bcc:' to send copies of your e-mail to recipients without your primary receiver knowing you did so. The bcc: recipients see the e-mail address of the primary recipient but not those of the other bcc: recipients. This protects the privacy of the bcc: recipients. If you had, instead, copied (cc:) them, their e-mail addresses would have been disclosed. If you wanted to protect the e-mail address of the primary recipient as well, you could bcc: that recipient, and send the message to yourself. Only your e-mail address would be public.

Bcc: also is useful in copying large numbers of people. If you had used cc:, you would have had a long and cumbersome list of e-mail addresses. Furthermore, the cc: list could be exposed to spammers and hackers.

Be extremely cautious in using bcc: It should not be used to share confidential information with someone without the knowledge of the primary recipient or to criticise someone without their knowledge.

Never click 'send' in a moment of anger or frustration. Careless use of e-mail could undermine your reputation as a responsible, trustworthy professional. It could have serious consequences. Your employer might call on you to account for violating company policies and procedures for use of e-mail. You could undermine important business relationships, hurt your chances for advancement, put your job at risk, or even expose you and your company to legal liability. Bottom line: Pay close attention to what you write.

Also keep in mind that e-mail is not a substitute for direct communication. Suppose you're angry with a colleague about an issue, such as how to manage project. You send them an e-mail that is highly critical of them. This is a way of avoiding a disagreeable exchange that could result from face-to-face communication or talking by phone. Even a well-worded, grammatically correct e-mail, in this instance, shows a lack of professional courtesy, and it could undermine a business relationship. Hiding behind e-mail can be seen as lacking in professional judgment and the ability to communicate appropriately.

Instant Messaging and Text Messaging

Instant messaging (IM) is the instant transmission of text messages over the Internet via computer, cell phone, or other transmission device. Many businesses are finding that IM is a convenient way to chat with other users without the disruption of a phone call. Senders and receivers must be online, although some IM services allow for messages to be delivered to receivers who are offline. IM can also be used to share files, web links, images and streaming content. Depending on the IM service, IM may include video calling features, voice over IP (Internet Protocol) and web conferencing services. Some social media services offer instant messaging features, one example being Facebook Chat.

In business, IM is attractive because it works in real time. It is flexible, allowing for conversation amongst different individuals or groups of people, such as between companies and customers and clients or amongst members of a team. Some companies use Enterprise Instant Messaging systems for internal communication amongst managers and employees. Some systems include gateways that allow communication with external IM users.

Text messaging (texting) is the typing and sending of text messages via cell phone or other mobile device. The messages may include video, images and sound content. In business, managers and employees use texting to quickly communicate with customers or clients or with others in the company; communicate company news, such as a new product or service; schedule meetings; and for instant reminders. Texting also can be used for communication in emergencies. Because the number of characters that can be seen on a cell phone screen is limited, texting has given rise to an entire vocabulary of acronyms.

As with other forms of online communication, IM and texting have their risks. They may expose a company to security risks, such as from hacking, viruses or the inadvertent sending of a message to a wrong party. They may create legal liabilities for a company, such as during disputes between a company and a client. They also could result in a loss of productivity if employees waste a lot of time on personal messaging and texting.

Memorandums

Memorandums, or memos, are informal communications within organisations. They are used for a variety of purposes, for example, to announce a policy, a signing of a major client or contract, manager and employee news, to provide instructions, to request information, and much more. A memo may be transmitted via e-mail and in most offices, e-mails have taken the place of traditional memos. However, hard copy memos have certain advantages, especially if they contain sensitive information that should not be stored online. Memos can be distributed widely (in addition to the designated recipients), and they be used as a physical record of communication. You can file memos that you sent or received for future reference, for example, to have a record of your performance in your current position.

As with all writing, you should be clear about your purpose in writing a memo, your audience, and what action, if any, you want the recipients to take. Your memo should be clear, concise, brief, well-organised, accurate and grammatically correct.

A standard memo format is the title of the company at the top of the page, the word 'Memorandum' below the company name, and the date, To, From, Subject, body of the text, and, if necessary, cc: and attachments (or enclosures).

XYZ COMPANY
MEMORANDUM

Date:

To:

From:

Subject:

Text (body of the memo)

cc:

Attachments (or Enclosures)

Many organisations have guidelines for writing memos and other documents, and a company's format for a memo may differ from this standard. (If your company does not have a standard, there are various software programmes for writing memos and letters that are available on the market, and Microsoft has templates that can be downloaded.) As shown below, 'Date' may be located after 'From.' Some companies ask the sender to initial or sign a printed memo to confirm that the sender is responsible for the memo. If the memo is sent electronically, it is not initialled or signed.

XYZ COMPANY
MEMORANDUM

To:

From:

Date:

Subject:

Text (body of the memo)

The memo usually begins with a statement of its purpose in one or two sentences, so the reader knows why you are writing. For example, a memo from the CFO might begin: 'Are you available to meet Friday at 10am with me and members of the finance team? The purpose is to discuss the team's progress in developing a system to more effectively manage the company's inventory.'

Like all writing, a memo should be clear and concise. Use headings and bullet points to help organise your memo and make it easier to read and understand. Include a conclusion if you wish to summarise key points or make a request.

The following is an example of a memo:

XYZ COMPANY
MEMORANDUM

Date: January 14, 2012

To: Robert Reed

From: Wendy Wright

Subject: Move to our new corporate headquarters to begin February 8.

Construction of our new corporate headquarters in downtown Pretoria will be completed February 1. Our company's move from our current headquarters will begin February 8.

A plan for the move is attached, including the schedule for your department's move February 10 between 9am and 6pm.

Could you please review the schedule and let me know by January 21 whether your department can move as planned? If you anticipate a delay for whatever reason, we can discuss this on the 21st.

I appreciate the thought and effort that you and your department have put into the planning of the move, and I will be happy to assist you in addressing any problems with relocating.

cc: Patrick Penn, Sandra Scribe

Attachments: Moving plan with department schedule

If the memo continues to the second page, put the name of the person to whom the memo is sent flush with the left margin, the page number in the centre, and the date in the right margin.

Memos can be printed and delivered by hand or mail, or they may be sent as attachments to e-mails.

Letters

Companies use letters to communicate with external parties, such as clients or customers, investors, creditors, suppliers or government regulators. In contrast to the informality of e-mail or instant messaging, letters create an image of authority and formality, and recipients may give them closer attention than e-mails. Letters can be printed and mailed or sent electronically.

Like memos, letters have a commonly used format: company letterhead at the top, including address, phone and fax numbers, e-mail and website; date, recipient's name and address, salutation, body, closing, signature, and other information, such as 'cc' list, enclosures, etc. Your company may prescribe a different format for a letter or have a standard template you can use.

The following is an example of a letter:

Balderdash Boilers Corporation

110 Vesuvius Avenue

Melbourne Victoria 3000

Australia

Phone: + 61 1 2345 6789

Fax: + 61 9 8765 4321

Email: balderdash@boom.com.au

www.balderdash.com.au

March 21, 2012

Mr. Brandon Burns

Burns Manufacturing Company

3 Arden Street

Hawthorn, Victoria 3322

Australia

Dear Mr. Burns:

This is to confirm that I will meet you at 9am on April 1 at your office to discuss replacing the boiler in your manufacturing plant.

As we agreed on our last phone call, I will do a presentation of different types of boilers that would meet your specifications. We can then discuss which boiler would best meet your needs.

I look forward to meeting with you on April 1. In the meantime, if I can answer any questions, please phone or e-mail me.

Sincerely yours,

Andrew Ashe

President

The same advice for memos and other written communications applies to letters. You should give thought to your reasons for writing a letter, your audience, your content and what action you want readers to take. Your writing is a reflection on you and your company, so give care to the drafting of letters. The next chapter gives some helpful advice for outlining and planning for any communication that you have to write.

PHONE

Although e-mail use has exploded, the telephone has not lost its value as a communication tool, and you should consider when to use the phone instead of e-mail or IM. Unlike e-mail, the phone provides instantaneous two-way communication without the hassle of typing. The phone can be faster means than e-mail for solving problems, discussing issues or identifying business opportunities because there is no waiting for a response. Unlike IM and e-mail, you can hear the tone of the other person's voice on the phone. Furthermore, the person you're communicating with may prefer that you use the phone, especially if you are exchanging sensitive information.[5] If a record of the call is desired, the call can be recorded or someone can takes notes, and a summary can be e-mailed to those on the call.

Voicemail is a useful tool for exchanging messages without the need to try and reach someone directly on the phone. To use voicemail efficiently, follow a protocol. Ensure that your greeting provides current information about your status, for example, whether you will be out of your office for the day or several days. Ask callers to leave a message including their name, organisation, contact information, and what they want and when. When leaving a message for someone else, make sure you, in turn, provide your contact information that tells callers the best way to reach you (in addition to leaving a recorded message). This could include your cell phone number, e-mail address and fax number.

CHAPTER SUMMARY

- Conversational skills are essential when meeting people at networking events and other venues, developing relationships, and building a network of professional colleagues, friends, advisers and mentors.

- Your e-mails, like all your communications, are a reflection on you. Demonstrate your professionalism and ability to communicate effectively by the quality of your e-mails.

- Use proper formatting when composing memos and letters.

Endnotes

1 Sherry Turkle, 'The Flight From Conversation,'
   The New York Times, 21 Apr. 2012 www.nytimes.
   com/2012/04/22/opinion/sunday/the-flight-from-
   conversation.html?pagewanted=all

2 Aaron Smith, 'Americans and Text Messaging,' Pew
   Internet & American Life Project [website], 19 Sept.
   2011 http://pewinternet.org/Reports/2011/Cell-
   Phone-Texting-2011.aspx

3 Martha Irvine, 'Is Texting Ruining the Art of
   Conversation?' *Bloomberg BusinessWeek*, Jun. 2012
   www.businessweek.com/ap/2012-06/D9V6AU682.
   htm

4 Peter Bergman, 'Coping With Email Overload,' HBR
   Blog Network [website], 26 Apr. 2012 http://blogs.hbr.
   org/bregman/2012/04/coping-with-email-overload.
   html

5 Michael Hess, 'When you should pick up the phone, and
   why,' *Moneywatch*, Mar. 2012 www.cbsnews.com/8301-
   505143_162-57399601/when-you-should-pick-up-the-
   phone-and-why/

5

WRITE FROM THE START

'Writing is easy,' Gene Fowler, Oscar-winning writer and director, once said. 'All you do is sit staring at a blank sheet of paper until drops of blood form on your forehead.' If you've ever stared at a blank page on a computer screen, you may know the feeling and the procrastinating that comes with it. This chapter is about how to go from a blank screen to writing a report or other communication. Both this chapter and chapter 6 focus specifically on writing reports to explain the writing process, but the same techniques can be applied to whatever communication you are writing.

PREPARING TO WRITE

You may think you are ready to put pen to paper or fingers to keys, but the best way to begin writing is to think and prepare. In his book, William Zinsser observes, 'All writing is ultimately a question of solving a problem. It may be a problem of where to obtain facts or how to organise the material. It may be a problem of approach or attitude, tone or style. Whatever it is, it has to be confronted and solved.'[1]

Solving a problem? That's what management accountants do: solve problems. Every day, someone in an organisation—a supervisor, a colleague, the head of a company—asks them to help solve problems. You can apply the same problem-solving strategies you use as a management accountant to solving the problem of writing. Start with a list of questions to consider with every writing project, large or small. This is not to suggest that writing is formulaic, but a list can help you to get organised and take a consistent approach to writing. Box 5-1 walks you through a list of questions and potential answers to consider as you prepare to write your business communication. You can refer back to it whenever you start a new project or need some guidance. The next sections walk you through the steps outlined in box 5-1.

Box 5-1: Writing: Questions to Consider

| 1. What is the purpose of the communication? | • Collaborate
• Consult
• Direct
• Educate
• Evaluate
• Inform
• Influence
• Innovate
• Market or sell
• Motivate
• Negotiate
• Persuade
• Recruit
• Report
• Request
• Solve problem
• Other | 3. Who is the audience? | • Board of directors
• Senior executives
  ◦ CEO
  ◦ CFO
  ◦ CIO
  ◦ Chief accounting officer
  ◦ Other
• Managers
  ◦ Operations: departments, divisions, units
  ◦ Service: finance, accounting, marketing, human resources, purchasing, other
• Supervisors
• Employees
• Co-workers
• Team members
• Customers and clients
• Shareholders and investors
• Suppliers and vendors
• Regulators
• Media
• Public
• Other |
| 2. What is the subject? | • Strategic
• Management
• Operations
• People
• Finance
• Accounting
• Technology
• Administrative
• Logistic
• Legal
• Other | | |

4.	What do you need to know about the audience?	• What is your relationship to the audience? • What does the audience know, or want to know, about you? • Who is the primary audience? The secondary audience? • How informed is the audience on the subject of the communication? • What are the characteristics of the audience? • How is the audience likely to react to the communication? • What action do you want the audience to take?

5.	Who is the author of the communication?	You? Or someone else?
6.	What is the timing?	When is the right time to deliver the communication?
7.	What is the form of communication?	• E-mail • Instant message • Text message • Memo • Letter • Fax • Presentation • Report • Blog • Web content • Social media • Webcasts and webinars

Purpose

Why are you writing your business communication? As shown in question 1 in box 5-1, there could be a variety of reasons. Regardless of the purpose, another way to look at why you are writing a report may be better considered as a means to an end. Thus, in the list of possible purposes that follows, *collaborate* is not an end itself, but a means to create a report. *Report* is not the end game; changing the company's compensation system is. This is not to say you will always accomplish your goal. Consider the *innovate* example in the list. Although your supervisor may decline to pass along your innovation for reducing manufacturing costs to senior management, you should still have a goal. Consider the following list of possibilities for why you are writing:

- *Analyse a problem.* You assist the CFO in writing a report that examines the reasons why the company's cash flow is not sufficient to cover its operating costs.

- *Ask for action.* You ask your supervisor whether you can attend a company training programme about communication.

- *Collaborate.* You work with a team to write a report about how a new accounting rule will change your company's financial reporting.

- *Consult.* You ask a colleague for advice on writing a report.

- *Deliver news.* The CFO sends a message to all employees that the company is increasing its performance bonuses for departments, teams and individuals.

- *Direct.* Your supervisor tells you to have the report ready by 8am on Thursday.

- *Educate.* You host a meeting with a group of managers to explain how the company uses cost accounting.

- *Inform.* You send an e-mail to your supervisor with the highlights of the report you will be presenting on Thursday.

- *Influence.* Your CFO writes a letter to the editor of a national newspaper arguing that Congress should extend a tax credit for investments in solar energy.

- *Innovate.* You send a memo to your boss about your idea for an innovation that will reduce the company's manufacturing costs.

- *Market* or *sell.* You assist the company's sales team in preparing an estimate of the costs of a new sales initiative.

- *Motivate.* Your supervisor tells people in your department they will receive a bonus this year if they meet certain performance goals.

- *Negotiate.* You assist a purchasing manager in negotiating a contract with a vendor to upgrade the company's information storage system.

- *Offer suggestions.* As the CFO, you send a memo to employees suggesting they volunteer for a community service programme of their choice. The company will give employees two hours of paid time off a month for volunteer work.

- *Persuade.* You convince your supervisor of the need for your department to hire another accountant. Your supervisor persuades the CFO to approve the hiring.

- *Problem-solving.* You join a team that is asked to help the company determine the causes of cost increases in a manufacturing process and how to eliminate them.

- *Provide solutions.* You assist the CFO with a report on how to increase the company's cash flow.

- *Recruit.* Your supervisor asks you to assist a company recruiter in writing a job description for the accountant that will be hired.

- *Report.* At your supervisor's request, you draft a report to the human resources director with some suggestions for revising the company's employee compensation system.

- *Request.* A colleague asks you for assistance in preparing a presentation.

Subject

What are you writing about? What is the general subject of your report or other communication? Management accountants are not just working in accounting anymore. They are working more frequently in other capacities throughout organisations, so you could find yourself writing about any subject from question 2 in box 5-1.

Say you are assisting a business line manager in managing an operating unit. The CFO has asked the manager to prepare a report on how the unit can expand into new international markets. It's a complicated strategic question, and the manager asks for your help with a piece of it. You must prepare a report on the estimated costs of going into a specific market. Next week, you could be asked to write about another business question or issue.

What this scenario suggests is that you should learn as much as you can about every aspect of a company's business. What are the company's most important strategic issues? What are its concerns in managing its people? Being well informed about a company will help you when deciding on the key messages in your communication.

Audience

The answers to question 3 in box 5-1 shows there are many possible audiences for your business communication. By deciding on the audience for your report or other communication, you can tailor your message accordingly. One way to think of your audience is as valued customers of your company. The book *Business Communications* indicates, 'Just as a company won't connect with its customers if it fails to understand them, their needs, and how they prefer to be served, you won't connect with your readers if you don't understand them, their needs, and how they prefer to receive information.'[2]

Imagine you are an account manager who is preparing a forecast of a company's cash flow for the next three months and an analysis of whether it will be sufficient to cover that company's various costs. Your audience, in this case, is the company's controller, who will use your report to prepare a cash management report and working capital analysis for the CFO. Or, say you're an accounting supervisor, and as part of your responsibilities, you supervise and train staff accountants in various company accounting policies and procedures. You write a checklist for staffers to use as a guide for following those procedures. It's a simple tool to help them do their work efficiently.

As these hypothetical scenarios demonstrate, your audience may determine the form of communication you need to write (see question 7 in box 5-1). The characteristics of that audience may also affect how you write your communication. The following list will help guide you in considering how best to reach your target audience.

What do you need to know about your audience to communicate effectively? First of all, you should understand your relationship with the audience and, conversely, the audience's relationship with you. Are you writing to someone you know well, such as a colleague in your department or your supervisor? Are you writing to a senior person in the organisation whom you do not know well? Or, are you writing to members of your team, some of whom you know better than others? The better you know your audience, the more likely you are to know how to best communicate with them.

Whether the people who constitute your audience are interested in what you write depends partly on how they perceive you. They may pay close attention to your writing because you are a recognised expert on the topic of your communication. They may not know you, and you have to capture their attention by writing an informed, thoughtful communication. Some people in your audience may be more important to you than others.

You should also think about who your primary and secondary audiences are. If you are writing to different people in your company, including the CEO, CFO or others in senior management, they would be the primary audience because of their power and authority. If you are submitting a business proposal to a customer or client, with copies to the CEO or CFO, the customer is the primary audience. If you are writing a letter to a consultant who is an expert on cloud storage systems to ask about a system for your company, with copies to the CFO or others, the consultant is the primary audience.

When considering who constitutes your primary and secondary audiences, especially if you do not know them well, take into account the background and knowledge they have. What is the professional background of your audience? Educational level? Position in your company? Beliefs, attitudes and biases? Assume you're an account manager who is writing a letter to your supervisor proposing that the company adopt a policy for the use of social media as a means of communication inside and outside the organisation. Despite your strong feelings about the value of social media, your memo lays out arguments both for and against the company's adopting such a policy. You conclude with your arguments about why the advantages outweigh any disadvantages. This will help your supervisor to consider both sides of the issue, as well as demonstrate that you can take a balanced approach in writing about an issue.

But what if you are writing to complete strangers? Suppose the editor of a prominent trade publication or professional journal has asked you to write an article. You can learn about your audience by asking the editor for background on the publication's readership, reading the publication's guide for submission of articles, reading past issues of the publication to see what interests readers and reading comments from readers on the publication's website.

Your audience's familiarity with the subject matter you are presenting will also affect how you communicate with them. If you are explaining what a new accounting rule means to an audience of people who are not accountants, you must write in a language they can understand. That does not mean you must dumb down your communication, but you must explain why your audience should care. For example, discuss the ruling's effect on the company's financial reporting, capital structure or operations.

Then again, your audience may have some knowledge of your topic. Perhaps you work for a global company whose executives are familiar with International Financial Reporting Standards (IFRS). If you are asked to write a report to senior management about some aspect of IFRS, you can do so without having to provide a lot of background information on IFRS, its purpose, how it differs from accounting principles generally accepted in the United States of America, and so on.

But suppose senior management wants to distribute your report to mangers and others in the company who may not be as knowledgeable about IFRS. For the benefit of this audience, you might write a brief article that provides background on IFRS. It can be included with, but distinguished from, the main article. Readers can decide whether to read this sidebar article.

The following are some other audience characteristics you will want to consider:

- *Management styles.* How managers and supervisors respond to what you've written depends partly on their management style. Some managers and supervisors want to know the essence of what you're writing about, and no more. For this audience, you might write a short article that highlights your key messages. Other managers may want you to go into great detail. For those managers, you could write an article that expands upon your key messages. If you are writing to managers who have different styles, you might write a short summary and then go into the details. The important thing is to be attuned to how your audiences want to receive information.

- *Cultural differences.* If you are writing for an international audience, there are cultural differences to consider. This might be the case if you are working for a global corporation or for a small business, such as an import-export firm that has international clients. In writing, you must be sensitive to language that might be acceptable in your culture but considered impolite or offensive in others. Avoid the use of idioms, jargon or other expressions that might not be understood by readers who are not fully conversant in English, and use a tone that shows a sensitivity to the views, perceptions and feelings of people of other cultures. If you are with a global organisation, you might ask people working in other countries to review and comment upon what you've written before it is sent to your audience. Or, you might consult with people in your organisation who are experienced in writing for a global audience. Faculty at colleges and universities, members of international professional and trade organisations, staff members of research institutions and employees of government agencies dealing with international business might also be of assistance.

- *Anticipated audience reaction.* Will readers be receptive, indifferent, or resistant? If you are suggesting ways the company might reduce its costs or increase its cash flow, readers might be interested. If you are writing about a new accounting rule, your audience might not be interested unless you clearly explain how it affects them. If you are sending a memo to a line manager about the unit's cost increase, the manager might not be happy to learn about the problem, but if you suggest steps to bring costs under control, the manager might welcome your ideas. The key is to show your readers how they can benefit from the information you've provided.

- *What you want to accomplish.* For you to accomplish your goal in writing, you need the commitment of your readers. 'When you start a letter or e-mail message, you are starting a relationship; you will need cooperation and agreement from the reader for the relationships to work,' writes Deborah Dumaine in *Write to the Top.*[3] 'It's best to begin by knowing what you want and by understanding what the other person expects.'

Delivery

Consider how, and by whom, your communication will be delivered. Questions 5, 6 and 7 in box 4-1 ask about authorship, timing and the form of your message.

Whether or not you do the actual writing, a key consideration is who is the right person to communicate the message? That depends partly on who will receive the message and the message itself. If a division president has put together a proposal for an acquisition and reviewed it with the CFO, the division president may be the best qualified to submit the proposal to the CEO. If the CFO has a plan to reduce the company's operating costs by 5%, the CFO may be the right person to communicate this to the CEO.

Another key consideration as you prepare to write is timing. When is the right time to deliver the message? If the company has just announced a major cost-cutting drive, this might not be the time to propose an acquisition. If the company's profits are growing at a rate of 15% and the company is flush with cash, senior management might be more receptive to your proposal.

Finally, what form your communication takes will steer you toward making many other decisions. How will you deliver your message? In an e-mail? In a letter sent by mail? In a report that you personally deliver to the CFO? Will you write a note and slip it under the CFO's office door?

When considering the right form or channel of communication, you should always start with the audience. Suppose you've written a memo to a business line manager in your company. Would the manager prefer to receive a printed memo or an electronic version? One benefit of a printed memo is that you can control the distribution: You personally give it to the manager. The manager may prefer to read it first and then decide whether to share it with others. With e-mail, there is always the risk that, for whatever reason, your memo could go to someone who shouldn't have seen it. But you may have to use e-mail if you need to quickly send the memo to people who work all over the world for your company. Also, e-mail enables recipients to respond quickly. Sometimes, you will communicate not just by writing but also by speaking, such as by making a presentation. Regardless of your platform, you would go through the same list of questions. Presentations are discussed in chapters 7 and 8.

THE WRITE MINDSET

Once you've decided on your purpose for writing, your subject, your audience and so on, you can begin the writing process—not by plunging into writing, but by planning first and then writing. As you outline and gather information, keep in mind a few of the 'Cs' of effective communication: clarity, consistency, conciseness and coherence. For the rest of this chapter, we will assume that you are writing a business report, although the same advice can be applied to any communication.

First, let's discuss clarity. In your report, there is probably a sentence or two, or perhaps a paragraph, that clearly states what the report is about. It is the message upon which the report is built. It may be the first paragraph of a report or the paragraph following an introduction. But it is there. So, whether you are writing a two-paragraph e-mail or a five-page report, your writing must have a message. Longer reports may begin with an executive summary, but the report itself should have that message.

Consistency is directly tied to clarity. Once you have stated your message, develop it and stay on message. If you lose focus, your writing could go off in different directions and turn into nothing more than a collection of notes.

According to *The Elements of Style*, 'Vigorous writing is concise. A sentence should contain no unnecessary words, a paragraph no unnecessary sentences, for the same reason that a drawing should have no unnecessary lines and a machine no unnecessary parts.'[4] In your writing, use the fewest words necessary to communicate. If you write a 500-word report, see if you can pare it to 400 words without losing the meaning.

For Amy Weinreich, CPA, clarity and conciseness means a single page. She is vice president, Finance and Administration, at Publishers Fulfillment Inc. She says the company's written communications are more concise than when she joined five years ago. 'For example, if I prepare a report for our senior executives, I summarise everything on one page, with just enough detail that they can make a decision. If they need more details, I can provide them with specifics.' (See interview 11 with Weinreich in appendix A.)

Finally, your report should be a coherent whole. It should be well-organised and have a logical structure. It starts at point A, continues through points B, C, D and E, and concludes with point F. Within each section of the report, you may choose to use different methods of organising your information. You may use a deductive method in one section, starting with the most important paragraph and continuing to the least important, and, in another section, the general to the specifics method, starting with a general statement and supporting it with specifics. Regardless of what form you use, there should be logic to your structure, so that your reader can easily glean your message.

Outlining is one of the best ways to build a coherent structure in your report. You probably learned how to outline in school, but it may have been many years since you have created a traditional outline. Read the next section for a refresher on outlining and other alternatives for giving your communications structure.

TRADITIONAL OUTLINING

One way to start the planning and writing process is by creating an outline. An outline can take different forms, but the important thing is to organise your thoughts. Once you begin writing, you may decide to reorganise your outline or add information, and you can update your outline accordingly. Keeping your outline current will help you to stay focused on your writing goal.

The traditional outline uses Roman and Arabic numerals and letters. It could be a short outline for documents such as e-mails, letters or memos, or a longer outline for documents such as reports or presentations. The short outline might simply list a few key topics; the long outline might list more topics and expand upon each one. If you and only a few others (such as members of your team) will see the outline, it could be informal, such as a bullet point list of the key ideas or issues. If you plan to circulate the outline to a wider audience, including senior management, you might use a formal outline of numbers and letters.

This is a short outline of a portion of chapter 1 of this book:

I. The changing role of the CFO

II. CFO responsibilities

III. Specific communication challenges CFOs face

Here is a longer outline of chapter 1:

I. The changing role of the CFO

    A. Management accountants traditionally at periphery

    B. Broad skills required

II. CFO responsibilities

    A. Finding insights in data

    B. Budgeting

    C. Measuring value

    D. Managing risk

III. Specific communication challenges CFOs face

    A. Explaining complex issues

    B. Communicating with investors

Here is a longer, even more detailed outline of chapter 1:

I. The changing role of the CFO

    A. Management accountants traditionally at periphery

        1. Typical CFO was a 'bean counter'

        2. CFOs stayed in their own departments

    B. Broad skills required

        1. CFOs provide analysis to help others make decisions

    2. More influence

    3. Communication skills are essential

II. CFO responsibilities

    A. Finding insights in data

        1. Help others make informed decisions

    B. Budgeting

        1. Many companies dissatisfied with traditional budgeting

        2. Alternative methods include rolling forecasts and others

    C. Measuring value

        1. How can value be measured?

        2. CFOs are called upon to measure the value of human resources and talent

    D. Managing risk

        1. CFOs measure risk in areas outside of finance

        2. Broad accountability leads to a balancing act

III. Specific communication challenges CFOs face

    A. Explaining complex issues

        1. Variety of audiences

        2. Different audiences have different goals

        3. Management accountants ensure business is performing as expected

    B. Communicating with investors

        1. Investors want more narrative reporting

        2. Rapid-growth markets present a challenge

The long outline is particularly useful for projects such as reports or presentations that cover a number of topics and issues. You can use the long outline to prioritise information, determine if there are any information gaps and decide whether more information is needed or some pieces of existing information could be shortened, revised or consolidated.

If you were preparing a presentation, you could note in the outline where visuals would be presented and include a brief description of each visual or the visual itself. (Presentations are discussed in chapters 7 and 8.)

ALTERNATIVES TO TRADITIONAL OUTLINING

Traditional Roman numeral outlines may not suit your mood or purpose, but there are many alternative ways to outline. Maybe you're spontaneous and want to write down whatever comes to mind. Maybe teachers forced you to write too many traditional outlines in school. Maybe your thoughts aren't organised enough yet. There are other choices.

Brainstorm Outline (Brainstorming)

Brainstorming is one way to begin the outlining process. Write down whatever comes to mind—about anything. As you write, you'll start to get the core ideas for your report, and you can forget about the other ideas. You can do this by yourself or with a team or other group. Brainstorming is especially useful for teams. The rapid-fire, back-and-forth dynamic of brainstorming helps in developing ideas for a report, including some that may not occur to individual team members if they had been working alone. Everyone has a chance to propose ideas and comment.

Whether alone or with a team, once you've finished brainstorming, you can organise related ideas into groups and discard those that are not relevant. You now have an outline to use in drafting your report or other communication.

Mind Mapping

Another approach to outlining is mind mapping. Write the central topic of your report in the middle of a sheet of paper or whiteboard. When an idea related to the central topic occurs to you, write it down. It becomes a subtopic. Draw a line from the central topic to the subtopic. Repeat this process with other subtopics. If you have ideas related to a subtopic, write them down and draw a line from the subtopic to these related topics. Repeat the process with other subtopics and so on. You now have a mind map you can use to help you draft your report.

Figure 5-1 is an example of a mind map outline using some of the elements of the traditional outline of chapter 1.

Figure 5-1: Mind Map

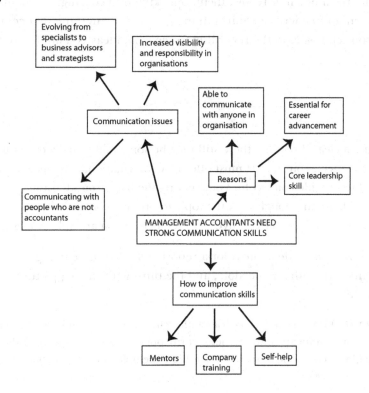

Questioning

Look at your report not just from your perspective but also from that of your readers. Imagine you are sitting in a room, facing an inquirer across a table. You're sweating under a hot light. The inquirer, concealed in the shadows, begins to interrogate you: 'What's your reason for writing this?' Followed by, 'Why should I care?'

The inquirer, representing your readers, asks you questions they might ask. Through this imagined question and answer process, you can determine what questions to address in your report, and you answers will provide a framework for writing. A team could use the same process for writing a report. For help, you might reach out to your colleagues, supervisor or others in your organisation. Tell them the concept or purpose of your report, and ask them what questions they have. They might think of a question or two that didn't occur to you.

Free Writing

What if you're trying to think of ideas for your report and you're drawing a blank? Are you so overwhelmed by the task of writing that you don't even know where to begin? This paralysing feeling is often called writer's block. So how do you get from idling on the block to producing ideas? You write your way out.

Free writing is a technique designed to help you overcome writer's block or self-criticism. Find a timer and commit yourself to writing nonstop for at least ten minutes. Write about anything that comes to mind, regardless of whether it's relevant to your topic. Don't stop to edit or revise. When the timer goes off, you're finished. Stop and look at what you've written. In the torrent of words, you may find ideas for your report. These ideas may lead you to think of other ideas. And then you can begin to organise them in an outline using one of the other techniques discussed previously.

Other ideas may come to you when you're away from writing, so you might jot them in a notebook or use your smartphone or tablet to write them down or record them. Speaking of recording, you could try free speaking as an alternative or supplement to free writing. Start talking and record anything that comes to mind for ten minutes or whatever time you set. Listen to the recording to see what ideas you might use for your report.

CONTEXT

Once you have an outline and a clear direction, there still may be some additional work you need to do. To capture the attention of your readers, your report must offer new information, insights and analysis, but 'new' compared to what? You need to provide context for your report—the background, framework or circumstances. In some instances, you may be familiar enough with the topic to provide context without doing any additional research. In other cases, you may need to do extensive research before you are able to begin writing your report.

Let's look at an example of how to provide context for a report. The first three paragraphs of the following quote provide context—the first two with an anecdote, and the third with the big picture: unemployment in the eurozone and the United States.

> For the past six years, VASCO Data Security has dealt with a chronic problem: It hasn't been able to easily recruit qualified workers for its software and internet security operations in Europe. And the plight hasn't gotten easier—even as a global economic crisis has led to high unemployment throughout the continent.

'It seems like in Brussels and in Zurich, both, we have a hard time when a spot opens up, filling it,' VASCO CFO Gary Robisch said. 'A lot of times we have to settle for somebody that doesn't exactly match the qualifications that we want.'

The economics don't seem to make sense. High unemployment, one would presume, would make it easier to fill jobs. The 17-country euro currency bloc hit a record in May when unemployment rose to 11.1%, while the rate across the EU was 10.1%, according to Eurostat, the EU's statistics office. US unemployment has hovered between 8.1% and 8.3% for the past six months.

Yet employers worldwide are still struggling to find workers with the skills to fill a wide variety of jobs. The situation is fuelling a human resources conundrum as employers ponder whether they should hold out and pony up for candidates with key skills or look to on-the-job training for promising candidates. [5]

If the article had simply been about high unemployment, it would have added nothing to what readers already know, except maybe to provide some statistics. But it goes on to dispel the notion that because of high unemployment, employers can easily find skilled workers. So, consider the context. This will help you to narrow the focus of your report and decide on your key message.

RESEARCH

To write a report and provide context, you must be informed about the topic. Even if you are an expert on the topic, you must keep abreast of new issues, developments and trends in your area of expertise. That will require research. You probably already have some experience with research from when you were in school or from earlier work in your company, and you can draw on that experience in doing your current research.

As with the rest of the writing process, focus on your key message—your theme—when researching. Otherwise, you could waste time stumbling across and fixating on fascinating but irrelevant bits of information, such as the Aldabra giant tortoise being one of the longest living animals.

You also may come across articles or images that will save you time and effort by already encapsulating the message you want to convey to your readers. Be careful to get permissions and properly cite the source of any previously published information. Just because something is posted on the Internet does not mean you have permission to use it.

The following are some good places to start your research:

- *Within your company.* Try starting with your own company. See what you can learn from company reports, articles, white papers, webcasts, the company library (if your company has one), and other sources of information, as well as talking to people in your company.

- *Outside your company.* See what has been written about your topic in books, newspapers, trade publications, professional journals and other print and online publications, or on webcasts, podcasts, online videos, online discussion groups and other sources.

- *Interviews.* Interview people inside and outside of your organisation who have the knowledge and experience to discuss your topic. They can speak from experience, provide insights and offer suggestions to readers. They might also be able to provide sound bites or quotes that you can use in your report to bolster your arguments.

- *Survey.* Another approach is to conduct a survey of knowledgeable people. The survey could be the basis for your report.

Of course, not every communication you write will require extensive research, but it may require at least *some* research. As you become more experienced in researching, you'll become more efficient, doing just what research is necessary and no more.

With your thoughts recorded, organised into an outline and supported by research, you are now ready to begin writing. The next chapter will discuss techniques you can use to write an outstanding report.

CHAPTER SUMMARY

- Using a standard list of questions concerning your audience, theme, subject and so on can help you to take a consistent approach.

- Always write your report with a specific audience in mind. What do readers expect from your report?

- Be clear about your purpose. What do you want to accomplish in writing the report?

- Your report starts with planning. Outline, provide context and do research in preparation for the actual writing process.

Endnotes

1 William Zinsser, *On Writing Well: An Informal Guide to Writing Nonfiction,* Fourth edition, (New York: Harper Perennial, 1999).

2 *Business Communication,* Harvard Business Essentials, (Boston: Harvard Business School Press, 2003).

3 Deborah Dumaine, *Write to the Top: Writing for Corporate Success,* (New York: Random House Trade Paperback, 2003).

4 William Strunk Jr. and E.B. White, *The Elements of Style,* Fourth edition, (White Plains, NY: Longman, 2000).

5 Ken Tysiac, 'Execs Battle Skills Gap in Hiring Despite High Unemployment,' *CGMA Magazine,* Jul. 2012 www.cgma.org/magazine/news/pages/20125850.aspx

6

WRITING THE REPORT

In chapter 5, you used the traditional techniques of outlining, brainstorming, creating a mind map or free writing, along with your research, to develop the ideas for your report. Now it's time to formally organise your information and ideas in a way that will interest your readers and enable them to easily read and understand what you've written, regardless of whether you're writing about a simple or complex theme.

In this chapter, I will give some general tips for good writing and then discuss report writing specifically. The standard elements of a report are the introduction, body and conclusion. Other components, such as an executive summary and recommendations, may be added as necessary, but this chapter will mostly focus on the core sections.

WRITING THE FIRST DRAFT

Start by writing your theme. Keep it at the top of your report as you write. You can decide later where to place it in your report, but writing it at the start and keeping it in a prominent place will help you stay focused. You can begin writing your report at any point you wish—so long as you begin. For example, if you've used the most-to-least important method of development and have six ideas to develop, each in a section of the report, you could start with the first one—the most important—or the fourth one. Whichever is easiest to write.

In the first draft, write each section from start to finish without stopping to rewrite sections or check grammar. Take short breaks as you wish, but keep writing until you've finished the report. You can make revisions the second time through.

Writing Your Theme

Your theme provides unity to your report. It explains why the story is being written and why your readers should care. Journalists call the paragraph containing the central message of a story the 'nut graf.' It could be a paragraph or several paragraphs or simply a sentence. Regardless of what form it takes, it is a thematic statement. 'I consider the main theme statement the single most important bit of writing I do on any story,' writes William E. Blundell, former features editor at *The Wall Street Journal*.[1]

Let's revisit an example we used in the last chapter to talk about context and look at it from the perspective of developing theme.

> For the past six years, VASCO Data Security has dealt with a chronic problem: It hasn't been able to easily recruit qualified workers for its software and Internet security operations in Europe. And the plight hasn't gotten easier—even as a global economic crisis has led to high unemployment throughout the continent.
>
> 'It seems like in Brussels and in Zurich, both, we have a hard time when a spot opens up, filling it,' VASCO CFO Gary Robisch said. 'A lot of times we have to settle for somebody that doesn't exactly match the qualifications that we want.'
>
> The economics don't seem to make sense. High unemployment, one would presume, would make it easier to fill jobs. The 17-country euro currency bloc hit a record in May, when unemployment rose to 11.1%, while the rate across the EU was 10.1%, according to Eurostat, the EU's statistics office. US unemployment has hovered between 8.1% and 8.3% for the past six months.
>
> Yet employers worldwide are still struggling to find workers with the skills to fill a wide variety of jobs. The situation is fuelling a human resources conundrum as employers ponder whether they should hold out and pony up for candidates with key skills or look to on-the-job training for promising candidates.[2]

The first two paragraphs discuss the difficulty of one employer in hiring qualified workers despite high unemployment in the euro currency bloc and United States. The third presents the broad unemployment picture. The nut graf is the first sentence of paragraph four. It notes the conundrum employers face in trying to find workers with the requisite skills.

As in journalism, every business communication should have a theme. This seems simple enough, but if you are not focused, your theme could become muddled or disappear in the writing process, leaving readers to wonder what the purpose of your piece was.

Building Your Report Paragraph by Paragraph

The theme is the foundation of your report. The paragraphs are the building blocks. Each paragraph has a topic sentence—usually the first sentence—that develops the theme. The topic sentence could be a statement, an instruction, an observation, a comment, a question, a definition, a request, a suggestion, a proposal, a summary or other communication. The remaining sentences build upon the topic sentence. The result is a seamless construction, with one sentence flowing logically to the next.

For the sake of variety, emphasis or other reasons, you can use other forms of paragraph construction. A paragraph might have an introductory sentence, the theme sentence and supporting sentences, or the theme sentence might go last or in the middle. Regardless of the construction, a paragraph usually only has a single idea or theme.

The following is a paragraph from a Morgan Stanley report on healthcare:

> Legislative and secular challenges are forcing a sea change in the U.S. healthcare sector. Whether or not U.S. healthcare reform is implemented as proposed, changes to the U.S. healthcare system over the next three to five years will be sweeping—and the investment implications broad. Only the players that can deliver more cost-effective or more progressive products and services stand ready to make the most of investment opportunities long term.[3]

The first two sentences provide context. The final sentence states the theme: Players that are best at delivering services will be the winners.

Your report will be more readable if you use short paragraphs, which can be accomplished by writing paragraphs of a few sentences or breaking up a long paragraph into two shorter paragraphs. But paragraphs of about the same length could become monotonous, so vary the number of sentences in a paragraph and the sentence length.

Use the Active Voice

When writing, most of the time you should use the active voice, in which the subject of the sentence acts. An example of a sentence that uses the active voice is, 'Joe presented the report to management at 10am today.' You should try to avoid the passive voice, in which something is done, but by whom is not always clear. An example using passive voice is, 'the report was presented to management at 10am today.' The active voice, as the term suggests, communicates action. It drives sentences and paragraphs forward. It is clearer and more concise and communicates actions and ideas more effectively.

That being said, there are some instances when you may use the passive voice, such as when you want to emphasise the action rather than who acts. For example, 'the deadline for filing the report is 5pm today,' rather than, 'the company has until 5pm today to file the report.' Passive voice can be useful if you want to be tactful, such as when correcting someone's mistake. For example, 'the office vault should have been locked before the office was closed for the weekend,' rather than, 'you should have locked the office vault before closing the office for the weekend.'

Use Transition Words

Every sentence in a paragraph should link to the next sentence, and every paragraph in a report should connect to the next paragraph. You can accomplish this with transition words, which are the bridges between sentences and paragraphs.

Your choice of transition words depends on the connection you want between sentences and paragraphs. Some examples of transition words are as follows:

- Compare: likewise, similarly, in comparison, compared to, compared with
- Contrast: however, nevertheless, on the other hand, but, still, yet, nor, although, conversely
- Amplify: also, moreover, furthermore, in addition, besides, too, again, besides, subsequently, last, finally
- Result: as a result, therefore, consequently, hence, so, thus, because
- Example: for example, for instance, to illustrate, such as, that is, specifically, thus
- Time: Now, previously, since, in the future, after, meanwhile, simultaneously, at the moment, before, often

The following are examples of transitions in a CGMA report example. Transition words are emphasised in **_bold italics_**:

Many major organisations' finance functions are being transformed to contribute more to their organisation's success by conducting their core activities more efficiently, providing better management information, and performing a more influential role in management.

Yet, the shift of finance professionals away from a sole focus on traditional tasks linked to the reporting cycle has been inconsistent across the business world. **_Often_**, finance professionals find it difficult to carve time away from their traditional duties and expand their scope within the company. They may lack the internal mandate to shoulder new responsibilities or are slow to acquire the new capabilities. **_Finally_**, they may need to develop new skills and leverage existing talent to apply their financial acumen to non-financial areas. [4]

Use the Appropriate Style

Style is the way you use language. It's not about what you write, but how you write. Everyone who writes has a style: how they communicate their thoughts in writing. Regardless of the style you use, you must use proper grammar, correct spelling and an economy of words.

Writing style is formal or informal. Scientists, professors, doctors, lawyers, accountants and others usually use a formal style of writing for technical and other issues for professional journals, legal reports, technical papers, research reports, lectures or presentations at meetings. Informal writing is conversational, relaxed and personal in tone.

When writing, you adapt your style to your audience, purpose, content and circumstances. For a report for clients and customers, a board of directors, or senior management, you might use a formal style. For a report to a supervisor, members of a team or others, you might use an informal style, or, perhaps, a blend of formal and informal.

If you are working for a large corporation, your company may have a style guide that prescribes the style to use in business communication. If you work for a small business, you may not have a style guide to use, but the business could use a particular style in its communication or defer to a well-known style guide, such as *The Chicago Manual of Style* or *The Economist Style Guide*.

Use Design Elements to Improve Readability

Like transitions, design elements make your report more readable. To quickly comprehend a report, readers usually browse through it first, looking for sections that particularly interest them, then they decide whether to read through the entire report. You can add design elements to help readers navigate a report or elements that particularly interest them.

Design elements include the following:

- *Headings and subheadings.* Use headings and subheadings to highlight sections of a report. For example, the heading for this section is 'Writing the First Draft,' the subheading for this section is 'Building Your Report Paragraph by Paragraph,' and the final subheading for this paragraph is 'Use Design Elements to Improve Readability.'

- *Numbered lists or bullet lists.* Use numbered lists to show steps in a process or to prioritise, such as in recommending a series of actions to take.

- *White space.* Make some space. Too many paragraphs or sentences on a page, words that seem squeezed together, sentences that seem to be sitting right on top of one another, or paragraphs that seem crowded together can all leave readers feeling claustrophobic. Open up your report through balanced use of white space.

- *Graphics.* Create charts, tables and other graphic elements to illustrate sections or elements of your report. Graphic elements serve many purposes: illustrating statistics, explaining complex subjects, showing a structure or sequence, setting priorities and much more.

- *Typography.* Use typography, which is the style and arrangement of type, to further enhance the readability of your report. This includes the typeface, font size, spacing between words, spacing between lines on a page and more. There are infinite choices in typefaces, sizes and other elements. However, your company may have a policy on document design that prescribes specific typefaces, such as Times New Roman.

With today's technology, you can create a beautifully designed report, but do you have the time? If you work for a large corporation, it may have in-house designers or employ freelance designers who can design the report for you. You might offer suggestions, but the designer does the work, freeing you to focus on the many demands of your job. A designer wouldn't necessarily work on every report you write, but for a major report, such as one you're sending to senior management, the designer is a resource. By contrast, if you're with a small business that does not have a budget for designers, you would write and design the report yourself, perhaps with the assistance of others in your organisation.

SECTIONS OF A REPORT

Body

The body of your report should contain all the information you want to present to your reader. You may find it easiest to begin writing this section first, even though it will be preceded by the Introduction. Use your outline to guide you while writing the body, and always keep in mind that the information should flow logically for the reader.

Depending on the interests of the audience and the content of the report, you may use different methods for developing the body of the report. They include the following:

- *Order-of-importance method.* This method sequences information in the order of most important to least important. See box 6-1 for an example of the order-of-importance method.

Box 6-1: Example of Order-of-Importance Method

An article in the Harvard Business Review lists the results of a survey on the 17 traits of organisational effectiveness and ranks them in order of importance.* The first paragraph explains the method of organisation in the article:

> Ranking the traits makes clear how important decision rights and information are to effective strategy execution. The first eight traits map directly to decision rights and information. Only three of the 17 traits relate to structure, and none of those ranks higher than 13th. We'll walk through the top five traits here.

The article is accompanied by a graphic, which also lists the traits in order of importance and colour-codes them by category. Together, the article and graphic use the order-of-importance method to quickly highlight and explain the results of the survey.

* Gary L. Neilson, Karla L. Martin and Elizabeth Powers, 'The Secrets to Successful Strategy Execution,' *Harvard Business Review*, Jun. 2008 http://hbr.org/2008/06/the-secrets-to-successful-strategy-execution/ar/2

- *Cause-and-effect (action and result) method.* Another method of development is cause and effect, or action and result. You explain why something happened or will happen. The cause-and-effect method could also be used to state a problem and suggest steps to solve it.

See box 6-2 for an example of the cause-and-effect method.

Box 6-2: Example of Cause-and-Effect Method

A case study on CGMA.org explained how one company benefited from outsourcing.[†] The article begins with a paragraph describing the cause and follows with a paragraph describing the effect:

> To improve customer service and consolidate its position in the Southeast Asia steel industry, Singapore-based Tata Steel International outsourced its logistics operation to Toll Global Logistics. Kevin Io, ACMA, CGMA, and Financial Controller, working with Andrew Heycott, Tata Steel International's General Manager for Southeast Asia, was tasked with finding the right logistics partner to help streamline the warehousing and shipping of steel to customers across the region.

> Managing a comprehensive facility for Tata, Toll carries out order processing, port clearance, customs documentation, and inventory management services for the company. 'By outsourcing the logistics division, we were able to divert our attention to our core competency, therefore increasing efficiency, achieving better order fulfillment and enjoying great savings,' says Io.

Cause: In the first paragraph, the first sentence describes the cause: Tata Steel outsourced its logistics operations to Toll to improve its customer service and consolidate its position.

Effect: The second paragraph describes the results of outsourcing. The first sentence, 'Managing a comprehensive facility...' tells what Toll does for Tata. The quote in the next sentence describes the benefits.

The article goes on to explain other benefits the company realised from outsourcing, how it quantified those benefits and how it evaluated third-party suppliers.

[†] Kevin Io, ACMA, CGMA, Financial Controller, Tata Steel International, Singapore, CGMA Case Study www.cgma.org/BecomeACGMA/WhyCGMA/DownloadableDocuments/TataCaseStudy_v4.pdf

- *Chronological method.* This method is used to show how something will happen or has happened. For example, a project report explains what is to be done, when it is to be done and who is responsible. The chronological method could also be used to track the progress of the project and help keep it on schedule. When was something done, and was it done on time?

- *Process method (sequential method).* Used to explain how something should be done, for example, the steps in constructing a building or servicing or repairing a piece of equipment.

- *Comparison method.* Used to explain an unfamiliar topic by comparing it with something familiar. Suppose an accountant is well versed in accounting principles generally accepted in the United States of America (U.S. GAAP) but has no knowledge of International Financial Reporting Standards (IFRS). Another accountant knows both IFRS and U.S. GAAP. This accountant might explain IFRS to the first accountant by first discussing some of the similarities between IFRS and U.S. GAAP.

- *Contrast method.* Used to explain the differences between ideas, concepts, or facts. Thus, the accountant knowledgeable about IFRS and U.S. GAAP could also explain some of the differences between the two to the first accountant who only knows U.S. GAAP.

- *General and specific methods of development.* Used to explain or persuade. Start with a general statement and fill in the specifics, or start with the specifics and come to a general observation. An Ernst & Young report on the need for collaboration in health care took the general to specific approach. It first noted that the dramatic changes in health care 'will require uncommon approaches that engage stakeholders to share knowledge, pool resources and synergistically enhance patient care—in essence, to collaborate.'[5] It goes on to provide specific ways in which policymakers, hospitals, health care professionals, health care organisations and others can collaborate.

- *Spatial method.* Used to describe the physical characteristics of an object: inside and out, top to bottom and so on. If you are writing a report on whether your company should acquire a manufacturing plant, it would include a physical description of the property.

- *Blending methods.* Rather than a single method of development, your report may blend several methods. For example, your report may use the general and specific method, but there may be a section in the report that uses the process method, and another that uses the chronological method. The point is, you are not bound to a single method in writing your report. You can use several different methods if the result is to create a report that is more readable and easily understood by readers.

Executive Summary

If your report has an executive summary, you can write it after you've finished drafting the body of the report. At that point, you'll have a much better idea of what to include in the executive summary than if you wrote it first, before the body.

The executive summary should capture the theme of your report, key messages, purpose, scope and context. Like the rest of the report, it should be clear and concise. It should be written for a specific audience: the CEO or CFO, other senior executives, line managers, project teams, or others in an organisation or for boards of directors, shareholders, investors and others outside the organisation.

The executive summary usually precedes longer reports, *longer* being defined as a report of five or more pages. There is no set length for an executive summary, although 10% of the length of a report has been suggested. Thus, a 20-page report would have a two-page executive summary. But the length can vary widely. For example, a 120-page report can have a two-page executive summary.[6]

In any case, busy executives and managers may want an executive summary even for shorter reports. It may be the only part of the report that some executives read, so you should give careful thought to writing it.

Introduction

As with the executive summary, you can write the introduction after you finish drafting the body of the report. The introduction describes your report, provides context, explains the purpose of the report and segues to the body of the report.

You can draw readers into the rest of your report in a myriad of ways. You could begin with a statement of purpose, a question, a problem, an anecdote, results of a survey, interesting facts, a forecast or a quotation. However it begins, the introduction must entice readers to read your report.

The following excerpt from a Deloitte report on decision making begins with a question. The rest of the report goes on to address the question:

> Bad decisions are made in organizations every day. Whether it's squishy goals, competing interests, bad assumptions, not enough time, insufficient information, or simply not enough talent, there are countless ways to miss the mark.
>
> On some level, making bad decisions is unavoidable. No one can always be right. But leading companies tend to make fewer bad decisions, especially when it comes to those that can drive or destroy significant value—decisions that matter.
>
> How do they do that? [7]

Giving Good and Bad News

It is worth taking a moment to reflect on how to introduce reports that contain bad news. If a report has obvious benefits, like a CFO's report detailing the company's plans to invest the company's substantial cash reserves in growing the business, increasing shareholder dividends, increasing employee pay, readers are going to be predisposed to read it.

But what if the CFO's report contains bad news? You may be tempted to use euphemisms or obtuse language to disguise the news, but you may end up confusing readers. It's best to be direct, but attempt to soften the blow by using neutral language to introduce the bad news. After you deliver the bad news, try to segue into something positive, such as congratulations for efforts made or offering suggestions for improvement. For example, a company has to reduce its costs by 10%, which could mean employee layoffs. One method for softening the blow is that the CFO could ask employees for suggestions about how the company can reduce costs in operating its businesses. The cost savings could reduce or eliminate the need for layoffs. Or, if layoffs are inevitable, the CFO's report might add that the company will offer workers severance packages or opportunities to work at other company locations.

Conclusion

Some reports end abruptly, leaving readers to wonder, What was that all about? Don't leave readers questioning your report. Provide a conclusion.

What do you want readers to remember about your report? What ideas should they should retain? The following sections offer some choices of conclusions that will help to drive home the message of your report.

Thematic Statement

Restate your theme. From reading your report, readers are, or should be, attuned to your theme, and a thematic statement reinforces your message. This type of ending will also bring your report full circle from the introduction, where you stated your theme for the first time.

Recall the beginning of the Deloitte report on decision making, which began with a question. That introduction went on to note that the CFO and CIO are two executives with the knowledge to help their organisations improve decision making. The report ends on the theme of collaboration that was stated at the beginning:

> For CFOs looking to improve the quality of decision-making in their organizations, there are plenty of peers who can help. But there may be no better door to knock on first than the one that says 'CIO.'[8]

This type of conclusion will neatly tie up the main message of your report and should provide readers with a sense of completeness.

Summary

Another option for concluding your report is to summarise key messages. If your report has an executive summary at the beginning that contains the same information, rephrase the executive summary to avoid repetition.

Call to Action

Conclusions with a call to action can help readers feel inspired to act on the information you have presented. For example, a CGMA tool on 'How to Develop a Strong and Independent Team' concluded with a checklist to help leaders evaluate the strength of their own teams.

Consider Questions

You might conclude your report by suggesting questions for readers to consider. PricewaterhouseCoopers concluded its 2012 global CEO survey by posing questions 'distilled from CEOs' insights [that] can help business leaders achieve the balance they'll need to grow their businesses in these volatile times.'[9] The questions tracked issues discussed previously in the report.

Offer Encouragement

A report from the CEO, CFO, business line manager, team leaders or others in the organisation could end on a note of encouragement. It could be encouragement to finish a project on schedule, help reduce costs, complete the work necessary to bid on a contract, or persevere through difficult times. This type of ending could be especially useful if your report has delivered some bad news or negative findings.

Recommendations

Typically, the Recommendation section follows the Conclusion and is written last, after you have completed the rest of the report. The Recommendation section should contain your suggestions to your audience based on the information you have presented in the report. This is one of the most important sections in the report because it offers suggestions and a call to action. This section is also where you can demonstrate your grasp of the issues by proposing solutions to problems.

Although it is unorthodox to put the Recommendations section at the beginning of the report, putting your recommendations earlier could grab your readers' attention. A Chartered Institute of Management Accountants (CIMA) report on sustainability[10] followed this format:

- Foreword
- Recommendations
- Executive Summary
- Purpose
- Methodology
- Definition of Sustainability
- Sections 1–5
- Conclusion
- About Us

EDITING

You've finished your first draft and typed the last word of your conclusion. But you're not done yet.

If you have the time—and time is a precious commodity in today's business world—save the draft on your computer, print a hard copy and go do something else. Writing is demanding work, and if you take a break, even a brief one, you'll be better prepared for the next step of editing what you've written.

After you've waited as long as possible, start the editing process. In addition to fixing the obvious typos and grammar, try to look at the report from the perspective of your readers. Look first at the big picture: structure, completeness, unity, context and conciseness. Do you need to restructure sections of the report? For example, if you've used a most-to-least important structure in writing sections of the report, should the sequence of the sections be changed to a more logical sequence? Do you need to add any content that you inadvertently left out? Have you put the report in the right context? You can revise your report to address these larger questions.

Next, look at your report close up, at the micro level. Read through it word by word to check for accuracy, proper usage of words, correct grammar and spelling, and proper attribution of sources. Make any revisions that are necessary.

Read through your report one more time as a final check. Are you satisfied with it? If so, you might ask people in your organisation to read the report and comment on its structure, completeness, conciseness and so on. Discuss their comments with them, make any necessary revisions and finalise the report. Use the following list as a guide to help you address all possible issues you can fix during the editing process:

- **Structure**
  - Is the report's structure consistent with the outline?
  - Are ideas in a logical sequence?
  - Is the theme clear?
  - Is the introduction strong?
  - Does the body of the report build upon the introduction?
  - Does the conclusion tie the report together?

- **Completeness**
  - Compare the content against the outline. Is anything missing in the content? An essential piece of information? A key observation? An important comment?

- **Unity**
  - Does the report have a sense of unity and purpose?
  - Do the sentences have the right mix of length and variety?
  - Do the transitions smooth the flow of sentences and paragraphs?
  - Are the design elements consistent?
  - Does the design make the report more readable?

- **Context**
  - Does the report provide the necessary background, conditions and circumstances for readers to understand its context? In this book, chapter 1 provided the context.

- **Conciseness**
  - Have you tightened your sentences? See appendix 6-1 at the end of this chapter for some suggestions on tightening sentences from the Plain English Handbook of the U.S. Securities and Exchange Commission.
    - Removed unnecessary words, phrases and sentences?
    - Shortened sentences and paragraphs wherever possible?

- Used the active voice (except where the passive voice makes sense)?

- Replaced weak verbs with strong ones?

- Avoided jargon and technical terms that readers may not understand.

- Explained any technical terms that cannot be avoided?

- **Accuracy**

  - Are facts and figures accurate?

  - Is the spelling correct?

  - Is the grammar correct?

  - Is the usage correct?

  - Is credit properly attributed to articles, books and other sources of information?

- **Style**

  - Is the style appropriate for the audience, purpose and content?

  - Is the style consistent throughout the report?

After you have a clean, final draft, you are ready to send it to others in your organisation to review, an in-house design and editing team, or directly to your readers.

A note about grammar and usage: A detailed discussion of grammar and usage is beyond the scope of this book; indeed, such a discussion would result in a book the same size as this one. There are a number of books, guides and other resources on the subject, and these are listed in the bibliography. For example, *Common Errors in English Usage* by Paul Brians explains the difference between *accept* and *except, cache* and *cachet, disinterested* and *uninterested,* and *imply* and *infer.*

You may use spelling and grammar software to check on your spelling and grammar, but these tools are not perfect. For example, typing 'Read it world by word...' would not be automatically corrected to 'Read it word by word.' Software is useful, but it cannot edit the report for you. At least not yet.

CHAPTER SUMMARY

- Use your outline as a guide in writing the first draft of your report.

- Edit your report for structure, content, style and so on.

- Take the same approach to writing, regardless of the audience, content or amount of time you have.

APPENDIX 6-1: SOME SUGGESTIONS ON HOW TO TIGHTEN AND STRENGTHEN YOUR SENTENCES

The following are suggestions from the Plain English Handbook of the U.S. Securities and Exchange Commission (SEC) that you can use to improve your writing.

Turn weak verbs into strong ones

Using strong verbs can help you sharpen your sentences and communicate ideas more effectively. As you edit your report, look for any form of the verbs 'to be,' 'to have,' or other weak verbs that could be turned into strong verbs. Here are examples from the SEC's Plain English Handbook.[11]

Before	After
We made an application	We applied
We made a determination	We determined
We will make a distribution	We will distribute
We will provide appropriate information to shareholders	We will inform shareholders
There is the possibility of prior Board approval of these investments	The Board might approve these investments in advance

Omit superfluous words

Superfluous	Simpler
In order to	To
In the event that	If
Subsequent to	After
Prior to	Before
Despite the fact that	Although
Because of the fact that	Because
In light of	Because
Owing to the fact that	Be
The following summary is intended only to highlight certain information contained elsewhere in this Prospectus.	This summary highlights some information from this prospectus.

Write in the positive

Positive sentences are easier to understand than negative ones. An example follows:

Before: Persons other than the primary beneficiary may not receive these dividends.

After: Only the primary beneficiary may receive these dividends.

Try personal pronouns

The pronouns to use are first- and second-person plural (we, us, our/ours) and second-person singular (you, your/yours). They keep your sentences short. They will also help you avoid abstractions and use more concrete, everyday language. In addition, you can use them to 'speak' directly to your reader, creating an appealing tone that will keep you reader reading.

Here is an example:

Before: This summary does not purport to be complete and is qualified in its entirety by the more detailed information contained in the Proxy Statement and the Appendices hereto, all of which should be carefully reviewed.

After: Because this is a summary, it does not contain all the information that may be important to you. You should read the entire proxy statement and its appendices carefully before you decide how to vote.

Concrete language

Always use specific, definite language rather than vague or abstract terms. If your readers are able to call up a specific image or concept associated with your words, you will be able to keep their attention and convey your message more effectively.

Before: The employees showed satisfaction as they took possession of their hard-earned rewards.

After: The employees grinned when they were handed their bonus cheques.

Other suggestions

- Keep the subject, verb and object close together.

- Make abstractions more concrete.

- Use parallel sentence structure.

Resources

The SEC handbook offers other suggestions for writing in plain English. It can be found online at www.sec.gov/pdf/handbook.pdf.

Another resource is *The Elements of Style*, a book by William Strunk, Jr and EB White. It covers elementary rules of usage, elementary principles of composition, a few matters of form, words and expressions commonly misused and an approach to style.

Other books and guides on communication and language use are listed in the bibliography.

Endnotes

1 William E. Blundell, *The Art and Craft of Feature Writing*, (New York: New American Library, 1988).

2 Ken Tysiac, 'Execs Battle Skills Gap in Hiring Despite High Unemployment,' *CGMA Magazine*, Jul. 2012 www.cgma.org/magazine/news/pages/20125850.aspx

3 'The US Healthcare Formula; Cost Control and True Innovation,' Morgan Stanley blue paper, Jun. 2011 www.morganstanley.com/views/perspectives/US_Healthcare.pdf

4 'New Skills, Existing Talents' CGMA Report, Sept. 2012 www.cgma.org/Resources/Reports/DownloadableDocuments/CGMA_new_skills_existing_talents.pdf

5 'Health Care Provider Industry Report 2012, New Horizons, Collaboration,' Ernst and Young [website] www.ey.com/Publication/vwLUAssets/New_Horizons_2012_health_care_provider_report/$FILE/New_horizons_2012_final_August_23.pdf

6 'Health Care Provider Industry Report 2012, New Horizons, Collaboration.' Ernst and Young [website] www.ey.com/Publication/vwLUAssets/New_Horizons_2012_health_care_provider_report/$FILE/New_horizons_2012_final_August_23.pdf

7 'CFO Insights; Making Decisions That Matter,' Deloitte [website], Oct. 2012 www.deloitte.com/assets/Dcom-UnitedStates/Local%20Assets/Documents/CFO_Center_FT/us_cfo_CFO-Insights_Making-decisions-that-matter_101112.pdf

8 'CFO Insights; Making Decisions That Matter,' Deloitte [website], Oct. 2012 www.deloitte.com/assets/Dcom-UnitedStates/Local%20Assets/Documents/CFO_Center_FT/us_cfo_CFO-Insights_Making-decisions-that-matter_101112.pdf

9 15th Annual Global CEO Survey 2012, 'Delivering Results: Growth and value in a volatile world,' PricewaterhouseCoopers [website] www.pwc.com/gx/en/ceo-survey/pdf/15th-global-pwc-ceo-survey.pdf

10 'Sustainability Performance Management: How CFOs Can Unlock Value,' Chartered Institute of Management Accountants in Association with Accenture www.cimaglobal.com/Documents/Thought_leadership_docs/Sustainability%20and%20Climate%20Change/sustainability_report_v7_web.pdf.

11 'A Plain English Handbook: How to create clear SEC disclosure documents,' U.S. Securities and Exchange Commission, Office of Investor Education and Assistance, 1998 www.sec.gov/pdf/handbook.pdf

PRESENTATIONS: PLANNING AND PREPARING

Knowing how to give good presentations is essential to achieving success in your organisation and career. That may not seem apparent if you just started in an entry-level position in a company, and most of the presentations you've made thus far were in school. But what you learned in school will help as you advance in an organisation and find yourself making more presentations to broader audiences. CFOs are in great demand as presenters. According to *CFO Magazine*, 'CFOs increasingly find themselves confronting eager audiences, as boards, Wall Street, and other constituencies call upon them for greater insight into corporate performance and strategy.'[1]

This chapter and the one that follows focus on presentations: their purpose, elements and structure, and how to use presentations to communicate effectively. In this chapter, we will discuss how to plan and outline your presentation. The next chapter will focus on designing and delivering slide presentations. Appendix E distils the considerations presented in these two chapters into a convenient checklist form.

So, what is a presentation? Simply put, it's showing and explaining something to an audience. What you present could be an idea, a solution, a service, a product, a project or something else. The audience could be an individual, such as your boss, a small group, such as members of your team, or hundreds of people.

There are many reasons for presentations, but they can be distilled into two main categories. The first reason is to inform: You provide the audience with new information or new insights. The second reason is to persuade: You try to convince the audience to support a plan or a cause, change their minds about an issue, or take action.

Presentations can be formal or informal. You could make a 20-minute presentation about a new product to your company's top executives. Or you could have three minutes to explain your product to a busy senior executive who missed your presentation and is hurrying out to a meeting. You could be called into a meeting on a moment's notice and asked to answer a question about the product. Whether you have 20 minutes to deliver a presentation or only a few minutes or whether you're presenting to top executives, your supervisor, or your colleagues, you have to be prepared, and that begins with planning.

PLANNING

In this book, an entire chapter is dedicated to planning and outlining before writing a report. Similarly, planning your presentation is an important step. This section summarises the questions you should ask while planning your presentation:

First, determine your purpose. Why are you making the presentation? Is it to inform or educate your audience about a topic, such as the business application of an accounting rule? Are you trying to convince your audience to support your plan to reduce costs, or change from opposition to support of a merger, or to buy a company product?

Next, identify the topic(s) of your presentation. Your topic could be about any aspect of a company's business: strategic planning, operations, finance, accounting, marketing, sales, human resources, logistics, research and development, education and training, and more. It could be about economic, social or other issues. Once you decide on your topic and learn about your audience, you can develop the key message for your presentation.

To determine your audience, think back to the discussion of audiences in chapter 5. Members of your audience might consist of people you work with every day; other people in your organisation, such as your supervisor, a business manager or the CFO; or people outside your company, such as customers or clients, investors, consultants, and others. It might include a mix of people from inside and outside your organisation and people from other countries. Your audience's familiarity with your topic might vary.

Ascertaining the needs and wants of your audience should be a top priority as you plan. 'During the planning phase of your presentation, always remember that it's not about you. It's about them,' writes communications coach Carmine Gallo. 'The listeners in your audience are asking themselves one question—"Why should I care?" Answering that question right out of the gate will keep your readers engaged.'[2]

Your presentation must be attuned to the needs, interests and concerns of people in your audience. To align your presentation with their interests, you must understand your audience first. What are their interests? Likes and dislikes? What motivates them? How are they likely to receive your presentation—with enthusiasm, indifference or hostility? Who are the influencers in your audience? These are the people who influence or make important decisions, and you will need their support for your ideas and initiatives. What can you say that will resonate with them?

Learning about your audience may require you to do some research. Assume you work for a large company, and you are speaking with managers across the organisation about development of an important product that will involve every manager and department. You want to know what questions they might ask. You could preview your presentation for one or two managers and solicit their questions. You might talk about your presentation with others in your organisation and get their questions. As a result of your research, you could decide to revise your presentation to address some of the questions, and you will be better prepared to answer others.

Some speakers, especially if they are new to making presentations, may be a little intimidated by the audience. An audience can be sceptical, ask tough questions, and maybe call you out if you make a mistake in the information you present. But the audience is on your side. 'In the real world, the average attendee at a conference or presentation has no interest in judging or critiquing you,' says author and speaker Justin Locke.[3] 'They all have one single thought uppermost in their mind and that thought is, "please, please, don't let this presenter bore me to death for the next hour."... Far from preparing to disdainfully judge you, the majority of the people in the audience are rooting for you like mad.'

Your last step in planning should be to investigate what the circumstances of your presentation will be. This includes the number of people in the audience, the size of the meeting room, the time of the presentation, the seating arrangements, your position in relation to the audience, the lighting and the comfort level of the room. If you are speaking to a large audience of several hundred people, you may have more of a challenge holding their interest than if you were speaking with ten people in a more intimate setting. Audiences may be more attentive in the morning than in the afternoon or evening. Uncomfortable chairs or too much or too little lighting may distract audiences.

OUTLINING YOUR PRESENTATION

Storyboard: A Visual Outline

When writing a report or other document, you begin by writing an outline. With a presentation, you start with a visual outline: a storyboard.

Although you can use PowerPoint, Keynote, Prezi or other software tools for this purpose, some presentation designers and consultants recommend you create an outline the old-fashioned way: by hand, using a pen or pencil and paper or a whiteboard. The reasoning is that the physical act of writing and sketching stimulates creative thinking, the free flow of ideas and a fresh approach to looking at problems or issues without working within the restrictions of software templates. In her book, *slide:ology: The Art and Science of Creating Great Presentations*, Nancy Duarte notes that much of today's communication has an intangible quality. 'Services, software, causes, thought leadership, change management, company vision—they're often more conceptual than concrete, more ephemeral than firm. And there's nothing wrong with that,' writes Duarte.[4] However, writing by hand can help to express your ideas so that they feel tangible and able to be acted upon.

You can jot ideas and sketch rough illustrations on a blank sheet of unlined paper, with one idea for each sheet. Or, if you prefer, you can write and illustrate on a whiteboard. Another option is to sketch on sticky notes and stick them to a whiteboard, a wall, a mirror or whatever else you want to use, as shown in figure 7-1. You can easily rearrange them as you organise your presentation, and their size limits the number of words you can write on a single note. This helps you to concentrate on the idea, not the wording.

At this point in planning your presentation, your aim is to sketch on paper or a whiteboard as many ideas as you can. The operative word is 'many.' Don't quit after jotting down a few ideas, keep going. Don't stop to try to organise your ideas. This is comparable to creating an outline for a written report or other document by brainstorming, mind mapping or free writing, as described in chapter 5. When you feel you truly have run out of new ideas, take a break and do something else or just relax. Time away from preparing your outline can give you a fresh perspective.

When you return to your outline with fresh eyes, study the paper, whiteboard or sticky notes containing your ideas and illustrations. Which ideas should you drop, which should you keep? Do any new ideas occur to you? Consider asking colleagues, friends and others to look at your ideas. They may offer new insights or raise new questions about what ideas to use. Get rid of papers or sticky notes containing ideas that you won't use, or file them for possible future use. Draw an 'X' through or erase ideas on your whiteboard. Through this process, you can identify, organise and develop the ideas that will form your presentation and start thinking about your key message.

Figure 7-1: Wall With Sticky Notes Outlining a Presentation

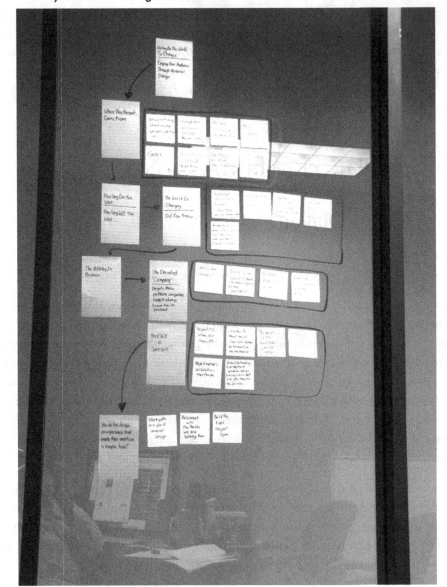

Source: Flickr (Credit: Kelsey Ruger). Whitney Quesenbery and Kevin Brooks, *Storytelling for User Experience*, (New York: Rosenfeld Media, 2010) www.rosenfeldmedia.com/books/storytelling/

Developing Your Key Message

In preparing your storyboard, think about your key message. Duarte writes, 'Your primary filter should be what I call your big idea: the one key message you must communicate. Everything in your presentation should support that message.'[5] One approach to developing your key message is to adapt a practice from journalism. To get started writing a story, some journalists write the headline first. This gets them thinking about the key message and how to capture it in a few words.

You could follow their example and write a headline for your presentation that captures your key message. It should be concise, specific and offer a benefit. In his book about Apple CEO Steve Jobs' presentation secrets, Carmine Gallo suggests headlines should be no more than 140 characters, the Twitter maximum. For example, in a 2007 presentation, Jobs introduced the iPhone to the world with the simple but powerful phrase, 'Apple Reinvents the Phone.'

Audience Memory Curve

Now that you've developed your key message, where should you place it in your presentation? A well-established principle, the audience memory curve, says that people are most likely to remember what was said at the beginning and the end of a presentation. So, state your key message at the beginning of the presentation, build upon it in the middle and reinforce it at the end (see figure 7-2 for an illustration of the audience memory curve). If there is one thing people should take from your presentation, it's that message.

Figure 7-2: Audience Memory Curve

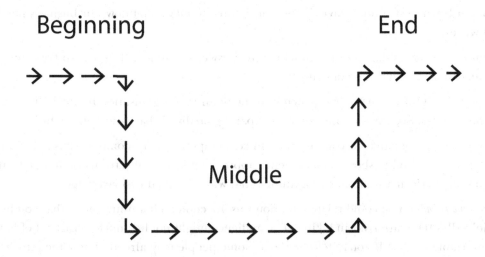

Introduction

Once you know your key message, you can decide on an introduction. Your audience may look alert and attentive at the start, but don't fool yourself. You have only a few minutes to engage people, otherwise, your audience will lose interest, so you need an introduction that will immediately get their attention. The following are some verbal examples of ways to immediately captivate your audience:

- *Explain why you're giving the presentation.* 'I'm here to explain how the software programme our company developed can help customers to better manage their inventories.'

- *Define a problem.* 'Our company's electricity costs increased faster than expected in the fourth quarter. Here are five steps we can take to control costs.'

- *Identify an opportunity.* 'We have an opportunity to enter a new market: Brazil. Should we take advantage of the opportunity and enter the market? Today I will discuss why we have that opportunity and suggest a decision-making process for determining whether we should enter the market.'

- *Make an attention-getting statement.* 'Over the next five years, one out of every five people in our company will retire. That means 5,000 people will leave our workforce. That's more than have retired in the past ten years. How are we going to recruit and train people fast enough to replace our growing number of retirees?'

- *Share a personal experience.* 'For the past few years, I've been working as a volunteer tutor in a community college programme. I've been tutoring an immigrant from China. When he arrived, he did not speak English, and he had no job skills. Now, he reads and writes English, he received his general equivalency diploma for secondary school, he's studying computer programming, and he plans to apply for citizenship. Today I want to talk about giving back to your community by working as a volunteer, the personal satisfaction you can get from volunteering and how you can learn more about volunteering.'

- *Share a quotation.* 'Henry Ford said, "Obstacles are the frightful things you see when you take your eyes off your goal." I'm here today to talk about goals, specifically, about three goals for our company: to increase sales by 10% a year, every year; increase profits by 7% a year; and increase our reinvestment in the company—in new factories, plants, and equipment and in hiring and training people—by 5% a year.'

- *Share an anecdote.* 'When a tidal wave hits, basically, three scenarios follow: Some people feel they have seen it all before, and they do nothing...and drown. Others will save themselves and evacuate (and when it's over, seldom have homes to return to). Finally, there are those who survive and say, "This is a tidal wave. I better learn to surf tidal waves." Tonight, I'd like to talk about how our business needs to learn to surf tidal waves.'[6]

- *Ask a rhetorical question.* Ask a question in which the answer is implied: 'If our cash flow continues to deteriorate, can we survive as a company?'

- *Ask a real question.* 'Our company has grown into the dominant organisation in our industry and markets in the United States. So, has the time come to expand globally? It has, and here's why.'

- *Surprise your audience.* 'Thanks to you, our magnificent employees, our company has made a terrific comeback this year. And to show management's appreciation for your hard work and dedication, we are reinstituting the performance bonus programme that was cancelled two years ago.'

- *Start with some humour.* You could relate a humourous anecdote, tell a funny story that you heard or read, or tell a joke. But there are risks in joking. The audience might not be amused. Instead of laugher, there is an uncomfortable silence. If you're telling a joke, some people may already know the punch line. Or, they may not appreciate your type of humour. If you want to start with humourous remarks, you might try them out first on some colleagues or friends.

- *Give a demonstration.* You could do a demonstration, for example, of a new product. Show the product on a screen and explain its features and benefits. But the product might still seem remote to the audience. They can see it, but they can't get close to it, touch it, handle it, or examine it. A solution might be to pass samples of the product around the room. At the introduction of its MacBook line of notebook computers in 2008, Steve Jobs discussed the design of a new aluminium frame that enabled production of lighter, thinner, more durable notebooks. Staff members passed out samples of the frames.[7]

  Of course, a live demonstration assumes the product can be easily shown and handled. A demo of your company's new rocket for launching satellites wouldn't work in a conference room—for obvious reasons. Maybe you could take the audience to a launching pad for a demo. That would certainly get their attention.

Which introduction should you use? As always, this depends on your audience. If you are making a presentation to top executives or business line managers, they'll want to know immediately why you're doing the presentation and why they should care. So, you could start with the reason for your presentation. Alternatively, you could start by defining a problem, stating a solution and then going into how to achieve the solution.

If you start with a quotation, anecdote or rhetorical question, segue quickly to the purpose of your presentation and why your audience should be interested. For example, in the preceding anecdote about the tidal wave, the speaker quickly goes on to tell the audience how to 'surf the tidal wave,' or how to manage through a crisis.

Don't wait until you have to make a presentation to start thinking about ideas for an introduction. When you come across an inspiring quote or relevant anecdote, file them away for future use. You can find ideas in many sources: books, articles, reports, blogs and other web content, the media and more. Some sources are listed in the bibliography at the end of this book.

Transitions

Build strong transitions between your introduction and your content, between the major elements of your content, and between your content and closing. They break the presentation into discrete but interconnected parts, making it easier for your audience to follow along as you move through your presentation. Box 7-1 shows where you can insert transitions during outlining to remind yourself to connect each piece of your content to the next.

Box 7-1: Presentation Outline With Transitions

Introduction
Transition
Content
Theme (Key Message)
Transition
Supporting argument #1
Transition
Supporting argument #2
Transition
Supporting argument #3
Transition
Conclusion

You can use a transition to look back in your presentation and then look forward. Let's consider an example. In the list of possible introductions in the previous section, the second point was this:

> Our company's electricity costs increased faster than expected in the fourth quarter. Here are five steps we can take to control costs.

The transition for this introduction is the second sentence. This transition can be carried throughout the rest of the presentation. After introducing the first step, discussing it, summarising it, and then looking back and then forward, the speaker's next transition could be, 'That was the first of my five suggested steps to control costs. Now, let's move on to the second step.' The speaker could use the same transition for each step. After discussing the five steps, the speaker might say, 'To summarise, these are the five steps I've suggested to control costs,' and then transition to the conclusion.

Guidelines for Content

Now that you've decided on your introduction, you can gather and outline your content. Recall that presentations generally have two purposes: to inform or persuade. Depending on the purpose of your presentation, you may choose to alter the content of your presentation to support your purpose.

When your purpose is to present information, you provide the information, explain why you are providing it and why the audience should be interested. For example, when speaking to a group of managers about a new system for cost accounting that the company is introducing, you could briefly explain the system, why it was introduced, how it will help managers in accounting for costs in their departments or business lines and how managers can help with managing the system.

When your purpose is to persuade, make your case for why the audience should support your point of view, commit to a plan, or take a course of action. Begin with your key message, support it with arguments, and back your arguments with statistics, examples, anecdotes, analogies and other support.

The advice in the rest of this section will help you to arrange your content to not only convey your information but also keep your audience interested.

Tell a Story

Telling a story through your presentation can be an unexpected but effective method for presenting your content. People can be captivated by a story, and no wonder. Humans have been telling and listening to stories for millions of years. Stories are our way of remembering, sharing and finding meaning in experiences. 'Everybody—regardless of age, race or gender—likes to listen to stories,'[8] writes Paul Smith, director of Consumer & Communications Research at the Procter & Gamble Company. Stories inspire people. Stories are memorable. Audiences are more likely to remember facts if they are woven into a story than if they are simply presented as facts. Stories are persuasive. An audience might resist a speaker who tells them what to do, but they could be won over with a story.

Executives are accustomed to using conventional language to persuade, building their case with facts, statistics and quotes from authorities. Even if they succeed, however, they've done so only on an intellectual basis, and people are not inspired to act by reason alone. Famed American screenwriting lecturer and coach Robert McKee discusses how storytelling can be a more persuasive technique than using rhetoric.[9]

> The other way to persuade people—and ultimately a much more powerful way [than rhetoric]—is by uniting an idea with an emotion. The best way to do that is by telling a compelling story. In a story, you not only weave a lot of information into the telling but you also arouse your listener's emotions and energy. Persuading with a story is hard. Any intelligent person can sit down and make lists. It takes rationality but little creativity to design an argument using conventional rhetoric. But it demands vivid insight and storytelling skill to present an idea that packs enough emotional power to be memorable. If you can harness imagination and the principles of a well-told story, then you get people rising to their feet amid thunderous applause instead of yawning and ignoring you.

By turning a presentation into a story, you greatly increase the chances that people will remember what you say, observes Nick Morgan, CEO of Public Words. According to Morgan, a CEO who gives rational arguments for increasing profits with lots of numerical support will only end up boring his audience. Furthermore, he or she is not likely to inspire employees to work to make those profits happen. 'If, on the other hand, he links our efforts (somehow) to finding the Holy Grail, or beating the Evil Empire, ...we're far more likely to remember—and act—upon what he's saying,' says Morgan.[10]

Big picture stories, like a company that was almost destroyed by the global recession and financial crisis managing to make a comeback, lend themselves to storytelling. But how can you tell stories about less dramatic things like getting inventories under control and reducing inventory costs?

In this case, you could tell stories about the ramifications of inadequate inventory control on people throughout the organisation, for example:

- The business line manager who cannot get the materials necessary to keep production on schedule
- The logistics manager who is trying to find space for an excess of inventory
- The failure of a team to complete a project on schedule because of a lack of parts and equipment
- The cost accountant who is trying to calculate the costs to the company of excess inventory

As you continue your presentation, you could describe the success of the CFO and financial managers in developing and implementing a plan to manage inventory more efficiently, thereby reducing costs and inefficiencies.

Creating a story will help your audience connect to your content, especially if your purpose is to persuade. Storytelling can be a useful technique if you need to put your numbers in context, as discussed in the next section.

Put Your Numbers in Context

Stephen Few, author of *Show Me the Numbers*, says, 'The information that's stored in our databases and spreadsheets cannot speak for itself. It has important stories to tell and only we can give them a voice.'[11] He describes this storytelling process as the 'statistical narrative.' When assembling a statistical narrative, one of the most important characteristics to address is context. A story cannot be told through numbers alone. Even if the numbers measure something important, they need to be presented in context.

Few contends that appropriate comparisons are a vital way to provide context for numbers. Examples of providing context include comparing the present to the past, examining targets and forecasts, looking at other things in the same category, such as competitors' products, and discussing norms and averages.

Numbers should be concrete, relevant and in context:

> XYZ company reports its profits increased 15% or $20 million in the current year versus last year. Profits increased because the company cut costs 5% and increased revenue 10%.

This statement is concrete and relevant to the company's investors and management, but there's no context. Add statements that provide context so that the reader can interpret the meaning of numbers. Compare the previous statement to the following one that gives more context.

> XYZ company reports its profits increased 15% or $20 million in the current year versus last year. The profits of XYZ's closest competitor increased only 5% or $5 million during the same period. XYZ is now the most profitable company in its industry. Of the $20 million profit, XYZ plans to reinvest half back into the company, use $5 million to pay down its debt and hold the remaining $5 million in a cash reserve.

Keep It Simple

If there's one overarching reason why presentations aren't effective at communicating content it's because they are unnecessarily complex. Keep your presentation simple. It's a rule not only for presentations but also for communication generally. David Duncan, president of Denihan Hospitality Group, echoes this sentiment in explaining his communication philosophy: 'Keep communication simple. Some people start with the details and soon get lost in complex technical discussions.' (See interview 12 with Duncan in appendix A.)

One way to keep your presentation simple is to separate the body of your presentation—your content—into three sections that develop your core message or theme. Why three? The rule of three is widely used in writing, storytelling, movies, books, cultures, history and organisations. Studies have shown that people have difficulty holding more than three things in short term memory, but they will remember units of three.[12] Julius Caesar said 'I came, I saw, I conquered.' Thomas Jefferson wrote of life, liberty and the pursuit of happiness. In 2011, Steve Jobs introduced the iPad2 as 'thinner, lighter, and faster' than the original.

Sometimes, it may make sense to have more than three sections of content. However, audiences could feel overwhelmed and start to tune out if you try to squeeze more sections and more details into a presentation. Also, audiences could grow impatient and sceptical. Instead of focusing on the information you are presenting, they will wonder why you can't communicate your ideas more efficiently or if you really understand your topic.

Deliver a Presentation, Not a Document

In making a presentation, you are speaking directly to your audience, which is entirely different from writing a report and sending it to people. But some presentations look and sound like reports. The presenter takes a page of a document, plugs the information into in a slide, puts the slide on the screen and reads the slide. Garr Reynolds, author of *Presentation Zen*, a book about presentation design and delivery, calls this type of presentation a 'slideument (slide + document).' The audience is struggling to simultaneously read a presenter's 'slideuements' and listen to the presenter. Before long, the audience gets frustrated and stops paying attention to the speaker and the slides.

Corporate presentation coach Jerry Weissman agrees that most slides tend to hinder rather than help presenters. 'The all-too-common complexity of the slides forces presenters either to skim over them or, in the worst case, read them verbatim.'[13] Weissman says he isn't recommending that presenters eliminate slides completely. He suggests designing slides that are simple and serve only to support the narrative of your presentation and do not distract from the presenter. See the section on designing effective slides later in the next chapter for tips on how to avoid creating overly complex, distracting slides.

Slides are one of the most common visual aids used in presentations, but whether you use slides, a flip chart or a whiteboard, your visuals should illustrate, illuminate and amplify your ideas. A single image or a line of text on a screen can communicate your idea with more power and eloquence than a screen full of words. Imaging is particularly effective with people who are oriented to learning and understanding through visual images. Let your visuals serve only as visuals and do not force them to be your entire presentation. Every element of your presentation should work together to reinforce your key message. By speaking, you connect with those in the audience who are attuned to learning by listening. If you want your audience to read a document supporting your presentation, it should be separate and not crammed into your slides.

Deliver a Meaningful Presentation

It seems obvious that you would want you presentation to be meaningful, but if you get engrossed in discussing facts and figures and preoccupied with your visuals, you may forget about why you're doing your presentation in the first place. There's also the risk you'll deliver a presentation that has little, if any, meaning for the audience—it could leave your audience confused and unenlightened. In planning your presentation, ask for a reality check from colleagues or others. Do they think your presentation will have value for your audience?

Establish Credibility With Your Audience

Whether your reputation precedes you, or you're an unknown quantity, you must establish credibility with your audience. In making an argument, present both sides and explain the reasons for your point of view. Demonstrate your mastery of detail. Back your presentation with solid research—look online for articles, studies, reports, statistics, web content and other sources of information. Talk to people in your company who are knowledgeable about the subject of your presentation and can offer observations and insights. Talk to people at trade groups, universities and other organisations about your topic.

Manage Your Time

Remember, based on the audience memory curve shown in figure 7-2, audience interest is lower in the middle of your presentation when you are delivering your content than at the beginning and the end. So, how can you keep the audience's attention? One way is to manage the time for your presentation. Can you complete your presentation in ten minutes? Or twenty minutes?

Sometimes, you may need to make a longer presentation because of the nature of the content or because you've been asked to make a 30-minute presentation. So, how do you keep your audience engaged? With a half-hour presentation, you might organise the presentation in three 10-minute segments. At the first 10-minute mark, introduce a new idea, concept or question, or make a challenging statement to reengage your audience, and then proceed to develop your idea or question for 10 minutes. At the second 10-minute mark, repeat the process. Use strong transitions to weave the sections together into a coherent whole.

Ensure Your Information Is Accurate

In the interest of providing your audience with credible information—and maintaining your credibility with your audience—make absolutely certain your information is accurate. This is a particular concern when you are presenting technical information, such as accounting and tax information, and your audience comprises other accounting professionals—or even customers and clients. In these circumstances, if you present inaccurate information, you can be certain someone will correct you, which is as unpleasant as it is embarrassing.

Create a Report

In addition to creating visuals and speaking, you can create a report to support your presentation. Your report can further develop the ideas, issues and questions you covered in your presentation, address questions raised by the audience following your presentation, provide more value to those who attended your presentation, and create a favourable impression of you because of your desire to serve the interests of your audience beyond delivering your presentation.

Your report should not be copies of your slides, which you designed to support and enhance your presentation, and not separate documents. You might include some of the information in your slides in your report if it helps to illustrate a point, provide an example, or serve another purpose. But slides are one thing, a report is another.

You can hand out your report after your presentation or send it to those who attended. If your report is heavy on quantitative information, you might consider distributing it beforehand.

Developing a Content Outline: An Example

Here's a simple example of how you might develop a content outline using the techniques discussed previously. In the list of possible introductions in the 'Introduction' section earlier in this chapter, the fourth option was 'make an attention-getting statement.' The example given was 'Over the next five years, one out of every five people in our company will retire. That means 5,000 people will leave our workforce. How are we going to recruit enough people to replace our growing number of retirees?' Let's use this scenario to develop a content outline, assuming your audience is a small group of your company's managers.

There are many ways to approach the presentation of content. You could begin by restating the 'How are we going to recruit' question. That question will frame this section of your presentation. Alternatively, you could begin with the solution to the question: 'Here is how we are going to recruit...'

Then put the question in context by providing some numbers:

- Number of people currently employed by the company

- Number who will leave because of

  ○ retirement

  ○ other reasons, such as taking another job

- Number who will need to be hired over next five years to

  ○ replace retirees

  ○ replace those who leave for other reasons

  ○ fill new positions created by the company's growth

Another way to approach the content is by looking at the issue from another perspective—the skills and experience of people who will be leaving because of retirement or other reasons. How many financial managers or accountants will leave over the next five years because of retirement or other reasons? How many line managers? How many machinists? This approach allows you to discuss not only the number of people but also the skills that will be needed. So, the question is not simply hiring a certain number of people but also hiring people with the right skill sets.

To put these departures in human terms, you could (with proper permission) include brief profiles of a few of the people who will be leaving: a controller who has been with the company for 25 years, an IT director with 10 years with the organisation, or others.

Now that you have sufficiently outlined and contextualised the problem, it is time to discuss your arguments for addressing the problem.

The first step in getting content might need to be information gathering. Do a study, perhaps with the assistance of a consultant, of general recruiting practices and those of the company's competitors. Find out what the best practices in recruiting are and which companies have stood out for their success in recruiting. Your study also might include asking employees who recently joined the company their reasons for joining and asking those who are leaving for other jobs the reasons they're leaving. Survey employees for their opinions about working for the company, what the company could do to create a more attractive work environment, and how it might recruit people.

A second step might be the development of a strategic plan for recruiting new employees. Use ideas and best practices in recruiting that were gleaned from the study to suggest creating and staffing a position for a company recruiter, taking steps to make the company a more attractive place to work, and creating a marketing campaign to attract new workers. Your plan might also include an initiative to reach out to certain workers to ask them to stay with the company for a period of time past their retirement date. The plan can include a budget for recruiting and hiring workers.

The third step might be outlining the implementation of the plan. This would include the specific phases of implementation, who will be responsible for implementation, their responsibilities and duties, a system for measuring progress toward implementation, and so on.

Some in your audience might be sceptical that your plan will work. To win them over, the last portion of your presentation can address their main concerns. You can anticipate their concerns by speaking with some audience members you know will be sceptics before your presentation or other people in your company. By doing your research in the development of your plan, you can show how other companies have implemented similar plans that were successful in recruiting more workers.

The Close

Based on the audience memory curve (figure 7-2), remember that your audience is most likely to remember the beginning and the end of your presentation, so give some thought to creating a memorable close. Rephrase and reiterate your key message. Summarise your arguments. Call your audience to action.

Let's go back to our example of recruiting enough people to replace retirees. In your close, you could hypothesise about what would happen if the company wasn't able to recruit enough people to replace its retirees and others. The company's growth could be less than expected and its profits reduced. It could have less money to reinvest in the business, hire and train workers, and maintain wage and compensation programmes that are competitive in its industry. Work could be slowed or disrupted by a shortage of key workers, and the stress on current managers and workers could increase. The company could lose workers to competitors who pay better and offer better working conditions, exacerbating the company's worker shortage.

Call your audience to action by having them complete a survey about working conditions at the company—what they like and what they don't like. Ask your audience to spread the word about the survey throughout the company. Ask what questions your audience has about the retirement issue and for suggestions on how to recruit people. Through this process, you can engage your audience, inform them about the issue and challenge them to help address it.

CHAPTER SUMMARY

- Be clear about your purpose in making a presentation.
- Know your audience: who they are, their interests, their concerns and why they should care about your presentation.
- Decide on a key message. Reinforce that message throughout your presentation.
- Create an outline of your presentation using pens and markers, paper and index cards, and sticky notes. These tools will spark your creativity and help you develop ideas and organise your presentation.
- Craft a strong introduction. Otherwise, you risk losing your audience.
- Craft a strong conclusion, with a call to action.
- Use the power of storytelling to engage, motivate and inspire your audience.

Endnotes

1 Laura DeMars, 'Uh, Is This Microphone On?' CFO.com, Mar. 2007 www.cfo.com/article. cfm/8759623/c_8766497

2 Carmine Gallo, *The Presentation Secrets of Steve Jobs: How to be Insanely Great in Front of Any Audience*, (New York: McGraw Hill, 2010).

3 Justin Locke, 'Presentation Skills 101: How to move away from trauma and perfect your skills,' *CPA Insider*, Feb. 2011 www.cpa2biz.com/Content/ media/PRODUCER_CONTENT/Newsletters/ Articles_2011/CPA/Feb/PresentationSkills101.jsp

4 Nancy Duarte, *slide:ology: The Art and Science of Creating Great Presentations*, (Sebastopol, California: O'Reilly Media Inc., 2008).

5 Nancy Duarte, 'Create a Presentation Your Audience Will Care About,' HBR Blog Network [website], Oct. 2012 http://blogs.hbr.org/cs/2012/10/create_ presentations_an_audien.html

6 Philip R. Theibert, *How to Give a Damn Good Speech*, (New York: Galahad Books, 1997), p. 91.

7 Carmine Gallo, *The Presentation Secrets of Steve Jobs: How to be Insanely Great in Front of Any Audience*, (New York: McGraw Hill, 2010).

8 Paul Smith, 'The Leader as Storyteller: 10 Reasons It Makes a Better Business Connection,' TLNT.com, Sept. 2012 www.tlnt.com/2012/09/12/the-leader- as-storyteller-10-reasons-it-makes-a-better-business- connection/

9 Bronwyn Fryer, 'Storytelling that moves people,' *Harvard Business Review*, Jun. 2003 http://hbr. org/2003/06/storytelling-that-moves-people/ar/1

10 Nick Morgan, 'How Do You Take an Ordinary Presentation and Turn It Into a Powerful Story?' Public Words blog [website], May 2012 http:// publicwords.typepad.com/articles/2012/05/how-do- you-take-an-ordinary-presentation-and-turn-it-into-a- powerful-story.html

11 Stephen Few, 'Statistical Narrative: Telling Compelling Stories with Numbers,' Perceptual Edge [website] Visual Business Intelligence Newsletter, Jul./ Aug. 2009 www.perceptualedge.com/articles/visual_ business_intelligence/statistical_narrative.pdf

12 Carmine Gallo, 'Thomas Jefferson, Steve Jobs, and the Rule of Three,' *Forbes*, Jul. 2012 www.forbes.com/ sites/carminegallo/2012/07/02/thomas-jefferson- steve-jobs-and-the-rule-of-3/

13 Jerry Weissman, 'Learning Presentation Skills by Learning to Swim,' *Harvard Business Review*, Aug. 2011 http://blogs.hbr.org/cs/2011/08/learning_ presenting_skills_by.html

8

PRESENTATIONS: DESIGNING AND DELIVERING

In the previous chapter, you wrote, sketched and organised your ideas for your presentation on paper, whiteboard or sticky notes (or you've developed and organised them using software). Then, you created a content outline. In this chapter, you will learn how you can use these resources to write notes and create visuals for your presentation. Your goal is to deliver a spontaneous, passionate, engaging presentation that resonates with your audience.

PREPARING NOTES FOR YOUR PRESENTATION

In contrast to a speech, you do not have to write the presentation in its entirety and deliver it verbatim. Nor do you have to memorise it word for word. If you do deliver it from memory, you risk appearing formal, stilted and lacking in conviction. And there is also the risk that you could forget something and stumble in your presentation.

Instead, for presentations, I recommend creating a set of notes—either written or printed on index cards or written in PowerPoint notes—and speaking extemporaneously. Write whatever number of notes you require, one for each slide, if necessary. Each note should be brief—just a few words that work as a memory key.

PREPARING VISUALS FOR YOUR PRESENTATION

One of the first things you should consider when preparing your presentation is whether you want to use visuals, such as pictures, graphs, tables or props. You may decide to make a presentation to your supervisor, members of your team, a senior executive or others inside or outside your organisation without using visuals. Some experienced speakers talk to large groups without any reference to visuals. Would it make any difference to your audience whether you used visuals?

Without visuals, the focus of the audience is entirely on you. You will not have to worry about finding or creating visual material, but to hold the attention of the audience during a presentation, you will have to excel at storytelling, explaining, informing, persuading and inspiring. You cannot depend on any visual information for support.

If you do decide to create visuals, which type should you use? Flip charts, whiteboards or paper handouts are suitable for a small audience in a conference room or other small venue. They lend themselves to the intimacy and informality of one-on-one meetings or small group discussions. Projectors or slide presentations work well for larger, more formal groups. A brief discussion of each type of visual follows.

Flip Charts

Flip charts—or large pads of paper sheets—are designed to be mounted on a stand or on wheels (for ease of transport) or to stand alone on a table. The presenter writes and draws on a sheet with a marker and flips over the sheet in order to start with a fresh sheet. The presenter has the option of creating charts in advance and creating more charts during the presentation, for example, to elaborate on an idea or answer a question from the audience. Flip charts can provide a permanent record of a presentation.

Whiteboards

Whiteboards are white glossy surfaces for writing and drawing with a non-permanent marker. Chalkboards or clear acrylic marker boards serve the same purpose. A presenter can write and diagram on a board, and, in moments of insight and spontaneity, add or erase what's on the board. If you use an interactive whiteboard, you can save what you've written on your computer and print a hard copy.

Paper Handouts

You could also create a presentation using sheets of paper—a deck or handout—that contains information and illustrations. Paper handouts typically are reserved for presentations to individuals or small groups, with copies given to each participant. You can go through the handout and discuss it with the participants.

Projectors

Overhead projectors are used in classrooms and conference rooms, but not as extensively today as in the past. Instead, presenters use video projectors that display data, images or video, as well as interactive whiteboards or computer projection systems. To be sure, some presenters still use overhead projectors. Among other reasons, transparencies can be easily organised and managed, and paper can be placed over part of the transparency to highlight or emphasise the exposed section.

Slides

For formal presentations, you can use computer and presentation software to create slides and a projector to show them on a screen. Properly designed and organised, slides illuminate, amplify and enhance presentations; they add depth, interest and variety.

But no matter how good they are, your slides are intended to support, not carry, your presentation. People planning to attend your presentation are not going to say, 'I don't know about the speaker, but I'm really looking forward to seeing the slides!' The audience is there to see and hear you, and it's up to you to engage, enlighten and persuade them. If you succeed, you can thank your slides later.

DESIGNING YOUR SLIDE PRESENTATION

The rest of this chapter will focus on creating an effective PowerPoint presentation. For better or worse, PowerPoint is the world's leading presentation software, with an estimated 95% market share. No doubt you have sat through your share of groan-inducing slide presentations. Perhaps you have also attended or watched videos of presentations that stood out for their power to engage, enlighten and inspire.

As might be expected for such a ubiquitous program as PowerPoint, it has its critics. One commentator writes that '…the software's users continue to prove that no field of human endeavour can defy its facility for reducing complexity and nuance to bullet points and big ideas to tacky clip art.'[1]

Part of the problem is that some users, particularly those who have little or no experience in designing slides, depend on PowerPoint's standard templates of charts, smart art, tables, themes and transitions to create presentations. Other users use the templates because it is standard practice in their organisation. Still, other users fall back on the templates because they are pressed for time or as a matter of expediency.

As a result, these various users limit their choices. They use templates to create not just some presentations but every presentation. The effect can be a certain sameness to presentations, including the ubiquitous use of bullet points and a disconnect between the design and function of the presentation. It's as if everyone in a community built houses using the same floor plan and materials. The houses get built, but they lack originality and practicality. They were not designed to meet the needs and tastes of individual owners.

On the other hand, a well-designed PowerPoint presentation can enhance your content. Some examples of the most creative uses of PowerPoint can be found in the winning entries in SlideShare's World's Best Presentation Contest.[2] If you are searching for some inspiration for your next presentation, take a look at some of the winning entries. In the 2009 contest, for example, the winning entry was 'American Health Care: a 4-Napkin Explanation.' Using sketches and napkins, the presentation sought to explain the state of US healthcare legislation. That 51-slide presentation was far easier to understand than the 1,000-page bills that were then winding their way through Congress. At their best, PowerPoint presentations will inspire and inform your audience. With a little effort, you too could design a winning presentation.

Whatever designs you, or someone else, creates for your slides, the aim is simplicity and clarity. With that goal in mind, this section offers some guidelines you can use to design your slides.

Mix of Slides

The following are some options for how to present information on slides. Your slides can contain

- text;
- pictures (photographs, illustrations, diagrams or clip art); or
- charts, graphs or tables.

'The most interesting and eye-catching, and therefore the most successful, presentations use a mix of the three methods of expression,' writes Deborah Dumaine.[3] Using different options creates variety for your audience, keeps them focused and persuades them to act.

Number of Slides

Your content will determine the number of slides you need, but there are some suggested guidelines you can follow to break up your content effectively. For slides containing text, some communication experts suggest a 7 x 7 rule, or seven lines per slide and seven words per line; or a 6 x 6 rule, or six lines per slide and six words per line. Another option is to let your outline guide your slide creation, such as one slide for each segment of your presentation: one for your introduction, one for the transition, one for the theme statement that begins the content, and so on. Your time limit might also determine the amount of slides you use. Former Apple employee Guy Kawasaki suggests a 10/20/30 rule for PowerPoint presentations: no more than ten slides in twenty minutes with no less than 30-point font.

The idea behind such guidelines is that each slide contains—or should contain—a discrete idea, and that there are only so many ideas, images and bits of information that an audience can comprehend. Furthermore, an audience wants to view a presentation for only so long. Beyond these visual and time limits, the slides could become a forgettable blur, and the audience could grow impatient.

Nancy Duarte, CEO of Duarte Inc., a presentation design and training company, says slides should pass the 'glance test.' 'A slide's message should come across in two or three seconds. An audience can only process one stream of information at a time, and you want them to hear what you're saying.'[4] If a slide is too complex, break it into multiple slides, each conveying a discrete message.

Above all, make sure your slides remind your audience of your key message. If your presentation has a powerful story, a logical narrative structure and slides that are seamlessly interwoven with your story, your audience may not know or care how many slides were shown. They'll remember your presentation—not the number of slides or the time taken.

Design Elements

If the information in slides is confusing, the problem usually isn't the information itself—it's the design. Edward Tufte, author of books on information design, said in an interview with *Advertising Age*, 'overload, clutter, and confusion are not attributes of information, they are failures of design.'[5] His solution for a cluttered slide presentation is to fix the design, not throw out the information.

Designing a slide involves a selection of design elements. One of the most important considerations when selecting elements is the 'back-of-the-room test.' Have you ever sat in the back of a large meeting room or hall and couldn't read the slides that the speaker put up on the screen? Maybe the speaker should have thought of that before the presentation. So, make sure your slides will be visible from any location. Sit in the back of your meeting room and put some test slides on the screen. Will people sitting in the back be able to see your slides? If not, you may need to reconsider the size of some of your design elements.

PowerPoint and Keynote, another presentation design program, allow you to design your own slide master as an alternative to using their templates. (The bibliography also lists books and articles on creating presentations, including visual design.)

The following are some design tips you will want to consider as you are developing your slides:

- *Determine a font size and type.* Use fonts that the audience can easily read. Presentation experts differ on which fonts to use, but seem to prefer 24- to 36-point size. As for font type, serif-type fonts like Times

New Roman are suggested for text and sans-serif fonts like Arial, Tahoma and Verdana for headlines. Use no more than two or three typefaces for slide presentations. Don't use delicate fonts that wash out.

- *Be consistent.* Be consistent in your use of fonts, font types and spacing. Every slide from your first to your last should be consistent.

- *Use strong contrasts.* Use strong contrasts between text, images and photos and the background of your slide.

- *Use engaging titles.* Put titles at the top of your slides to capture the point of each slide, enable your audience to quickly understand the purpose of the slide, and provide transitions between slides.

- *Write phrases, not sentences.* Use the fewest number of words to communicate your idea or message, but be specific. 'Profits declined' is short but too general. 'Profits increased 20% to $5 million in 2012' is specific. This might go with a bar chart showing the dollar amount in profits in 2012 versus 2011.

- *Skip the jargon.* You understand the technical terms used in accounting or finance, but don't assume everyone in your audience does.

- *Use capitalisation sparingly.* AVOID WRITING SENTENCES SUCH AS THIS ONE IN WHICH EVERY WORD IS CAPITALISED. Avoid Using Sentences Such As This One With All Initial Caps. Such sentences are difficult to read. Instead, use sentence case, capitalising only the first letter of the first word and any proper nouns.

- *Limit the number of bullet point slides.* Sometimes you may find yourself struggling to come up with an idea for a slide. 'Well, I'll put in some bullet points and be done with it,' you say to yourself. Don't default to bullet points. Consider alternatives such as graphs, charts, diagrams, photos and illustrations. You may find better ways to communicate the information in your slide than bullet points. This is not to say you shouldn't use bullet points, but they should be used modestly, for specific purposes such as explaining technical subjects.

- *Junk the chartjunk.* 'Chartjunk' is a term coined by information design guru Edward Tufte in his book *The Visual Display of Quantitative Information.*[6] It consists of visual elements in charts and graphs that are not necessary for the viewer to comprehend the information represented. With today's presentation software, you can easily create razzle-dazzle slides filled with chartjunk. But chartjunk only serves to distract, confuse or annoy your audience.

- *Value empty space.* In contrast with chartjunk, empty space is integral to a slide. Some presenters don't seem to appreciate this. In *Presentation Zen,* author Reynolds says, 'One of the biggest mistakes typical businesspeople make with presentation slides (and documents) is going out of their way to seemingly use every centimetre of space, filling it with text, boxes, clip art, charts, footers and the ubiquitous company logo.'[7] Reynolds notes that empty space suggests elegance and clarity and gives the few elements on a slide their power.

Colours

Like images and words, colours define your presentation. They set the tone, shape your message, distinguish your brand and guide your audience through your presentation. They add richness, context and variety to your presentation.

What colours should you choose? As always, start with your audience. What are their preferences? What is the purpose of the presentation? If you were making a formal presentation to an audience of several hundred business executives, it might be best to stick to conservative foreground colours, such as blue. If you were making a presentation to a group of employees to get them fired up to start a project, you might use foreground colours such as red, orange or yellow that stimulate your audience.

When creating slides, consider the relationship of your background and foreground colours and the relationship of foreground colours to one another. You could choose any variation of colours for your background—or you could go for a white or black background. If you are doing a formal presentation, you might choose a white or black background that would set your foreground colours in sharp relief. Or, to set a more informal, relaxed tone, you might choose a different background.

Ensure that your foreground colours contrast well with your background. Choose foreground colours to create a complementary or contrasting colour mix or a combination of complementary and contrasting colours. Experiment. Try different colours and relationships on some slides and test them using the projector and screen you will use for your presentation. You don't have to rely on the pre-chosen PowerPoint colour schemes either. Try online tools at sites like colourcombos.com or colourlover.com, where you can browse colour schemes.

Presentation Design Example

Armed with your new design knowledge, let's return to our example from the list of possible introductions in the 'Introduction' section in the last chapter. The example given was 'Over the next five years, one out of every five people in our company will retire. That means 5,000 people will leave our workforce. How are we going to recruit enough people to replace our growing number of retirees?' Let's use this scenario to develop sample slides to illustrate some of the points about designing slide presentations that were previously discussed.

The title for a slide should be engaging and short. For our example, some potential slide titles might be

- 5,000 people: gone in five years.
- 5,000 people: gone by 2017.
- Talent drain: 5,000 employees to retire by 2017.
- Retirement rate will double over next five years.

The slide's content should be visually appealing, making good use of white space and using bullet lists and long text sparingly. An effective use of space could be an illustration that shows that 2,500 people retired in the past ten years while 5,000 people, or twice as many, will retire over the next five years, or in half the time.

If you want to play on your audience's emotions, drive home the message of loss. Begin with a slide that shows a crowd of people with the title, 'Here today.' On the next slide, leave that space blank with only the title 'Gone by 2017.'

To showcase the talent that will be walking out the door, you might have an illustration or chart that gives a sense of the skills loss. For example, 1,000 production line supervisors and workers will retire, along with 500 people in accounting and finance and 200 people in sales and marketing or a slide with some combination of the loss in numbers and skills. See figure 8-1 for a simple slide that can accomplish that purpose.

Figure 8-1: Example of an Effective PowerPoint Slide

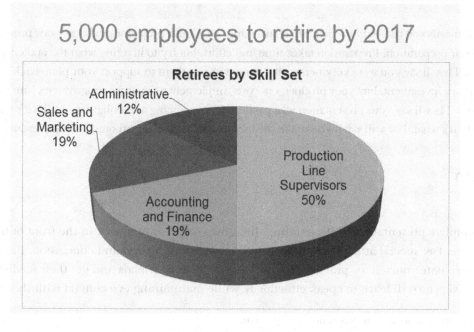

You could continue the presentation with slides that show how the company will find replacements for the workers who are retiring or otherwise leaving by convincing some people to postpone retirement, hiring new workers and so on. Other slides could explain how people in the audience can help address the problem, for example, by helping to recruit new workers.

For an example of what *not* to do, see figure 8-2. This slide breaks nearly every rule of good slide design.

Figure 8-2: Example of an Ineffective PowerPoint Slide

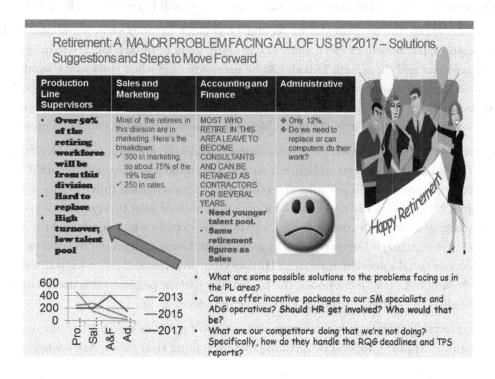

DELIVERING YOUR PRESENTATION

Whatever type of visuals you use—whiteboard, flip chart, paper handouts, projector or slides—your presentation is only as good as your preparation. Preparation takes time and effort, but try to imagine what the audience will say after your presentation. They'll say you were very persuasive in convincing them to support your plan, back your project, raise capital, make an investment, buy your product, cut costs, implement a new reporting system, hire more people or achieve other goals. They'll say your presentation was passionate, convincing and enlightening. That's what you want them to say, and that's what they will say if you make the investment in creating an outstanding presentation.

Preparation

Practise

Practise your complete presentation while standing. Imagine you are on stage or in the front of the room with your audience. Pay special attention to delivering a strong introduction and conclusion. Practise in front of a mirror and evaluate yourself, or practise in front of colleagues or friends and get their feedback. As you continue to practise, you will learn to speak effortlessly while maintaining eye contact with the audience.

The following are some considerations when using visual tools:

- *Flip chart.* If you are using a flip chart, you could prepare the charts in advance, using coloured markers. Include blank pages among your completed pages so you can write more information or create additional charts during your presentation. Practise flipping pages while you speak so you don't have to stop, turn a page and resume talking. Or have someone flip pages and create new charts or add to existing charts for you.

- *Whiteboard.* Use a variety of coloured marker pens that stand out. Make sure erasers are available. Ensure that your words and illustrations are clearly visible. You may want to practise, especially if you haven't done any drawing since grade school. If you are using an interactive whiteboard, remember to save and print a copy before you erase information on the board so you will have a record for possible future use.

- *Overhead projector.* Make sure the projector works and won't block anyone's view. Stand next to the screen so you don't impede the audience's view, and you can easily point to the screen. Try to minimise walking between the projector and the screen. This should be necessary only when you change overhead sheets. Or, you could have someone change the sheets at your direction. Make sure the sheets are properly positioned on the projector, otherwise, the information on the projector could appear tilted on the screen, or part of the information on the overhead may not be visible on the screen. Instead, it could end up on the wall.

- *Paper Handouts.* Before, during or after the presentation? That's the question to consider regarding when to distribute handouts to your audience. You may distribute handouts beforehand if you want the audience to read your material in advance and come to your presentation fully informed and prepared to ask questions. Or, you may distribute the handout at the start of your presentation if you want to go through the material along with your audience. In any case, explain why you created the handout and how you will present it, that is, are you going to go through the entire handout in sequence or concentrate on specific sections or take another approach? During your presentation, try to keep the audience focused on you, not the handout. Ask them to open the packet to a specific page and discuss it with them. Try to maintain eye contact as you are speaking. Encourage questions.

- *Slides.* Get comfortable operating the computer and projector you'll be using. Practise going through your slide show until you appear effortless in speaking and presenting your slides. Ask some colleagues or other observers to critique your presentation and provide feedback. Have someone make a video of your presentation so you can evaluate it yourself.

Meeting Venue

Before your presentation, check out the conference room, auditorium or other venue where it will be held. Meet with the technicians who will provide technical support. Work with them to make sure the venue is properly lit. The lighting can usually be adjusted for your presentation. Also, make sure the room is comfortable. Don't use a podium, unless you're required to do so by your company or other organiser of your presentation. Instead, speak directly to your audience, just as if you're having an informal conversation with some colleagues or friends. Be prepared. Have a contingency plan in case of equipment failure or other problem. Will there be replacements available if equipment crashes? Or will you have to continue your presentation without your slides or a microphone? Save a copy of your presentation on a disc and print a hard copy. Finally, arrange for someone to record a video of your presentation. .

If possible, do a complete run-through of your presentation at the meeting venue. If you will be using a microphone, check that it's working properly, and that you can speak comfortably. Check the time of the run-through against the time you planned (or allowed by a sponsoring organisation) for your presentation. Can you complete it within your time limit? Do a back-of-the-room test of your decks, transparencies, flip charts, slides or whiteboard to make sure your presentation can be seen properly. These preparations will help you familiarise yourself with the venue and get comfortable in making your presentation.

Presentation Day

Dress for the Occasion

Before you speak the first word of your presentation, the audience will judge you based on your appearance, so dress to convey the right professional image. If you are making a presentation to people in your company, you will know or can inquire about the proper attire for a presentation. If you are making a presentation to people outside your organisation, such as members of a professional society or other organisation, you can find out from the organisation's directors or one of its members. In any case, it's better to exceed than to fall short of the appropriate attire for the presentation.

Relax

American Comedian Jerry Seinfeld jokes about people fearing public speaking more than death, saying, 'This means to the average person, if you go to a funeral, you're better off in the casket than doing the eulogy.'

You may not be *that* afraid of speaking, but you may be nervous. It's not uncommon. Even experienced speakers can get the jitters. To relax, get a good night's sleep before your presentation. Before your presentation starts, get some physical exercise, such as taking a walk, or lie down in a quiet room and rest for a few minutes. Do some breathing exercises. Relax your vocal chords by taking a hot shower and drinking warm liquids. Warm up your voice by humming or singing softly. Put yourself in a positive mental state. Imagine you're telling a story, and people are crowded around to hear you. They are totally immersed in your narrative.

You're On!

You know your subject inside and out. You've practised and then practised some more. You have a story to tell, and you're excited about telling it. You know that you can win your audience over. You walk confidently on stage. You begin your presentation.

So how do you get from an auspicious beginning to the conclusion of a successful presentation? Through the process of facing your audience, moving about the stage, maintaining eye contact and using your voice.

When facing your audience, stand straight, with your feet about shoulder width apart. But don't stay rooted to the same place. Move about, but with intent. Walk slowly toward another area of the stage, and stop to make a point, or start a new section of your presentation. Repeat the process over the course of your speech, but do not move so often or so quickly that it becomes distracting. Glance only briefly at the screen when introducing or commenting on a slide, and then quickly resume looking at the audience. If you are using a computer and projector to present visuals, you can look at the slides on your computer, and you only need to glance at the screen occasionally to make sure the visuals are being presented correctly.

Maintain eye contact with the audience throughout your presentation. Look at one person in one part of the room and then another person in another part. Continue to look at people in different areas: those in the front, in the middle, and the rear, and those off to one side or the other. Some people may be smiling, some frowning, some may have blank faces. Regardless, make brief eye contract with them, and then move on. Through this process, you will connect with people throughout the room and pull your audience into your presentation.

Use your voice to communicate your enthusiasm and energy and establish credibility. Speak in a natural and conversational tone. Speak at a measured pace—not so fast that you appear to be hurrying through your presentation but not so slow that the audience is starting to look at their watches. Speak loudly enough that you're heard in the back of the room, but without shouting. Use voice inflection—the alteration in the pitch and tone of your voice—to emphasise a point, delineate transitions in your presentation, or introduce a question.

After your presentation, follow up by talking to members of your audience (or contact them later). Ask for feedback. What did they like or dislike? Do they remember your key message or your call to action? Watch the video of your presentation (assuming you arranged to have one recorded) and think about how to improve your presentation and how to plan for your next one.

Questions

Think also about how you will respond to questions during the presentation and afterward. The circumstances may dictate the timing of your responses. If you are presenting to a single manager or small group, such as your supervisor or members of your team, or a few senior executives, you can expect them to ask questions during your presentation. If you are speaking to a large audience, you may ask that they hold their questions until you are finished, or you may decide to take questions during your presentation.

A risk in taking questions while you are speaking is that complicated, irrelevant or extraneous questions could sidetrack your presentation, or you could get blindsided by a hostile questioner. A risk in taking questions at the end is that you are preventing some people from leaving, and some may even head for the exit anyway, so you might take only a few questions at the end, conclude the presentation, and speak personally with questioners or communicate with them later.

CONCLUSION

It takes creativity, focus and discipline to develop a presentation that will stand out from the ordinary, resonate with your audience and communicate your message. But the result will hopefully be a presentation that achieves your goal, whatever that goal may be: to sell your boss on a new idea, motivate your team to complete a project, sell a product or service, enable your company to reduce costs or increase revenue, or something else. There is more at stake than just achieving your goal. Your presentation is a reflection on you as a professional. Your ability to deliver a winning presentation will add to your communication skills, build your reputation as a communicator and help you advance in your career, whether you work for a corporation or small business or become an entrepreneur. You can use your use your presentation skills to give back to your community, such as by raising funds for your favourite cause or teaching a class that helps high school students learn a skill or prepare for college. Your presentation skills give you the power to effect change in your organisation, your career and your life.

RESOURCES

There are many resources available for learning to make presentations or building on your existing knowledge and skills:

- *Your company*. Your organisation may have in-house designers and other communication specialists who can assist you in developing your presentation. Your company may have formal training programmes on presentations, or you may be able to find an experienced presenter who can mentor you. Your company may also have a set of instructions for creating presentations that prescribes company standards for presentations but perhaps allows you to exercise your creativity and judgment within those standards.

- *Community resources*. You could join organisations, such as Toastmasters, that help you develop your public speaking and presentation skills. Or, sign up for a class on presentations at a local community college or other institution.

- *Online education*. You can find many outstanding presentations on the Internet. For some of the best, go to TED's website. (TED stands for Technology, Entertainment, Design.) Another online resource for presentations is YouTube.com (search under 'presentation skills training'). You can also search other sites, such as Quora.com (search under 'presentation skills').

- *Professional societies*. Some professional societies and organisations, such as the AICPA or CIMA (Chartered Institute of Management Accountants), state accounting organisations, such as the Maryland Association of Certified Public Accountants (MACPA), and other organisations offer education and training for presentations.

- *Designers, design consultants, communication consultants*. You (or your company) could hire a designer or design or communication consultant to assist you in preparing your presentation, if the cost were justified by the importance of the presentation, your desire to improve your presentation skills, or other reasons. Some designers and consultants are listed in the bibliography. You can also get advice on making presentations on the websites of consultants who write blogs or produce videos on the subject.

- *Books and articles*. There are excellent books and articles on communication, presentations and design. Some of these are listed in the bibliography.

CHAPTER SUMMARY

- Presentations often fail because they're too complex. Keep yours simple.

- Know quantification, or how to present numbers so your audience understands.

- Prepare thoroughly for your presentation. Know your subject.

- Prepare your visuals (if you use visuals).

- Practise.

- Face the audience, maintain eye contact and move with a purpose. Use your voice, and speak from the mind—and heart.

Endnotes

1 Bob Parks, 'Death to PowerPoint!' *Bloomberg Businessweek*, 30 Aug. 2012 www.businessweek.com/articles/2012-08-30/death-to-powerpoint

2 SlideShare's World's Best Presentation contest was last held in 2010. Winning entries can be viewed at http://blog.slideshare.net/2010/12/10/the-convenient-truth-wins-worlds-best-presentation-contest-2010/

3 Deborah Dumaine, *Write to the Top: Writing for Corporate Success*, (New York: Random House Trade Paperback, 2003).

4 Nancy Duarte, 'Avoiding the Road to PowerPoint Hell,' *The Wall Street Journal*, 22 Jan. 2011

5 Michael Carmichael, 'The Ad Age Stat Q.&A.,' Adage.com, Nov. 2011 http://adage.com/article/adagestat/edward-tufte-adagestat-q-a/230884/

6 Edward Tufte, *The Visual Display of Quantitative Information*, 2nd edition, (Cheshire Connecticut: Graphics Press Inc., 2001).

7 Garr Reynolds, *Presentation Zen: Simple Ideas on Presentation Design and Delivery*, 2nd edition, (Berkeley, California: New Riders, 2011).

9

SOCIAL MEDIA IN BUSINESS

As a management accountant, you could be called upon—now or in the future—to help your company determine or refine its goals for communicating both inside and outside the organisation, develop strategies for accomplishing those goals, and evaluate whether those strategies are working. You could be asked to assist with new initiatives, such as integrating social media into your company's business plan and operations. Management accountants can apply the same technical knowledge, financial expertise and critical thinking skills to communication management that they have applied to other areas, such as advising a company on managing operations more efficiently and at lower costs or evaluating plans to enter new markets or acquire other companies. This chapter will discuss some of the benefits and risks of using social media, summarise the features of some popular social media platforms, and explain why your company should have a social media policy.

Social media refers to interactive platforms where individuals or groups (such as companies) can create, share, discuss and modify user-created content. Employees of corporations and businesses are probably well-accustomed to using social media sites, such as LinkedIn, Twitter, Facebook, Pinterest and Google+.[1] Individuals spend more time on social media sites than anywhere else on the Internet.[2] According to an MIT Sloan/Deloitte survey and research study, the main reasons people participate in social media at work are to network with others, work more effectively and voice opinions.[3] Among other reasons are to feel more connected to the organisation, improve personal reputation and develop skills.

By contrast, many companies are still in the early stages of incorporating social media into their business models and operations. The potential to use social media in business is enormous, including improved customer relationship development and market research. One of the biggest potential benefits for companies is the ability to communicate with customers through social media. Corporate leaders have been hesitant to adopt social media, which may explain why their companies are not pursuing social media. Seven of ten CEOs reportedly have no presence on major social networks.[4] Concerning the use of Twitter, some executives say they don't have the time or don't see a direct correlation with sales. But advocates of CEOs using Twitter and other social media say they provide an inexpensive and effective means of connecting with customers, clients and employees.

Companies that do use social media have seen benefits in the area of communication. Internal and external networking and social media tools can be used to speed access to knowledge, cut communication costs and reduce time to market for products and services. As companies find new uses and applications for social media, they are expanding their goals for social media from specific objectives (such as cost savings) to strategic goals (such as increasing the rate of innovation through collaboration).[5] Finance professionals, typically sceptical about social networking, are starting to see the value of social media for interacting with investors, employees, customers and stakeholders.

Because social media platforms are continuously evolving, some companies may find it difficult to grasp the benefits and risks of using social media. According to a Financial Executive Research Foundation report, 'many companies are just now starting to take a serious look at the benefits of social media in business, and they are looking even more closely at the risks involved, such as fraud, theft, defamation, cyber-bullying and invasion of privacy among others.'[6] The report ultimately found that many of the executives surveyed believed the risks can be mitigated or are outweighed by the benefits. Let's examine the benefits and risks of using social media as a business communication tool.

BENEFITS

Among other benefits, social media platforms such as Facebook, Twitter and LinkedIn empower companies to

- broaden, deepen and strengthen relationships with audiences, including current and prospective customers and clients, current and prospective employees, shareholders and investors, business partners, vendors, suppliers and service providers.

- communicate with a wider market of prospective customers and at a lower cost than may be possible through traditional means, such as print advertising.

- develop their own social business applications or acquire applications from third party providers to write plans for incorporating social media into the organisation, create metrics for measuring the value of social media, manage social media more efficiently and evaluate the performance of social media.

- increase the company's visibility in the marketplace and promote its brand using platforms such as Facebook or Twitter and communication channels such as blogs, videos, webcasts and podcasts. In the UK, a wide range of small businesses, including a hotelier, a dentist, a business coach and a bookbinder have used social media to attract customers and increase sales.[7]

- put a human touch on an organisation through blogs, tweets, videos and other communication from senior executives and others in the company.

- inform and educate existing and prospective customers and clients about the company's products and services, launch of new products and other news about the company, and get customer feedback, for example, through polls of customers on social media sites.

- learn more about customers and clients based on their comments left on company social media sites, online conversations with them, and market research using social media and other sources of information and intelligence.

- study the social media sites of competitors and other organisations to learn about best practices, competitors' social media initiatives, social media trends and other information.

- use internal networks based on social media models like Yammer to enable managers and employees to communicate and collaborate within the organisation.

- foster innovation in the organisation through collaboration, sharing of knowledge, testing of ideas, and research and development.

A further benefit of the increased visibility generated by social media is in hiring. As you may recall from chapter 2, the next generation of management accountants has required some companies to re-think many of their policies. Anoop Mehta, vice president and CFO of Science Systems and Applications, Inc., has observed that technology has affected the communication skills of recent graduates. 'Companies will have to adapt to [young people's] expectations if they expect to recruit and retain talented young people, which is why we are looking at the possible use of Facebook and other social media tools in our company.' See interview 13 with Mehta in appendix A.

RISKS

Although social media offers exceptional opportunities for companies to communicate, collaborate and reach global markets, it also carries serious risks. A few of these risks are explained in the following list:

- *Loss of control.* A company's postings on its social media sites or comments about a company on its sites or other sites could go viral, reaching millions of people almost instantaneously.

- *Damaging comments.* Comments about a company from people inside or outside the organisation can seriously damage a company's reputation.

- *Security breaches.* Protection of sensitive or proprietary information could be breached because of inadvertent or deliberate disclosure by employees or others or in the event an employee accidentally loses his or her smart phone, tablet, or other mobile device containing company information.

- *Hacking.* Social media sites are vulnerable to malware attacks and hacking that could result in loss of company information and data.

- *Loss of productivity.* Employees could spend time using their personal or professional social media accounts for purposes that are not related to work.

- *Regulatory transgressions.* A company could violate governance and compliance laws and regulations for corporate social media sites.

MANAGEMENT ACCOUNTANTS AND SOCIAL MEDIA

Although business leaders may have questions and concerns about social media, they generally agree on its growing importance to their organisations. To investigate the effects of social networking and social software on business, Deloitte and *MIT Sloan Management Review* collaborated in a global research project.[8] While just 18% of all survey respondents believe social business is important to their organisation today, 63% say it will be important in three years. Similar results were found in a separate IBM study of CEOs worldwide.[9]

Breaking down the results of the Deloitte study further, 28% of CEOs, presidents and managing directors say social business is important to their organisations today compared with 14% of CFOs, treasurers and comptrollers.[10] The gap persists looking ahead: 71.3% of CEOs, presidents and managing directors believe that social business will be important to their organisations in three years, compared with 56.3% of the CFOs surveyed. That CFOs place less value on social media may be because they tend to focus on returns on investment, and few companies measure the results of their social initiatives. Many CFOs seem inclined to hold back on adopting social business until the technology matures and there is more evidence to support its business value. However, now is an opportune time for CFOs to take the lead in the social business of their companies. Embracing social media could enhance the strategic role of CFOs in the organisation and enhance their companies' competitive edge.

Although social media can help to improve communication with external customers, increase productivity and achieve other corporate goals, it has limits and is not an appropriate substitute for all other forms of communication. A Deloitte survey of the role of social media in building workplace culture found that nearly half of executives surveyed believe social media has a positive effect on workplace culture while only a quarter of employees surveyed agreed.[11] There was a similar divide when executives and employees were surveyed about their thoughts on if social media allows for increased workplace transparency. 'Our research suggests executives are possibly using social media as a crutch in building workplace culture and appearing accessible to employees,' said Punit Renjen, chairman of the board, Deloitte LLP. 'The norms for cultivating culture have not changed, and require managers to build trust through face-to-face meetings, live phone calls and personal messages.'

Another difficulty that companies face when determining the value of social media as a communication vehicle is developing metrics to measure the return on their investment. One question is whether traditional metrics can capture the true value of social media, or whether new metrics need to be developed to measure its value in reaching a global audience, building relationships with current and prospective customers, converting those relationships to sales, or fostering innovation in an organisation. Management accountants may be called upon to help determine if an investment in social media is practical. See box 9-1 for ways that management accounts can contribute to social media projects. Despite the uncertainties surrounding social media, this much seems certain: Measurement could become even more important if social media causes companies to make significant changes in their practices, processes, measurement systems and information systems.[12]

Box 9-1: CGMA: Role of Management Accountants in Web 2.0 Projects

According to a CGMA report, there is comparatively little data on organisations' experiences with social media tools and implementation of web-based collaborative approaches (web 2.0). A lack of publicly available information on the costs and benefits makes it difficult to advance the business case for web 2.0 projects.* This is where management accountants come in.

'Management accountants have a significant role to play in web 2.0 projects, particularly the creation of the business case and the implementation and evaluation of the project against objectives,' the report noted.

The CGMA report includes a tool for helping companies go through the process of establishing a business case. The following are highlights of this process:†

1. Determine the objective of the company's social media/web 2.0 projects.
2. Identify the opportunities.
3. Outline the assumed benefits (measure of success).
4. Identify the risks.
5. Gather data on initiatives similar to the company's project.
6. Determine what information needs to be purchased to support business case.
7. Determine what use can be made of internal information in making assumptions, estimates.
8. Test assumptions. What weight should be given to the assumptions underlying the project?
9. Consider alternatives, for example, the effect if the organisation did not implement the project.
10. Address uncertainty. Use techniques such as modelling to simulate different outcomes.
11. Decide how to integrate all the information about a project to help decision-makers.
12. Determine if project expenditures can be capitalised.
13. Ensure information about usage could be captured.
14. Set benchmarks to measure success.
15. Conduct post-completion audit to determine if project has achieved its objectives and contributed to the company as intended.
16. Provide feedback to project participants. Ensure any lessons are captured that could be applied to future projects.

* CGMA (Chartered Global Management Accountant), 'How to make a business case for Web 2.0' www.cgma.org/resources/tools/pages/make-a-business-case-for-web20.aspx
† For more details, including corporate case studies, see the report on the CGMA website at www.cgma.org/resources/tools/pages/make-a-business-case-for-web20.aspx.

SOCIAL MEDIA CHANNELS

Assuming a company has established a business case for using social media or has reviewed and validated an existing business case for its use, a company must consider which social media channels to use or evaluate its existing use of channels. The following sections summarise the social media channels most actively used by businesses today. We will start our examination of social media platforms with LinkedIn, one of the most popular tools for professional networking. LinkedIn will be discussed as both a personal and business tool, whereas other sites—Twitter, Facebook, Google+ and YouTube—are discussed as business tools only.

LinkedIn

LinkedIn operates the world's largest professional network on the Internet. As of September 30, 2012, LinkedIn had more than 187 million members in more than 200 countries and territories. More than two million companies have company pages on LinkedIn. On its page, a company can tell its story, highlight its products and services, engage with followers, including current or prospective customers, and share career opportunities.

Author Jan Vermeiren says the most powerful concept behind LinkedIn is that it finds the right people and the connections that you, the user, have with them.[13] These features make it possible for you to connect with your primary network: the people you know. More than that, they enable you to build on those connections to associate with other people and other networks.

Your LinkedIn Profile

Creating a profile on LinkedIn gives you visibility in the business and professional community, promotes your personal brand, and showcases your work experience, knowledge and expertise. Furthermore, you can enhance your reputation by getting recommendations to add to your profile. The more detailed your profile, the easier it is for someone to find you.[14]

If you work for a global organisation, people in your own organisation who work in distant offices may learn about you through your LinkedIn profile. You may use LinkedIn to find people in your organisation with the expertise you need to help you with a project or join your team. You also can develop long-term relationships with others in your company. If you work for a small business, you can use your profile to connect your business to a global audience. In return, professional colleagues, professionals in other industries and others can find you through your profile.

Groups and Answers

By joining and actively participating in LinkedIn Groups, you can meet people with skills and interests similar to yours, learn about trends and issues in your company's industry and markets, and build a reputation as a knowledgeable and thoughtful participant in group discussions. Likewise, by actively participating in LinkedIn Answers, you can develop a reputation as a knowledgeable source of information in your area of expertise. These interactions will strengthen your profile and enhance your professional credentials. They might also help impress future employers and recruiters.

Company Page

When you create a LinkedIn profile, you select the company for which you work. Your profile is then automatically added to the company page. Employee profiles on the company's page serve to showcase the talents, skills and experience of its workforce to customers and clients, investors, business partners and others. They also show an organisation's human resources. Through LinkedIn, employees can help their organisations to provide customer service, provide customer feedback, identify prospective customers, develop business partnerships, recruit people, track competitors or find experts who may help a company to address a business problem.

Twitter

More companies, from small businesses to corporate giants, are setting up Twitter accounts and tweeting, and some CFOs who are at the forefront in using social media are active Twitter users. As with other social media, a company should first consider how using Twitter fits into the organisation's strategic goals and business plan. Twitter could help to support specific goals, such as building relationships with customers or prospects, improving customer relations, sharing ideas, promoting its thought leadership or other purposes. But the purposes for using Twitter should be clear.

Twitter is one of many ways a company can communicate, and it should be integrated with the organisation's other communication platforms. The company should develop a plan for Twitter usage, including its goals, target audience, tweet topics, responding to questions and asking questions of followers.[15]

In a large company, a full-time 'social media specialist' might be dedicated to managing the organisation's Twitter account. In smaller organisations, managing Twitter might be part of (many) other responsibilities. Regardless, the company should have designated people managing the account. If multiple employees are managing the account, some companies use the company name as a Twitter handle, and, in the profile information, they list the real name of the employees who manage the account.[16]

Facebook

If Facebook were an actual country, it would have the world's third largest population. With more than one billion users,[17] it is one of the most popular social networking sites. Businesses, from large corporations to small businesses, are networking with current and prospective customers and clients and marketing and selling products and services on Facebook. Businesses can draw on a wealth of advice from Facebook and other sources to promote their brands.

Facebook has a 'Social Business Blueprints' section that offers suggestions on building a page and promoting a brand, the success stories of some well-known corporations, and more. It also has a best practices guide for managing a Facebook account. Other organisations also have produced guides.[18] These guides can be useful resources for developing your company's social media presence.

Because it is free (if you don't advertise), Facebook enables small businesses to market to a global audience at no cost. To make the most of Facebook, provide robust company information, make it a point to respond to every question from followers, make it easy to share content and partner with other small businesses. Small businesses are having success on Facebook. The National Federation of Independent Businesses profiled three such businesses on its website: a computer repair firm, a carpet and flooring business, and a photography company.[19] The owners of each company describe how Facebook has allowed them to provide better communication with customers and quickly resolve customer service issues.

Google+

Google+ is a social networking and identity service operated by Google Inc. It has 500 million registered users of whom 235 million are active across Google.[20] Google describes it as an overarching layer that integrates many of its online services, such as Google Mail (Gmail), Maps, Profiles and Picasa.

Google+ also includes new services such as Circles, Hangouts and Sparks. Circles enables users to share information and ideas with friends, colleagues and others. Hangouts lets up to ten users join an online video meeting. Users can add a Hangouts event to their Google calendar, join the meeting directly from Gmail and open a Google document in a meeting. Using Hangouts, workers could efficiently collaborate in a virtual meeting and embed in a calendar future work commitments and follow-up. Sparks enables users to find articles and videos of interest on the Internet, sort them by topic, and share them. By creating Google+ Pages, businesses can share information that interests customers, prospects and others, promote their brand, and increase their visibility in the marketplace.

YouTube

Founded in 2005, YouTube allows billions of people to discover, watch and share original videos. YouTube provides a forum for people to connect, inform and inspire others across the globe. It acts as a distribution platform for original content from creators and advertisers large and small. More than 800 million unique users visit YouTube each month, and more than four billion hours of video are watched each month on YouTube.[21]

In contrast with some other social media, YouTube does not have a platform specifically designed for businesses. Even so, businesses large and small are creating branded channels on YouTube to which they upload videos they've created on a variety of topics, such as video annual reports or short videos that highlight a company's financial results. (A channel is the YouTube home for a company's brand. It is similar to a Facebook page or Twitter profile.) Creating a channel enables businesses to build relationships with clients and prospects and other viewers, build their brands, and market products and services.

Businesses and professionals are using YouTube to search for and view videos for a variety of purposes: (1) as a means of competitive analysis, (2) for garnering information that could be helpful in managing the business and (3) as a way to help employees develop their skills. Businesses also are using YouTube to participate in communities focused on issues of common interest. They are also leveraging their YouTube videos to achieve higher rankings on Google and other search engines.

INTERNET

In addition to social media platforms, the Internet offers many different ways for a company to build relationships with customers and clients, build its brand, increase its presence in the online marketplace, market products and services, obtain feedback from viewers on the company or its products and services and realise other benefits. Social media features can be integrated into a company's online presence to allow clients and customers to further increase communication.

As with social media, a company needs to develop a plan for using the Internet. The plan includes the reasons for online communication, the audiences, a risk assessment, resources required and management responsibilities. Here again, as a management accountant, you could be asked to assist your organisation in writing and implementing a plan, and you might develop new skills or build upon existing skills in using the Internet to communicate in various ways.

Some online options available to a company are discussed in the sections that follow.

Company Website

A company's website is the centrepiece of its communication online. Many businesses, from Fortune 500 corporations to small businesses, have websites. Some sites contain a brief description of the company, contact information and not much else. Others are robust sites that include detailed information about the company, its principals, products and services and their benefits, articles and reports of interest to customers and others, and much more. Companies use their own employees or contract with outside designers, writers, videographers and others to design and produce content for their sites.

With so many business websites, the challenge for a company is to produce fresh, quality content that attracts interest, stands out in the marketplace, builds relationships with its audience, and helps to market its products and services, and increase rankings on search engine websites.[22] Blogs and podcasts, discussed in the sections that follow, are excellent options for generating content to make a company's website more robust.

Blogs

In a small company, one or two people may write a company blog. In large corporations, people at different levels in the organisation may write blogs. For example, the CFO may write a blog and ask management accountants to contribute or write their own blogs. Company blogs may cover broad business, economic and other issues, as well as company news, stories about how its products or services help customers and clients, interviews with employees or others, and other content. To keep content fresh, new content is posted on a regular basis. Content may be linked or posted to a company's social media channels and other outlets. In addition to their own blogs, some small businesses and companies write and post content on microblogging sites, such as Tumblr, that enable users to post text, photos, quotes, links, music and videos.[23]

Podcasts

Podcasts provide another way for small businesses and corporations to engage their audiences, and they provide a more personal connection than words on a page. A company may create an original podcast or convert its blog content into a podcast (or both). In addition to hosting the podcast on its own site, a company distributes the podcast through iTunes (subject to Apple's acceptance) or other channels. Like blogs, podcasts can cover a variety of content, and people from all levels of the organisation may participate in creating podcasts.

Video

Technology has made video production affordable for small businesses, as well as large corporations. Depending on their budgets and other considerations, businesses can produce videos on their own or use professional talent on their staff, or they can use outside service providers. Quality videos have the power to make a strong connection with audiences, and videos can enhance a company's search engine optimisation.

Search engines often display video content along with text pages, and videos that incorporate target key words can achieve higher listings in search results.[24] But especially with businesses that are new to producing video, close attention must be paid to the production process, from a selection of a simple topic to keeping the video brief and concise, to incorporating a call to action.[25]

Web Conferencing (Webinar)

In a web conference or webinar, persons in different locations participate in meetings, conferences, lectures, training and presentations. Communication is by text messaging, voice and video. It is point-to-point, or between two locations, or multicast, or between a sender and multiple locations. A webinar may be between only a presenter and an audience, in which case it is sometimes called a webcast. It also may be collaborative, with members of the audience offering comments and asking questions or completing surveys. If you are making a presentation on a webinar, many of the same rules apply (see chapters 7 and 8 for more on presentations). What is your goal? Who is your audience? What is your key message? What is your call to action? But you also must adapt your presentation to the web platform. For example, to keep your audience engaged, you may want to use more slides than in a live presentation. As always, make sure that you are prepared for the presentation: what you will say, what slides you will present, whether the equipment and services to support your presentation are working correctly, and so on. Rehearse your presentation so that when the webinar goes live, you feel confident conducting the programme.

MOBILE DEVICES

People are accessing the Internet more frequently using mobile devices, and businesses and corporations have taken notice. More businesses are harnessing the power of smartphones, tablets and other mobile devices to communicate with customers and clients through mobile websites and mobile applications (apps). If you own a smartphone, you can take advantage of the apps from many of the social media sites previously discussed. If you are called upon to advise your business when it considers its mobile strategy, you will need to consider many of the benefits and risks of tackling new forms of social media.

As with any form of communication, businesses should determine the purpose of their mobile strategy if they choose to create or adapt content for mobile devices. Is it to bring in new business? Provide better service to existing customers and clients? Keep up with the competition in an increasingly mobile world? Achieve other business goals? Businesses also need to consider the value of a mobile strategy versus the costs.[26] That is where management accountants, led by the CFO, come in. You may be asked to determine if certain technology is an appropriate investment. Your experience with metrics can assist your company with decisions about adopting mobile strategies.

SOCIAL MEDIA POLICY

If your company has not already done so, it should consider adhering to a social media policy. Social media policies provide guidelines or a code of conduct for employees who post content online as part of their job or private life. As a management accountant, you might be asked to help your company develop and implement a plan for social media usage or evaluate an existing plan. This could be an opportunity for you to get experience in the management of social media in business—experience that could prove valuable if, as expected, business use of social media continues to grow. And of course, as an employee, you should know how to comply with the policy.

Social media is about communicating, and the company and its employees are communicating regardless of whether a company has a policy. Likewise, customers and clients and others outside the organisation, as well as employees themselves, are communicating about the company. The difference is that if there is no policy, the risks of damage to a company's reputation, legal liability and other risks could be greater than if it had a policy. With a policy in place, a company may be more likely to realise the benefits of social media, such as developing deeper relationships with customers and clients, converting those relationships into new business, fostering innovation within the organisation and other benefits.

Some companies have published specific policies for the use of social media by their managers and employees, whereas others have only general guidelines for usage or nothing at all. More companies are expected to write policies as corporate use of social media continues to grow. For ideas and guidance, companies can look to firms that have such policies.[27] Some regulatory agencies also have issued guidelines. For example, the Australian Department of finance and deregulation issued a 'Social Media 101' guide for Finance employees.[28]

Among the considerations for a company that is writing or reviewing a plan are

- how social media can help the organisation to achieve its business goals.
- the investment of capital, employee time, and other resources to start and manage social media channels.
- how to manage the risks in the use of social media.
- how to establish criteria for measuring the effectiveness of a company's social media channels.
- who the social media audience is. In addition to customers and clients, the audience could include prospective customers, investors, business partners, the media, the public, employees and other audiences.
- whether to begin using channels such as Facebook that are new to the company.
- who in the organisation will be responsible for helping to manage social media and their responsibilities.
- how will policies and procedures for use of social media be developed and by whom.

Social media policies often are the result of a collaborative effort across the company. Employees offer experience in using social media; marketing defines the scope of messaging; IT outlines social technologies and devices; and the legal or compliance department ensures guidelines meet the necessary regulatory criteria. As a management accountant, you may be asked to help quantify and explain the value of social media data. In addition to your technical and communication skills, you may already be experienced in using social media for personal use, and you can apply that experience when assisting your company to fine tune its policy.

CHAPTER SUMMARY

- As a management accountant, you could be called upon to help your company determine its goals and implement strategies for communicating inside and outside the organisation.

- You can apply the same technical knowledge, financial expertise and critical thinking skills to communication management that you've applied in other areas of the business.

- If you are asked to help your company develop a plan for the use of social media or evaluate an existing plan, it could be an opportunity for you to get experience in social media management in your organisation.

- You could also be asked to assist your organisation in implementing a plan for communicating on the Internet through blogs, podcasting, video, or other ways. In the process, you might develop new skills or build upon existing skills for communicating online.

Endnotes

1 Ignite Social Media, a social media marketing firm, has published '2012 Social Network Analysis Report: Demographic—Geographic and Search Data,' a statistical analysis of a number of social media. Go to www.ignitesocialmedia.com/social-media-stats/2012-social-network-analysis-report/.

2 'State of the media: The social media report 2012,' nielsenwire.com http://blog.nielsen.com/nielsenwire/social/2012/, accessed 9 Dec. 2012

3 David Kiron, Doug Palmer, Anh Nguyen Phillips and Nina Kruschwitz, 'Social Business: What Are Companies Really Doing? The Growing Importance of Social Business,' *MIT Sloan Management Review*, May 2012 http://sloanreview.mit.edu/feature/social-business-value-key-findings/

4 Leslie Kwoh and Melissa Korn, '140 Characters of Risk: Some CEOs Fear Twitter,' *The Wall Street Journal*, 26 Sept. 2012. http://professional.wsj.com/article/SB10000872396390444083304578018423363962886.html?mg=reno64-wsj. The article cites a recent report by CEO.com and analytics company Domo.

5 Josh Hyatt, 'Putting Social Networks to Work,' CFO.com, Aug. 2012 www3.cfo.com/article/2012/8/it-value_social-networks-collaboration-companies-cfo-research?currpage=1

6 Thomas Thompson Jr., Jan Hertzberg and Mark Sullivan, 'Social media and its associated risks,' Financial Executives Research Foundation report sponsored by Grant Thornton, Nov. 2011. www.grantthornton.com/portal/site/gtcom/menuitem.91c078ed5c0ef4ca80cd8710033841ca/?vgnextoid=324b4c0939f73310VgnVCM1000003a8314acRCRD&vgnextfmt=default&vgnextrefresh=1

7 Alison Coleman, 'How social media can benefit small businesses,' *The Guardian*, Aug. 2012 www.guardian.co.uk/small-business-network/2012/aug/14/small-business-benefit-social-media

8 David Kiron, Doug Palmer, Anh Nguyen Phillips and Nina Kruschwitz, 'Social Business: What Are Companies Really Doing? The Growing Importance of Social Business,' 2012 Social Business Global Executive Study and Research Project, *MIT Sloan Management Review*, May 2012 http://sloanreview.mit.edu/feature/social-business-value-key-findings/

9 Mark Fidelman, 'If You Don't Have a Social CFO, You're Going to Be Less Competitive,' *Forbes*, May 2012 www.forbes.com/sites/markfidelman/2012/05/22/ibm-study-if-you-dont-have-a-social-ceo-youre-going-to-be-less-competitive/

10 David Kiron, Doug Palmer, Anh Nguyen Phillips and Nina Kruschwitz, 'Social Business: What Are Companies Really Doing? Who Values Social Business Today May Surprise You,' *MIT Sloan Management Review*, May 2012 http://sloanreview.mit.edu/feature/social-business-value-key-findings/

11 'The Social Divide: Employees, Executives Disagree on the Role of Social Media in Building Workplace Culture: Deloitte Survey,' Deloitte [website], Jun. 2012 www.deloitte.com/view/en_US/us/press/Press-Releases/917ed0b3d26e7310VgnVCM2000001b56f00aRCRD.htm

12 David Kiron, Doug Palmer, Anh Nguyen Phillips and Nina Kruschwitz, 'Social Business: What Are Companies Really Doing?' *MIT Sloan Management Review*, May 2012 http://sloanreview.mit.edu/feature/social-business-value-putting-social-business-into-action

13 Jan Vermeiren, *How to Really Use LinkedIn*, (Charleston: Booksurge, 2009).

14 Robin M. Hensley, 'LinkedIn Tips for CPAs,' *Journal of Accountancy*, Mar. 2011 www.journalofaccountancy.com/Issues/2011/Mar/20103310.htm

15 'Best Practices,' Twitter for Business, Twitter.com https://business.twitter.com/basics/best-practices/

16 Jill Duffy, 'How to Use Twitter for Business,' PCMAG.com, Nov. 2012 www.pcmag.com/article2/0,2817,2383442,00.asp

17 Mark Zuckerberg, 'One Billion Users on Facebook,' Facebook Newsroom, Oct. 2012 http://newsroom.fb.com/News/457/One-Billion-People-on-Facebook

18 'Facebook Guide Book—How To, Tips and Instructions by Mashable' http://mashable.com/guidebook/facebook/

19 '3 Everyday Companies Using Facebook to Provide Better Customer Service,' National Federal of Independent Businesses [website]

Endnotes continued

www.nfib.com/business-resources/business-resources-item?cmsid=56293

20 'Google+: Communities and photos,' Google Office Blog, Dec. 2012 http://googleblog.blogspot.com/2012/12/google-communities-and-photos.html

21 'Statistics,' YouTube.com www.youtube.com/t/press_statistics

22 Gregory J. Wright, 'Six SEO Tips for CPAs,' AICPA Insights, Dec. 2011 http://blog.aicpa.org/2011/12/6-seo-tips-for-cpas.html#sthash.jGoOJgp6.dpbs

23 Laura Drell, 'The Quick and Dirty Guide to Tumblr for Small Business,' Mashable, Feb. 2012 http://mashable.com/2012/02/18/tumblr-small-biz-guide/

24 AJ Kumar, 'Five Ways to Optimize Video for Search Engines,' *Entrepreneur*, Mar. 2012 www.entrepreneur.com/article/223195

25 Gail Goodman, 'How to Use Video to Market Your Business,' *Entrepreneur*, Apr. 2011 www.entrepreneur.com/article/219524#

26 Michael Millar, 'Does your firm need its own mobile app?,' *BBC News*, 7 Apr. 2011 www.bbc.co.uk/news/business-13000883

27 Corey Eridon, '5 Noteworthy Examples of Corporate Social Media Policies,' HubSpot's Inbound Internet Marketing Blog, Dec. 2011 http://blog.hubspot.com/blog/tabid/6307/bid/29441/5-Noteworthy-Examples-of-Corporate-Social-Media-Policies.aspx

28 'Social Media 101: A beginner's guide for Finance employees,' Apr. 2010 http://agimo.govspace.gov.au/files/2010/04/social-media-101.pdf. See http://socialmediagovernance.com/policies.php for more examples of social media policies.

BIBLIOGRAPHY

AICPA, 'Core Competencies from CPA Vision Project Final Report' www.aicpa.org/research/cpahorizons2025/cpavisionproject/pages/cpavisionproject.aspx

AICPA, 'Presentation Tips and Tricks That Work' www.aicpa.org/interestareas/youngcpanetwork/resources/leadership/pages/presentationtipsandtricks.aspx

AICPA, '12 Tips to Better Power Point Presentations' www.aicpa.org/InterestAreas/YoungCPANetwork/Resources/Leadership/Pages/12TipstoBetterPowerPointPresentations.aspx

AICPA and Chartered Institute of Management Accountants (CIMA), 'CGMA Report: The Fast Track to Leadership: The challenges, opportunities and action plan' www.cgma.org/Resources/Reports/DownloadableDocuments/CGMA_Fast_Track_to_leadership.PDF

AICPA and CIMA, 'CGMA Report: Poor Talent Management Stifling Innovation, Capping Financial Growth,' AICPA and CIMA press release, Sept. 2012 www.aicpa.org/press/pressreleases/2012/pages/poor-talent-management-stifling-innovation.aspx

AICPA and CIMA, 'CGMA Report: Rebooting Business: Valuing the Human Dimension,' www.cncima.com/uploads/docs/CGMA_launch_report_-_REBOOTING_BUSINESS__VALUING_THE_HUMAN_DIMENSION.pdf

Amato, N., 'Memo to finance professionals: Broaden your horizons, take a broader role in your company,' *CGMA Magazine*, Aug. 2012 www.cgma.org/magazine/features/pages/20126136.aspx?cm_mmc=CGMANL-_-24Aug12-_-MostRead-_-leadership&utm_source=cgmanl&utm_medium=24Aug12&utm_term=mostread&utm_content=leadership&utm_campaign=cgmanl

Amato, N., 'To ascend to CFO role, controllers must take a broader look at business,' *Journal of Accountancy*, Nov. 2012 www.journalofaccountancy.com/News/20126797.htm

Banham, R., 'Let It Roll: Why more companies are abandoning budgets in favor of rolling forecasts,' *CFO Magazine*, May 2011 www.cfo.com/article.cfm/14570220/1/c_14570395

Barnes, N. G., Lescault, A. M., and Andonian, J., 'Social Media Surge by the Fortune 500 2012: Increased Use of Blogs, Facebook, Twitter and More,' Charlton College of Business Center for Marketing Research, University of Massachusetts Dartmouth [website], 2012 www.umassd.edu/cmr/socialmedia/2012fortune500/

Bavor, C., 'Bringing Google+ to Work,' Official Google Enterprise Blog, Aug. 2012 http://googleenterprise.blogspot.com/2012/08/bringing-google-to-work.html

Belicove, M. E., 'Finally, Guidance on Employer Social Media Policies,' *Forbes*, Jul. 2012 www.entrepreneur.com/blog/223951#

Bennett, S., 'Employee Use of Social Media Is On the Rise (And Twitter Leads the Way),' Mediabistro.com, Oct. 2012 www.mediabistro.com/alltwitter/office-social-networking_b30133

Berglas, S., 'Learning the Art of Listening,' *Forbes*, Jul. 2009 www.forbes.com/2009/07/09/how-to-listen-entrepreneurs-management-berglas.html

Bergman, P., 'Coping With Email Overload,' HBR Blog Network [website], 26 Apr. 2012 http://blogs.hbr.org/bregman/2012/04/coping-with-email-overload.html

Bergstrom, R., Batchelor, S., and Marcotte, G., 'The Future Used to be Easier: Planning for Success in a Dynamic Environment,' Accenture [website] www.accenture.com/SiteCollectionDocuments/PDF/Accenture_The_Future_Used_To_Be_Easier_Palnning_Success_Dynamic_Environments.pdf

Blundell, W. E., *The Art and Craft of Feature Writing*, (New York: New American Library, 1988).

Bolchover, D., 'Plugging the Skills Gap: Shortages Among Plenty,' *The Economist*, Economist Intelligence Unit, 2012 www.managementthinking.eiu.com/sites/default/files/downloads/EIU_SuccessFactor.pdf

Bolten, R., *Painting With Numbers: Presenting Financial and Other Numbers So People Will Understand You*, (Hoboken: John Wiley & Sons Inc., 2012).

Business Communication, Harvard Business Essentials, (Boston: Harvard Business School Press, 2003).

Bryant, A., 'He Wants Subjects, Verbs and Objects,' *The New York Times*, 25 Apr. 2009 www.nytimes.com/2009/04/26/business/26corner.html

Brynjolfsson, E. and McAfee, A., 'Big Data's Management Revolution,' *Harvard Business Review*, Sept. 2012 http://blogs.hbr.org/cs/2012/09/big_datas_management_revolutio.html

Buck, S., 'Managing Millennials: Why Generation Y Will Be Running the Country by 2020 [Infographic],' Mashable.com, Jun. 2012 http://mashable.com/2012/06/28/millennials-work-jobs/

Cain, S., *Quiet: The Power of Introverts in a World That Can't Stop Talking*, (New York: Crown Publishers, 2012).

Carmichael, M., 'The AdAge Stat Q&A,' Adage.com, Nov. 2011 http://adage.com/article/adagestat/edward-tufte-adagestat-q-a/230884/

Charan, R., 'The Discipline of Listening,' *Harvard Business Review*, Jun. 2012 http://blogs.hbr.org/cs/2012/06/the_discipline_of_listening.html

Chasan, E., 'Economic Volatility Heats Up War for Finance Talent,' CFO Report, *The Wall Street Journal*, Sept. 2012 http://blogs.wsj.com/cfo/2012/09/17/economic-volatility-heats-up-war-for-finance-talent/?mod=wsj_valetleft_email

Chui, M. et al., 'The social economy: Unlocking value and productivity through social technologies,' McKinsey Global Institute [website], Jul. 2012 www.mckinsey.com/insights/mgi/research/technology_and_innovation/the_social_economy

Chartered Global Management Accountant (CGMA), 'From ledgers to leadership: A journey through the finance function,' Chapter two: the competencies required of finance professionals www.cgma.org/Resources/Reports/Pages/ledgers-to-leadership.aspx

CGMA, 'How to make a business case for Web 2.0' www.cgma.org/resources/tools/pages/make-a-business-case-for-web20.aspx

CGMA, 'CGMA Report: New Skills, Existing Talents,' Sept. 2012 www.cgma.org/Resources/Reports/DownloadableDocuments/CGMA_new_skills_existing_talents.pdf

CGMA, 'Talking Head, Jim Morrison, CFO, Teknor Apex,' CGMA.org www.cgma.org/Resources/Reports/DownloadableDocuments/ledgers-jim-morrison.pdf

CGMA, 'CGMA Report: New Skills, Existing Talents: The new mandate for finance professionals in supporting long-term business success,' Sept. 2012 www.cgma.org/Resources/Reports/DownloadableDocuments/CGMA_new_skills_existing_talents.pdf

CGMA, 'CGMA Tool: How to Develop a Strong and Independent Team,' Jul. 2012 www.cgma.org/Resources/Tools/DownloadableDocuments/HowToDevelopaStrongAndInterdependentTeam.PDF

Chartered Institute of Management Accountants (CIMA) in association with Accenture, 'Sustainability Performance Management: How CFOs Can Unlock Value' www.cimaglobal.com/Documents/Thought_leadership_docs/Sustainability%20and%20Climate%20Change/sustainability_report_v7_web.pdf

CIMA, 'How Management Accounting Drives Sustainable Success' www.cimaglobal.com/Global/CGMA/Role_Of_Management_Accounting.pdf

Clegg, A., 'Number cruncher to co-pilot,' *Financial Times*, Sept. 2010 www.ft.com/intl/cms/s/0/4ff60000-bb90-11df-89b6-00144feab49a.html#axzz24wwuh9es

Coleman, A., 'How social media can benefit small businesses,' *The Guardian*, Aug. 2012 www.guardian.co.uk/small-business-network/2012/aug/14/small-business-benefit-social-media

DeFelice, A., 'Social Media Panel Outlines Tips for Accountants,' *Journal of Accountancy*, Jul. 2009 www.journalofaccountancy.com/Web/20091830.htm

Deloitte [website], 'As the Importance of Social Business Grows, So Does the Need for C-Suite Support,' *CFO Journal*, Dec. 2012 http://deloitte.wsj.com/cfo/2012/10/18/as-the-importance-of-social-business-grows-so-does-the-need-for-c-suite-support/

Deloitte [website], 'CFO Insights; Making Decisions That Matter,' Oct. 2012 www.deloitte.com/assets/Dcom-UnitedStates/Local%20Assets/Documents/CFO_Center_FT/us_cfo_CFO-Insights_Making-decisions-that-matter_101112.pdf

Deloitte [website], 'Generation Y: Powerhouse of the Global Economy' www.deloitte.com/view/en_US/us/Services/consulting/human-capital/organization-and-talent/a90f49642dff0210VgnVCM100000ba42f00aRCRD.htm

Deloitte [website], 'The Social Divide: Employees, Executives Disagree on the Role of Social Media in Building Workplace Culture: Deloitte Survey,' Jun. 2012 www.deloitte.com/view/en_US/us/press/Press-Releases/917ed0b3d26e7310VgnVCM2000001b56f00aRCRD.htm

DeMars, L., 'Uh, Is This Microphone On?' CFO.com, Mar. 2007 www.cfo.com/article.cfm/8759623

Drell, L., 'The Quick and Dirty Guide to Tumblr for Small Business,' Mashable.com, Feb. 2012 http://mashable.com/2012/02/18/tumblr-small-biz-guide/

Duarte, N., 'Avoiding the Road to PowerPoint Hell,' *The Wall Street Journal*, 22 Jan. 2011 http://online.wsj.com/article/SB10001424052748703954004576090053995594270.html

Duarte, N., 'Five Presentation Mistakes Everyone Makes,' *Harvard Business Review*, HBR Blog Network, Dec. 2012 http://blogs.hbr.org/cs/2012/10/create_presentations_an_audien.html

Duarte, N., *slide:ology: The Art and Science of Creating Great Presentations*, (Sebastopol: O'Reilly Media Inc., 2008).

Duffy, J., 'How to Use Twitter for Business,' PCMAG.com, Nov. 2012 www.pcmag.com/article2/0,2817,2383442,00.asp

Dumaine, D., *Write to the Top: Writing for Corporate Success*, (New York: Random House Trade Paperback, 2003).

DuPraw, M. E. and Axner, M., AMPU Guide: 'Working on Common Cross-cultural Communication Challenges,' PBS.org www.pbs.org/ampu/crosscult.html

Eridon, C., '5 Noteworthy Examples of Corporate Social Media Policies,' HubSpot's Inbound Internet Marketing Blog, Dec. 2011 http://blog.hubspot.com/blog/tabid/6307/bid/29441/5-Noteworthy-Examples-of-Corporate-Social-Media-Policies.aspx

Ernst & Young [website], 'A tale of two markets: Telling the story of investment across developed and rapid-growth markets' www.ey.com/Publication/vwLUAssets/CFO_A_tale_of_two_markets/$FILE/CFO_A_tale_of_two_markets.pdf

Ernst & Young [website], 'CEOs rely more on CFOs to develop strategy, support growth and operations initiatives, according to exclusive interviews with Ernst & Young LLP,' press release, Jun. 2012 www.ey.com/US/en/Newsroom/News-releases/CEOs-rely-more-on-CFOs-to-develop-strategy-support-growth-and-operations-initiatives

Ernst & Young [website], 'Finance forte: the future of finance leadership,' Mar. 2011 www.ey.com/GL/en/Services/Assurance/Finance-forte--the-future-of-finance-leadership

Ernst & Young [website], 'Preparing tomorrow's leaders: nine steps that CFOs can take now to prepare for the future' www.ey.com/GL/en/Services/Assurance/Finance-forte--the-future-of-finance-leadership---Nine-steps-for-CFOs-to-prepare-for-the-future

Ernst & Young [website], 'Views. Vision. Insights. The evolving role of today's CFO,' Jun. 2012 www.ey.com/Publication/vwLUAssets/Americas_CFO_ViewsVisionInsights_062012/$FILE/Americas_CFO_ViewsVisionInsights_062012.pdf

'Everyday Writing: Memos, Letters, and E-mail,' *Harvard Business Essentials: Business Communication: 9 Steps to Help You Engage Your Audience*, (Boston: Harvard Business School Press, 2003).

Facebook, 'Best Practices for your page and media strategy,' Facebook.com http://ads.ak.facebook.com/ads/FacebookAds/Best_Practices_Guide_3.01.12.pdf

Facebook, 'Social Business Blueprints,' Facebook.com www.facebook.com/business/fmc/guides/whitepapers

Few, S., *Show Me the Numbers: Designing Tables and Graphs to Enlighten*, (Oakland: Analytics Press, 2004).

Few, S., 'Statistical Narrative: Telling Compelling Stories with Numbers,' Perceptual Edge [website], Visual Business Intelligence Newsletter, Jul./Aug. 2009 www.perceptualedge.com/articles/visual_business_intelligence/statistical_narrative.pdf

Fidelman, M., 'IBM Study: If You Don't Have a Social CFO, You're Going to Be Less Competitive,' *Forbes*, May 2012 www.forbes.com/sites/markfidelman/2012/05/22/ibm-study-if-you-dont-have-a-social-ceo-youre-going-to-be-less-competitive/

Fogarty, M., 'Small Business Podcasting: 7 Tips to Grow Your Listener Base,' Mashable.com, Jul. 2011 http://mashable.com/2011/07/21/podcasting-tips-small-business/

Freed, R. C., Freed, S., Romano, J., *Writing Winning Business Proposals Landing the Client, Making the Sale, Persuading the Boss*, 3rd edition, (New York: McGraw-Hill Companies, 2010).

Fryer, B., 'Storytelling that moves people,' *Harvard Business Review*, Jun. 2003 http://hbr.org/2003/06/storytelling-that-moves-people/ar/1

Gallo, C., 'The World's Best Business Presentations,' *Bloomberg BusinessWeek*, September 2009 www.businessweek.com/smallbiz/content/sep2009/sb20090929_495291.htm

Gallo, C., *The Presentation Secrets of Steve Jobs: How to be Insanely Great in Front of Any Audience*, (New York: McGraw Hill, 2010).

Garfield, S. *Get Seen: Online Video Secrets to Building Your Business*, (Hoboken: John Wiley & Sons Inc., 2010).

Gartner, Inc. [website], 'Gartner Identifies Seven Critical Questions to Ask Before Developing a Social Media Policy,' Feb. 2011 www.gartner.com/it/page.jsp?id=1544814

Gillin, P., *Secrets of Social Media Marketing*, (Fresno: Quill Driver Books, 2009).

Gonzalez, A., 'New MACPA White Paper Outlines Future CPA Leaders' Vision for the Industry,' *Going Concern*, Nov. 2011 http://goingconcern.com/2011/11/new-macpa-white-paper-outlines-future-cpa-leaders-vision-for-the-industry

Goodman, G., 'How to Use Video to Market Your Business,' *Entrepreneur*, Apr. 2011 www.entrepreneur.com/article/219524#

Google, 'Google+: Communities and photos,' Google Office Blog, Dec. 2012 http://googleblog.blogspot.com/2012/12/google-communities-and-photos.html

Grant Thornton [website], 'The evolving accounting profile: CFO strategies for attracting, retaining and retaining accounting professionals,' Summer 2010 www.grantthornton.com/staticfiles/GTCom/Grant%20Thornton%20Thinking/Whitepapers/Accounting%20talent%20WP/Accounting%20talent%20-%20FINAL.pdf

Groysberg, B., Kelly, L. K., and MacDonald, B., 'The New Path to the C-Suite,' *Harvard Business Review*, Mar. 2011 http://hbr.org/2011/03/the-new-path-to-the-c-suite/ar/1

Groysberg, B., and Slind, M., *Talk, Inc.: How Trusted Leaders Use Conversation to Power Their Organizations*, (Boston: Harvard Business Review Press, 2012).

Grumet, L., 'Quantity Over Quality: How to Improve Accounting Education,' *The CPA Journal*, Jan. 2007 www.nysscpa.org/cpajournal/2007/107/perspectives/p7.htm

Hadley, A. and Chapman, C. C., *Content Rules: How to Create Killer Blogs, Podcasts, Videos, Ebooks, Webinars (and More) that Engage Customers and Ignite Your Business*, (Hoboken: John Wiley & Sons, 2012).

Hagel, J., 'As role evolves, CFOs must brush up on communication skills and strategic thinking,' *CGMA Magazine*, Jun. 2012 www.cgma.org/magazine/news/pages/20125884.aspx

Hardy, Q., 'Google Plus Goes to the Office,' Bits, *The New York Times*, Aug. 2012 http://bits.blogs.nytimes.com/2012/08/29/google-plus-goes-to-the-office/

Hensley, R. M., 'LinkedIn Tips for CPAs,' *Journal of Accountancy*, Mar. 2011 www.journalofaccountancy.com/ Issues/2011/Mar/20103310.htm

Hess, M., 'When you should pick up the phone, and why,' *Moneywatch*, Mar. 2012 www.cbsnews.com/8301-505143_162-57399601/when-you-should-pick-up-the-phone-and-why/

Holmes, R., 'Social Media Compliance Isn't Fun, But It's Necessary,' HBR Blog Network, *Harvard Business Review*, Aug. 2012 http://blogs.hbr.org/cs/2012/08/social_media_compliance_isnt.html

Hood, T., 'Are You a Digital CPA? Insights from the Digital CPA Conference,' Maryland Association of CPAs [website], Dec. 2012 www.macpa.org/blog/3100/are-you-a-digital-cpa

Hyatt, J., 'Putting Social Networks to Work,' CFO.com, Aug. 2012 www3.cfo.com/article/2012/8/it-value_social-networks-collaboration-companies-cfo-research?currpage=1

Ignite Social Media [website], '2012 Social Network Analysis Report: Demographic—Geographic and Search Data' www.ignitesocialmedia.com/social-media-stats/2012-social-network-analysis-report/

Irvine, M., 'Is Texting Ruining the Art of Conversation?' *Bloomberg BusinessWeek*, Jun. 2012 www.businessweek.com/ap/2012-06/D9V6AU682.htm

Keiley, E., 'How to Work a Room and Make Lasting Connections,' Boston.com [website], Apr. 2012 www.boston.com/business/blogs/global-business-hub/2012/04/how_to_work_a_r.html

Kerby, D. and Romine, J., 'What's Ahead for Management Accountants?' *New Accountant* www.newaccountantusa.com/newsFeat/ip/ip_whatsahead.html

Kim, J., 'Obstacles facing management accounting professionals as they seek to step up as global leaders,' CIMAstudy.com, Jun. 2012 www.fm-magazine.com/feature/depth/obstacles-facing-management-accounting-professionals-they-seek-step-global-leaders

Kiron, D., Palmer, D., Phillips, A. N., and Kruschwitz, N., 'Social Business: What Are Companies Really Doing? The Growing Importance of Social Business,' *MIT Sloan Management Review*, May 2012 http://sloanreview.mit.edu/feature/social-business-value-key-findings/

Kumar, A. J., 'Five Ways to Optimize Video for Search Engines,' *Entrepreneur*, Mar. 2012 www.entrepreneur.com/article/223195

Kwoh, L. and Korn, M., '140 Characters of Risk: Some CEOs Fear Twitter,' *The Wall Street Journal*, 26 Sept. 2012 http://professional.wsj.com/article/SB10000872396390444083304578018423363962886.html?mg=reno64-wsj

Lamoreaux, M. G.,'CFO 101: Five Prerequisites,' *Journal of Accountancy*, Sept. 2009 www.journalofaccountancy.com/Issues/2009/Sep/20091501.htm

Lehman, C. M., DuFrene, D. D., *Business Communication*, 15th edition, (Mason: Thomson South-Western, 2008).

Lidwell, W., Holden, K., and Butler, J., *Universal Principles of Design*, (Beverly: Rockport Publishers Inc., 2010).

LinkedIn Help Center, Company Page—Overview http://help.linkedin.com/app/answers/detail/a_id/28406

Livermore, D., 'How impatience undermines cross cultural effectiveness,' management-issues.com [website], Jun. 2012 www.management-issues.com/2012/6/19/opinion/how-impatience-undermines-cross-cultural-effectiveness.asp

Locke, J., 'Presentation Skills 101: How to move away from trauma and perfect your skills,' *CPA Insider*, Feb. 2011 www.cpa2biz.com/Content/media/PRODUCER_CONTENT/Newsletters/Articles_2011/CPA/Feb/PresentationSkills101.jsp

Mankell, H., 'The Art of Listening,' *The New York Times*, 10 Dec. 2011 www.nytimes.com/2011/12/11/opinion/sunday/in-africa-the-art-of-listening.html

Marks, G., 'Your Business Checklist: a Website, a Phone Number, a Mobile App,' *Forbes*, May 2012 www.forbes.com/sites/quickerbettertech/2012/05/07/your-business-checklist-a-website-a-phone-number-a-mobile-app/

Martin, J. S. and Cheney, L. H., 'Communication Skills Needed for Successful Integration With America's Largest Trading Partners,' Association for Business Communication [website] http://businesscommunication.org/wp-content/uploads/2011/04/PABC-2009-03-MartinandChaney.pdf

Martin, S., 'Being Persuasive Across Cultural Divides,' *Harvard Business Review*, Dec. 2010 http://blogs.hbr.org/cs/2010/12/being_persuasive_across_cultur.html

Mashable, 'Facebook Guide Book—How To, Tips and Instructions by Mashable' http://mashable.com/guidebook/facebook/

May, C.B., and May, G.S., *Effective Writing: A Handbook for Accountants*, Ninth edition, (Upper Saddle River: Prentice Hall, 2012).

McCann, D., 'For CFOs, There's No Place Like Home,' CFO.com, Mar. 2012 www3.cfo.com/article/2012/3/job-hunting_heidrick-struggles-cfo-turnover

McKee, R., *Story: Substance, Structure, Style and the Principles of Storytelling*, (New York: HarperCollins Entertainment, 1997).

Millar, M., 'Does your firm need its own mobile app?' *BBC News*, 7 Apr. 2011 www.bbc.co.uk/news/business-13000883

Molinsky, A., 'Leveling the Playing Field on Cross-Cultural Teams,' HBR Blog Network [website], Apr. 2012 http://blogs.hbr.org/cs/2012/04/leveling_the_playing_field_on.html

Morgan, N., 'How Do You Take an Ordinary Presentation and Turn It Into a Powerful Story?' Public Words [blog], May 2012 http://publicwords.typepad.com/articles/2012/05/how-do-you-take-an-ordinary-presentation-and-turn-it-into-a-powerful-story.html

Mullaney, T., 'Social media is reinventing how business is done,' *USA Today*, May 2012 http://usatoday30.usatoday.com/money/economy/story/2012-05-14/social-media-economy-companies/55029088/1

Munter, M., *Guide to Managerial Communication: Effective Business Writing and Speaking*, Ninth edition, (Upper Saddle River: Prentice Hall, 2012).

Murphy, M., 'The Inside/Outside Pay Gap,' *CFO Journal*, Sept. 2012 http://blogs.wsj.com/cfo/2012/09/11/the-insideoutside-pay-gap/

Murray, J. W., *The Complete Guide to Writing Effective and Award-Winning Business Proposals*, (Ocala: Atlantic Publishing Group Inc., 2008).

National Federation of Independent Businesses [website], '3 Everyday Companies Using Facebook to Provide Better Customer Service' www.nfib.com/business-resources/business-resources-item?cmsid=56293

Navarro, J., *What Every BODY Is Saying*, (New York: Harper-Collins Publishers, 2008).

Neilson, G. L., Martin, K. L., and Powers, E., 'The Secrets to Successful Strategy Execution,' *Harvard Business Review*, Jun. 2008 http://hbr.org/2008/06/the-secrets-to-successful-strategy-execution/ar/2

O'Connor, F., '10 Questions for Quest Software CFO Scott Donaldson,' CIO [website], Aug. 2011 www.cio.com/article/688018/10_Questions_for_Quest_Software_CFO_Scott_Davidson?page=3&taxonomyId=3157 (See question 3, 'What are the biggest challenges facing CFOs today?')

Office of Investor Education and Assistance, A Plain English Handbook: How to create clear SEC disclosure documents, U.S. Securities and Exchange Commission, Aug. 1998 www.sec.gov/pdf/handbook.pdf

O'Reilly, T. and Milstein, S., *The Twitter Book*, (Sebastopol: O'Reilly Media Inc., 2009).

Peberdy, D., 'PowerPoint Skills: Creating Effective Slides,' *Insight*, Chartered Institute of Management Accountants, May 2011 www.cimaglobal.com/Thought-leadership/Newsletters/Insight-e-magazine/Insight-2011/Insight-May-2011/PowerPoint-skills-creating-effective-slides/

PricewaterhouseCoopers [website], 15th Annual Global CEO Survey 2012, 'Delivering Results: Growth and value in a volatile world' www.pwc.com/gx/en/ceo-survey/pdf/15th-global-pwc-ceo-survey.pdf

Quint, K. D. and Butler, T. C., 'Boards and the Expanding Role of the CFO,' *Bloomberg BusinessWeek*, Sept. 2009 www.businessweek.com/managing/content/sep2009/ca20090922_634820.htm

Raice, S., 'Social Networking Heads to the Office,' *The Wall Street Journal*, Apr. 2012 http://professional.wsj.com/article/SB10001424052702304459804577285354046601614.html?mg=reno64-wsj

Reynolds, G., *Presentation Zen: Simple Ideas on Presentation Design and Delivery*, 2nd edition, (Berkeley: New Riders, 2012).

Rhode Island Society of CPAs [website], 'Internal Cross-Training on a Budget,' Rhode Island Society of CPAs newsletter, 2012 www.what-counts.org/aicpa-national-topic/62-internal-cross-training-on-a-budget

Rikleen, L. S., 'Creating Tomorrow's Leaders: the Expanding Roles of Millennials in the Workplace,' Boston College Center for Work & Family [website], Jan. 2011 www.bc.edu/content/dam/files/centers/cwf/research/pdf/Millennials%20presentation%2011_29_11.pdf

Ritsema, C. M. and Manly, T. S., 'Creating Slides for Effective Presentations,' *The Tax Adviser*, Nov. 2011 www.aicpa.org/publications/taxadviser/2011/november/pages/c2c_nov2011.aspx

Roam, D., *The Back of the Napkin: Solving Problems and Selling Ideas With Pictures*, (New York: Penguin Group (USA), 2009).

Robert Half International, 'Social Media in the Workplace: What are the Opportunities and Risks for Your Firm,' CPA Insider, Jul. 2011 www.cpa2biz.com/Content/media/PRODUCER_CONTENT/Newsletters/Articles_2011/CPA/Jul/SocialMediaWorkplace.jsp

Ross, S. and Carberry, J., *The Inside Track to Careers in Accounting*, (New York: American Institute of Public Accountants Inc., 2010).

Sagian, R., 'This Is Generation Flux: Meet the Pioneers of The New (And Chaotic) Frontier of Business,' *Fast Company*, Jan. 2012 www.fastcompany.com/1802732/generation-flux-meet-pioneers-new-and-chaotic-frontier-business

Sant, T., *Persuasive Business Proposals: Writing to Win More Customers, Clients and Contracts*, (New York: American Management Association, 2012).

Schiavone, K., 'Hone Your Business Communication Skills,' *Chicago Tribune*, 4 Aug. 2012 www.chicagotribune.com/classified/jobs/chi-business-communication-skills-20120804,0,5670679.story

Seligson, H., 'For American Workers in China, A Culture Clash,' *The New York Times*, 23 Dec. 2009 www.nytimes.com/2009/12/24/business/global/24chinawork.html?_r= 0

Shellenbarger, S., 'This Embarrasses You and I,' *The Wall Street Journal*, 19 Jun. 2012 http://professional.wsj.com/article/SB10001424052702303410404577466662919275448.html?mg= reno64-wsj

Smiciklas, M., *The Power of Infographics*, (Indianapolis: Que Publishing, 2012).

Smith, A., 'Americans and Text Messaging,' Pew Internet & American Life Project [website], Sept. 2011 http://pewinternet.org/Reports/2011/Cell-Phone-Texting-2011.aspx

Smith, P., *Lead with a Story: A Guide to Crafting Business Narratives that Captivate, Convince and Inspire*, (Saranac Lake: AMACOM Books, 2012).

Smith, P., 'The Leader as Storyteller: 10 Reasons It Makes a Better Business Connection,' TLNT.com, Sept. 2012 www.tlnt.com/2012/09/12/the-leader-as-storyteller-10-reasons-it-makes-a-better-business-connection/

Stevens, S., 'Doing Business Better—Critical Communication Skills,' Oregon Society of CPAs [website] https://secure.orcpa.org/about/doing_business_better/3/1229-critical_communication_skills

Stringfellow, A., '10 Tips on Using Facebook to Boost Business,' American Express Open Forum [website], Apr. 2012 www.openforum.com/articles/10-tips-on-using-facebook-to-boost-business/

Strunk, Jr., W. and White, E. B., *The Elements of Style*, Fourth edition, (White Plains: Longman, 2000).

Taylor, G., *The Ultimate Guide to Marketing Your Business With Tumblr*, (CreateSpace, 2012).

Theibert, P. R., *How to Give a Damn Good Speech*, (New York: Galahad Books, 1997).

Thompson Jr., T., Hertzberg, J., and Sullivan, M., 'Social media and its associated risks,' Financial Executives Research Foundation report sponsored by Grant Thornton, Nov. 2011 www.grantthornton.com/portal/site/gtcom/menuitem.91c078ed5c0ef4ca80cd8710033841ca/?vgnextoid= 324b4c0939f73310VgnVCM1000003a8314acRCRD&vgnextfmt= default&vgnextrefresh= 1

Tingum, J., 'When to Use a Business Report to Communicate Instead of a Business Letter,' *Houston Chronicle* http://smallbusiness.chron.com/use-business-report-communicate-instead-business-letter-22593.html

Tuffe, E., *The Visual Display of Quantitative Information*, 2nd edition, (Cheshire: Graphics Press Inc., 2001).

Turkle, S., 'The Flight From Conversation,' *The New York Times*, 21 Apr. 2012 www.nytimes.com/2012/04/22/opinion/sunday/the-flight-from-conversation.html?pagewanted= all

Twitter, 'Best Practices,' Twitter for Business https://business.twitter.com/basics/best-practices/

Tysiac, K., 'Execs Battle Skills Gap in Hiring Despite High Unemployment,' *CGMA Magazine*, Jul. 2012 www.cgma.org/magazine/news/pages/20125850.aspx

Vermeiren, J., *How to Really Use LinkedIn*, (Charleston: Booksurge, 2009).

Warrell, M., 'Is It Past Time You Engaged in a "Courageous Conversation?"' *Forbes*, Nov. 2012 www.forbes.com/sites/margiewarrell/2012/11/13/courageous-conversation/

Warrell, M., 'Hiding Behind Email? Four Times You Should Never Use Email,' *Forbes*, Aug. 2012 www.forbes.com/sites/margiewarrell/2012/08/27/do-you-hide-behind-email/

Weissman, J., 'Learning Presentation Skills by Learning to Swim,' *Harvard Business Review*, Aug. 2011 http://blogs.hbr.org/cs/2011/08/learning_presenting_skills_by.html

Wiens, K., 'I Won't Hire People Who Use Poor Grammar. Here's Why,' *Harvard Business Review*, Jul. 2012 http://blogs.hbr.org/cs/2012/07/i_wont_hire_people_who_use_poo.html

Williams, G. B. and Miller, R. B., 'Change the Way You Persuade,' *Harvard Business Review*, 1 May 2002.

Wilkie, H., *Make Your Words Count: A Short Painless Guide to Business Writing for Accountants*, (CreateSpace, 2001).

Wolstenholme, N., and Bennett, S., 'Sharpening an FD's soft skills,' *Financial Director*, Jan. 2012 www.financialdirector.co.uk/financial-director/feature/2142534/sharpening-fds-soft-skills

Wong, D. M., *The Wall Street Journal Gide to Information Graphics*, (New York: W.W. Norton Co., 2010).

Wright, G. J., 'Six SEO Tips for CPAs,' AICPA Insights [blog], Dec. 2011 http://blog.aicpa.org/2011/12/6-seo-tips-for-cpas.html#sthash.jGoOJgp6.dpbs

Young, R., 'Eight Ways to … Use social media,' *CIMA Financial Management Magazine*, Mar. 2011 www.fm-magazine.com/feature/list/8-ways-use-social-media

YouTube, 'About You Tube' www.youtube.com/t/about_youtube

Zelazny, G., *Say It With Charts: The Executive's Guide to Visual Communication*, Fourth edition, (New York: McGraw-Hill, 2001).

Appendix A

INTERVIEWS

INTERVIEW 1: JIM MORRISON, CFO OF TEKNOR APEX

Jim Morrison is the chief financial officer of Teknor Apex Company, a diversified material science company headquartered in Pawtucket, Rhode Island. Prior to joining Teknor in 2000, he was the CFO of ANGUS Chemical Co. (1990–2000). Before that, he worked at Monsanto for 16 years (1973–1989), where he started his career as a management accountant. He advanced to division controller/plastics at Monsanto and, subsequently, to Singapore-based director of planning, Asia Pacific Region. Morrison is chair of the AICPA's Business and Industry Executive Committee and a member of the board of the Rhode Island Society of CPAs. He is also on the board of the new AICPA-CIMA joint venture to promote the discipline of management accounting worldwide.

What is your approach to communicating?

It begins with trust. I've shown trust in people, regardless of their level or function in an organisation. And they have trusted me not to blindside them. Because of this mutual trust, I've been able to serve not only as a CFO but also as an adviser to people on company and professional development matters.

Another aspect of my approach is that I don't overcomplicate things. You have to explain things to businesspeople in their language. If you get bogged down in accounting details, you won't get through to them. I've learned this from experience.

How did you learn?

At Monsanto, if you were in the accounting department, you physically stayed there—even if you were a financial analyst who was supporting a business manager. That was my situation when I was named manager of financial analysis in the plastics division, responsible for supporting the vice president of the division, which, at the time, had $800 million in worldwide sales. I asked, and the company approved, my moving from the accounting department into business operations. As a result, I had the opportunity to work more closely with the division president and other managers and learn how to improve communication with them. I also had the opportunity to become a speechwriter, and, in the process, to learn more about communicating.

How did you become a speechwriter?

Every quarter, Monsanto's vice presidents, including my boss, would make presentations to a management team about how their business line was performing. My boss asked me to help with one of these presentations. So, I prepared answers to some financial questions that he might be asked. I thought he would simply use them as background, but he included them in a speech that he wrote. Unfortunately, his speech did not go over well. So, he asked me to write a speech for him. To help engage the audience, I added a little humour.

What was the speech about?

At the time, there was a big debate in accounting and business about whether accountants should have earnings goals. One side of the argument held that accountants are not on the operating line and do not generate any income; they essentially are number crunchers who do not make tactical or strategic decisions. The other side—the one I took—was that businesses depend on the quality of information that accountants provide. The better the quality, the better the decisions made by management. I wrote about this issue of the value of accountants for his speech, and he used it word-for-word. Knowing your audience and connecting with them was key. This was a speech not just to the accounting department but also to the company's entire management. The speech was well received. He thanked me and told me I was his speechwriter from then on.

Any tips on speechwriting and making presentations?

I've used humour in speeches and presentations I've made in my company, or for the AICPA, the Rhode Island Society of CPAs and other organisations. You can add a little humour to a speech if it's relevant to your topic. Humour helps to entertain and engage the audience, explain complex subject and make a point. You can be self-deprecating, but careful not to offend others.

As for presentations, don't make the mistake of simply throwing a bunch of numbers together and calling it a presentation. Your presentation should have a theme—a story—and elements that support and develop the theme. Those elements should come together in a logical, coherent structure. Also, do thorough research for your speech, and be prepared to answer questions.

What's an example of providing a clear, simple explanation of a complex subject?

In the late 1970s, during my time at Monsanto, the world was going through a second oil crisis, with another run-up in oil prices causing a sharp increase in inflation. Because the company was using LIFO accounting for inventory valuation, the oil-price spike significantly reduced earnings and undermined the company's efforts to achieve its business performance goals. Yet LIFO's effects remained mostly a mystery to many business managers. To clarify matters, I wrote a one-page description of LIFO: what it is, how it is calculated and why it is important to business. I concluded with an example. If you want to know how LIFO will impact earnings, watch prices at the gas pump. If the price went up 5%, you could expect a charge to inventory on the financial statements. In a company of Monsanto's size, that charge would have been so many millions of dollars.

How are you using your communication skills in your current position?

Part of my role now is to help facilitate and drive conversations. For example, in meeting with our company's senior management team, I lead discussions of financial reviews. I may be presenting the numbers, but I'll ask the VPs in manufacturing or marketing to comment on what is driving the company's performance. I listen as much as I talk. I want to lead the group to a consensus, to agree on a way forward. I use the same approach with other topics, such as getting the opinions of senior managers about the risks of a possible acquisition.

How do you embed good communication in the culture of a company?

A lot of it depends on the company's leadership. Some companies take a paternalistic approach to communicating with employees, meaning the company tells its people what it wants them to know, and no more. So, employees may be kept in the dark, for example, about details of the company's financial condition. Other companies are very transparent. When I worked at ANGUS, my boss was a former Monsanto executive who thought everyone should be aware of our performance. But the trend is toward more transparency in companies. That's partly the result of more young people moving into management positions. They are very comfortable with openness in an organisation. In any case, the important thing is to put yourself in the audience and determine how the information will be received. Do not mislead, but be sure the outcome of the message is a positive one or has a direction forward.

What's your advice for management accountants who are just starting their careers?

You should learn not just the company's accounting system but how that system informs and supports its business operations. Try to work in different parts of the company so you get front-line experience in its operations. Develop relationships with line managers; learn about their jobs and the issues that concern them. Look for opportunities to learn about areas of the organisation that you are not familiar with. At Teknor, I established a Finance Academy[1] about five years ago. Its mission is to facilitate the sharing of ideas, skills and knowledge among employees across areas of specialty. Employees who are knowledgeable about a subject offer instruction to other employees who want to improve their knowledge of that subject. Topics of our instruction have included transfer pricing, insurance, accrual concepts, credit evaluation, international finance and advanced tax. The academy has enabled the company to use internal resources, at a reasonable cost, to broaden and refine the skills of its employees.

INTERVIEW 2: KENNETH KELLY, SENIOR VICE PRESIDENT OF MCCORMICK & CO.

Kenneth Kelly is Senior Vice President & Controller of McCormick & Company, a global company with more than $3.5 billion in sales. McCormick manufactures, markets and distributes spices, seasoning mixes, condiments and other flavourful products to the entire food industry. In his years with McCormick, Kelly has held senior level finance positions at both corporate and operating units.

You've said that management accountants and finance professionals 'have to go from counting the beans to growing the beans.' Could you elaborate on that?

Finance professionals have moved beyond simply reporting and record keeping to serving as strategic advisors to management. Today, the key question for finance professionals is how to work with management to grow the business. We can do this by helping the organisation to go from data to information to insights formed from that information. We can present the information to management and offer our insights as to what it means. Through this process, we help management to make informed business decisions.

How does this process of supporting management relate to the traditional finance function?

As always, we must maintain our objectivity and independence, exercise financial discipline, and be forthright in our communication with management and other stakeholders, for example, in communicating the risks in business decisions. We have to help the organisation to strike the right balance between growing the business and maintaining a financially sound business.

What is the company's communication philosophy?

We are more of a consensus building than a command-and-control organisation. Communication is central to creating a consensus. People accomplish things through other people in the company, and that requires everyone to know how to communicate effectively, build relationships, share ideas and present their point of view. Because of the need for consensus, it may take longer to get a project going than with the command-and-control model, but with everyone on board, the project has momentum.

What is your approach to communication?

Communication should always be open and honest. That doesn't mean you have to communicate everything you know. It depends on the needs of your audience, whether that audience is the board, senior management or others in the company. I always suggest to people that as they advance in the organisation, they should seek the advice of others—including how to communicate with different audiences.

In terms of communication, what do you expect of people who report to you?

I expect people to filter their information so they tell me only what I need to know—no more and no less. In meetings with people, I will tell them on the spot whether they are providing too much or too little information. As they learn from this experience, they should be better attuned to my expectations. But they should learn not just from me but also from everyone with whom they communicate in the organisation. Always try to get feedback, to learn and to get better at communicating.

How does the company promote effective communication in the organisation?

We have a global competency model for the organisation. We define competencies that are common across the organisation, such as leadership, teamwork, innovation, business sense, strategic leadership and handling complexity. Another corporate-wide competency is communication.

How does the communication competency apply to finance?

In finance, everyone must have technical, communication and other competencies. These competencies would be adjusted to their level in the organisation. To get down to specifics, we divided finance into four levels and detailed the competencies required at each level, including communication skills. We also spell out the outcomes we want at each level, such as the ability to speak to different audiences. Through this process, people have a clear understanding of communication at each level and the competencies required to communicate effectively.

How do you train finance professionals and others in the company to develop and improve their communication skills?

One of the ways we develop communication skills is through what we call 'multiple management boards.' These are self-governing, cross-functional boards established at different locations in our global company. Anyone can ask to join any board they choose. Each board takes on a different business project and creates teams to work on different aspects of a project for a six-month period. During that time, every team member must make a presentation to the team, and everyone eventually takes a turn as team leader. The primary purpose of the boards and teams is to help participants develop their leadership, teaming, communication and other skills. Team members receive feedback from their peers on their performance, including how well they did in communicating. Team members are ranked based on their performance by the rest of the team.

What are your suggestions for communicating globally?

One thing I have learned from my experience is to keep your communication simple and concise. Your message should be direct and on point. This helps people for whom English is not their native language. If necessary, go over what you said. Make sure you are understood. Ask the people you're communicating with to tell you what they think you said or wrote. This can be time consuming, but you have to learn to be patient. Otherwise, there is the risk of miscommunication.

Final thoughts?

As someone once told me, accounting is the language of business. And communication is central to accounting and finance. As a finance professional, you must be able to communicate effectively, explain complex concepts to those who are not accountants or finance experts, and help managers to make well-informed decisions. Your communication skills are as important to your success as your technical skills.

INTERVIEW 3: SARAH VAUDRAIN, BUSINESS ANALYST, TEKNOR APEX

Sarah Vaudrain is a business analyst (financial analyst) with Teknor Apex, a diversified material science company headquartered in Pawtucket, Rhode Island. In 2008, she graduated from Providence College with a bachelor of arts, Economics. In 2010, she began studies for a master of business administration at the University of Rhode Island. She graduated in 2012.

What was your first job?

In my senior year of college, I worked 20–25 hours a week as a customer service representative for Fidelity. After I graduated, I got a job as a junior accountant, administration of hedge funds, in the Boston office of Kaufman Rossin Fund Services.[2] After one year, I was then promoted to a semi-senior accountant within the firm.

How did you learn accounting?

I hadn't taken any accounting courses as an undergraduate. So, to get up to speed at Kaufman, I learned about accounting through reading and studying on my own. I also got on-the-job experience in working at Kaufman. After about two years there, I joined Teknor in 2010 as a cost accountant. That same year, I enrolled in the MBA programme at the University of Rhode Island. I took some accounting courses as part of that programme.

Why did you go to work for Teknor?

I hadn't planned on a career in accounting. But I got interested in it from my experience in working at Fidelity and Kaufman. However, I wasn't interested in continuing to work for financial services firms. I wanted to work in accounting within a business. In looking at online job sites, I came across an announcement of a job opening placed by a recruiter. It was for a cost accountant position at Teknor. I applied and got hired.

What did you do as a cost accountant?

I worked with business analysts who supported some of our company's business lines. This gave me the opportunity to learn about the company's businesses and how the analysts helped managers to solve problems. For example, the analysts would analyse financial statements to see if there were any problems with the accounting entries that needed to be resolved. Or, they would look at our sales, costs and other information to verify the numbers or determine whether there were any variances that needed to be addressed.

What are your responsibilities as a business analyst?

As a business analyst, I support our nylon division, which designs and manufactures nylon compounds that have broad industrial and consumer applications. I am part of the business team, working with different departments and managers, talking to people all over the company, and helping to investigate problems, for example, why a customer isn't buying as much as in the past, or why certain costs aren't in the system. I participate in monthly meetings with senior executives and others where we review the numbers and discuss how we can improve the business. I try to help make things easier for people so they can do their jobs more efficiently and with less stress. I strive to be a valued partner within the business and provide the team with support to assist in making strategic decisions for the future.

Did you take communication classes as part of your studies for a master's degree?

There wasn't a separate class in communication, but communication was stressed in classes in organisational analysis, small business management and other subjects. With the benefit of hindsight, a communication class would have been helpful, for example, in learning how to write effective e-mails, memos and other types of business communication.

What have you learned about communicating since you started at Teknor?

I have learned to be clear and concise in communicating with managers and others in our departments. I try to phrase requests in terms they can understand, not in technical accounting terms, and to be very precise in explaining what I need. I also consider the impact of what I am requesting. Will this make things more difficult for a department or not? Initially, I would sometimes make decisions without thinking through the effects on the departments. Now I try to look at my request from the department's perspective. In any case, the important thing is to be open and direct in communicating with people.

Whom do you go to in the company for advice?

I talk to my boss, other supervisors, my peers and others in the company if I am concerned or uncertain about something. I bounce questions off them and try to get their perspective and draw on their experience in resolving issues.

Where do you see yourself in five or ten years?

I grew up in Rhode Island. Once in a while, I went by Teknor, but I didn't know much about the company. And I certainly had no idea that I would be working for Teknor one day. Yet here I am. I would like the opportunity to advance in the organisation, and to be challenged in whatever position I am in, whether it is in the finance department or in a business unit.

INTERVIEW 4: DONNA VIENS, ASSISTANT PROFESSOR AT JOHNSON & WALES UNIVERSITY

Donna Viens is an assistant professor and chair of the department of accountancy and finance at Johnson & Wales University, Providence, Rhode Island. Before joining the university's faculty, she spent 15 years in manufacturing and construction accounting. She worked as a raw materials clerk, an accounts payable manager, a cost accountant, an assistant controller, a controller and a chief financial officer.

When you worked in manufacturing and construction, what did you learn about communication?

In construction, when you are on a job site, a lot of the communication is verbal. You talk with supervisors or other workers about different things, and the conversations tend to be very brief. Construction people usually are very skilled at their jobs, but, depending on the person and their level of education, their communication skills may not be as good as their technical skills. Sometimes you speak with people who are not as fluent in English as in their native Spanish, Portuguese or other language.

How did you deal with these communication issues?

Regardless of whom you're speaking with, you have to be very clear in speaking with them. Make sure that you are understood and that you understand them. I sometimes couldn't completely understand what others were saying, but I usually could infer what they said. You have to be patient in communicating with people. Impatience can lead to misunderstandings.

Another issue is that communication in construction tends to be informal. When I became a manager for a construction company and started working in an office, I still wore jeans because I never knew when I might have to go out to a job site. But this informality can make some people too comfortable with you. At some point, you may have to tell them that you worked hard to become a manager, and you expect to be treated like one.

How did communication at the management level compare with communication on the job site?

When you move into management—the controller level or above—you communicate more in writing. Regardless of whether you are speaking or writing to someone about financial topics, you have to do so in such a way that you are understood. You not only have to know the numbers but also be able to explain them, sometimes to executives who are highly educated and experienced but who do not have backgrounds in finance. I once worked with a CEO who rolled his eyes whenever I started to talk about financial issues. So, I started making graphs and charts for him, and he understood—he got it. He was very visually oriented.

How do you help your students to develop the communication skills to work in accounting?

Every student in our accounting programme is required to take a class in business communication that is offered by our English department. In addition, in all of our accounting classes, students are required to complete some type of writing assignment: e-mails, correspondence, presentations, client letters, audit opinions and other communications. They also work on writing their resumés, letters to prospective employers and so on. Through a process of having their work critiqued by their teachers and rewriting and revising, they learn to improve their writing skills. We ask students to keep copies of everything they write, from initial drafts to finished product. When they graduate, they can review their writing projects and see how their skills have developed.

Do you have any particular concerns in helping students with their oral communication?

One concern is helping students to improve their skills in making presentations. Some accounting professionals lack the confidence to make presentations to senior executives, a management committee or a board of directors. We help students to develop that confidence while in school, so they are prepared for the time in their careers when they are called upon to make high-level presentations.

How do you help them to develop skills and build confidence?

We use various means, such as discussions, debates or role playing. We may ask students to discuss something they've seen in the news and to have a debate on an issue that's relevant to the class they're taking. For example, the debate might be about an issue of ethical behaviour in accounting and business. In debating, students learn to treat each other as equals and to conduct themselves in a civilised, professional manner. We've also introduced into our programme exercises for students in explaining financial statements to people who are not accountants. Students might participate in role playing in which one student plays an accountant who is trying to explain the numbers to another student who plays a boss who is struggling to understand. The whole purpose of these various programmes is to prepare students as much as possible to go into the world of accounting and business.

INTERVIEW 5: JAMES J. BENJAMIN, PROFESSOR AT MAYS BUSINESS SCHOOL

James J. Benjamin is the Deloitte Foundation Leadership Professor and Head of the Accounting Department in the Mays Business School at Texas A&M University. He joined the faculty at Texas A&M in 1974, and he has served as department head since 1982. Dr Benjamin received his MBA and DBA degrees from Indiana University, and he is a CPA. He previously served as the PhD coordinator for the Mays School and the director of the College Honors Program.

Through the Mays School of Business, Texas A&M offers a bachelor of business administration (BBA) in accounting, a master of science in accounting and a doctoral programme in accounting. In addition, it offers the Professional Program, a two-and-a-half-year programme that students enter in the spring semester of their junior year. Upon completion of the programme, they earn a BBA in accounting and a master of science in one of the following: accounting, finance, management information systems, marketing or entrepreneurship.

How has the accounting programme helped students to develop their communication skills?

We originally introduced communication into our programme in 1982, when we worked with the university's College of Liberal Arts to teach oral and written communication to accounting students. After a few years, the college was unable to continue with this communication course. We decided to reach outside the university to hire a communication expert to join our faculty and create a course. We've had the course ever since. It's a required course that focuses on written and oral communication, but it also encompasses broader skills that managers need, such as the ability to build relationships, work with people, actively listen and learn from criticism.

How would you characterise the communication skills of students when they begin the accounting programme?

As you might expect, the communication skills of students vary widely. Some students are quite polished, while others have rudimentary skills. We do some diagnostics to identify students who need help. Among other resources, these students can make use of a communications lab in our business school. The lab has software to help students improve their writing, videotaping equipment and other facilities.

Besides the required communication course, how do you help students to develop their communication skills?

All of our courses require some writing and oral work, and two of these courses are writing intensive. Students in our Professional Program participate in teams that work on case studies. The experience is similar to participating on a team in the working world. As team members, students work on improving their communication skills, including taking the required communication course at the mid-point of the programme. As students progress in the programme, their level of communication practice increases. In the final year of the programme—students' fifth year at the university—the student teams participate in case competitions in which every team member has to make a presentation. For students interested in the energy field, we offer an energy accounting course and an energy case competition.

Do students in the Professional Program work as interns?

The 250 students in the programme work as interns, mainly at public accounting firms. Candidates for internships typically interview with several firms, and they almost always are awarded internships. They usually complete audit or tax internships during the firms' busy season in the spring and systems audit or advisory internships in the fall. If, for some reason, a candidate is not offered an internship, it's a wake-up call that they need to improve their communication and other skills.

How do you help students to develop the communication skills to be ready for future employment?

We help them to develop self-confidence and build their personal brand. It is important that they are able to tell stories about themselves. They can use these skills in interviewing for jobs. Beyond that, they can continue to develop these skills in public accounting, where most of our students start their careers. If they later decide to go into corporate accounting or some other sector of accounting, they will have developed a foundation of communication skills from their experience in public accounting.

What skills do employers require of students?

Regardless of whether an employer is a Big 4 firm or a Fortune 500 company or other organisation, employers want graduates to pass the CPA exam and to have the communication and other skills required for a job.

What feedback do you receive from employers about the communication skills of today's accounting graduates?

I hear a lot about the informality of students in communicating, such as in writing e-mail or text messages or sending an e-mail to someone rather than walking down the hall to talk to them. There is a tendency to use social media as a substitute for face-to-face communication. And students carry these habits into the business world. In helping students to improve their communication skills, we try to teach them the appropriate use of technology, the value of personal communication, and the importance of strong writing and speaking skills.

INTERVIEW 6: CHRISTOPHER J. PAPA, EXECUTIVE VICE PRESIDENT AND CFO, POST PROPERTIES, INC.

At some point in their careers, some CPAs who are partners in public accounting move into the corporate sector and become CFOs. Christopher J. Papa, executive vice president and CFO of Post Properties, Inc., a leading developer and operator of upscale multifamily communities, made the transition. Papa joined Post Properties as CFO in 2003. Before that, he was an audit partner at BDO Seidman, LLP, CFO of Plast-O-Matic Valves, Inc., and an audit partner at Arthur Andersen, LLP, where he spent ten years.

In terms of communicating, how did you manage the transition from public accounting to CFO?

When I joined Post Properties, I started by getting to know people inside and outside of our company. I met one-on-one with key executives in our organisation. I joined other executives and managers in town hall-style meetings with associates in property management, accounting, information technology and other parts of our company. I sought feedback from people throughout our organisation. Externally, I began to build relationships with representatives of our primary lenders and bankers, rating agencies, as well as tax advisers and other key constituencies. It helped that I already knew some of these people from my prior experience in public accounting. It also helped that I had a broad background in business from having worked closely with executive management and boards of my public accounting clients, firms, investment bankers and other organisations.

What is your approach to communicating?

I aim to be as transparent and as collaborative as possible—being open, accessible, willing to listen to and consider other ideas, while providing an atmosphere where issues are easily surfaced, discussed and resolved. I believe in being straightforward, honest and direct, while exhibiting a strong tone from the top and adhering to strong ethical standards. I try to promote a team environment, to have an open door policy, and to be available to discuss any issues. I also hold regular meetings with people to discuss where we are as a company or department, talk about problems that have come up, and get regular updates on what they are working on. I want to hear everything about our company, whether good or bad.

How have you applied your experience in public accounting in your current position?

When I was in public accounting, I learned to think strategically, beyond the boundaries of compliance functions. As CFO, I have taken the same strategic approach. I rely on a strong network of other company executives, attorneys, bankers, tax advisers and others for ideas, insights and advice. I have learned to be balanced in providing leadership and oversight while relying on the professional judgment of our controller, tax directors and other direct reports to manage their individual areas of responsibility.

How do you manage your time in communicating with many different constituencies?

In public companies today, senior executives are spending more time meeting with analysts, shareholders, prospective investors and others to update them on the state of the company, listen to their comments and answer questions. People want more face time with the CEO and CFO. Meanwhile, you have to maintain internal communication with managers, auditors and others.

What's the benefit of this intensified communication?

Over time, you strengthen relationships with people inside and outside of your organisation, and people feel comfortable talking with you about issues. But there are also more and more demands on your time. You receive a constant stream of requests for meetings, phone calls and so on. It is important to have a very strong executive assistant to help you effectively manage the multiple requests for your time.

INTERVIEW 7: GREG CONDERACCI, PRESIDENT AND FOUNDER OF GOOD GROUND CONSULTING

Greg Conderacci is president and founder of Good Ground Consulting, a private consulting firm that helps organisations and teams discover and defend their good ground—the fertile market niche where their productivity peaks. In other words, he helps them answer their clients' question, 'Why should I do business with you?' He teaches marketing at the Johns Hopkins University Carey School of Business. He also is a senior fellow with the Maryland Association of CPA's Business Learning Institute.

In the 1990s, Conderacci held senior marketing positions with Price Waterhouse, Prudential and Deutsche Bank Alex. Brown. In the 1980s, he created and marketed several innovative programmes for the poor of Maryland, including the state's largest soup kitchen. In the 1970s, as a reporter for *The Wall Street Journal*, he covered business and economics. He is a magna cum laude graduate of Princeton University. He holds a master in public policy from Harvard University.

What's the biggest communication challenge for management accountants in moving up the corporate ladder?

When they are at a lower level in an organisation, accountants are narrowly focused on the numbers. Upon advancing to CFO or other senior position, they find themselves dealing with complex issues and advising top management in making decisions that will affect the future of the company. They must have the skills to communicate clearly and work with senior executives from every business line and department in the company. And they must have a different image of themselves. They must see themselves not as number crunchers sitting in cubicles, but as strategic advisers to senior management.

Are accountants up to the challenge?

Most CPAs can discuss accounting principles or methodologies in great detail. But they do not always explain the reasons for the principles or why anyone should care. It's analogous to explaining the inner workings of a car's engine but not how to operate the car. To succeed at the highest levels of an organisation, accountants must have strategic vision, the ability to articulate ideas succinctly and the skill to sell their ideas.

How has the perception of CPAs changed as more of them move from accounting and finance to the highest levels of organisations?

People in an organisation trust accountants, especially those who have the CPA credential. At the CFO or other senior management level, CPAs are seen not only as the financial experts but also as ethical leaders within the organisation. CFOs are expected to know the right thing to do financially, and, more than that, whether the right thing also is the moral thing to do. Because of how they are seen, CFOs have greater authority and influence, and with that authority comes the responsibility to communicate clearly about complex ethical and moral issues and to provide guidance as to how organisations can address those issues.

What are accountants doing, or what could they be doing, to increase their value to organisations—and their opportunities to move up the corporate ladder?

CPAs who aspire to move into senior management, whether with a public accounting firm or a company, must have the ability to sell—if only their ideas. In public accounting, CPAs learn about sales and marketing and business development early on. Frequently, business development is the path to promotion. In corporations, management accountants often do not have the same early opportunities. When they reach the top echelons of management, they usually are not involved in direct selling. But they must know about the marketing and sales of the company's products and services, and even be prepared to suggest sales-related ideas, such as pricing and how to reduce the costs of sales. The most successful CFOs know how to work with the marketing and sales department in their sales efforts.

So how can management accountants learn about sales and marketing?

Look for every opportunity inside and outside your organisation to learn, whether through reading, classes, talking with sales and marketing people, or other ways. In the classes I teach, I am seeing a whole new interest in sales and marketing on the part of some accountants and others who, not long ago, wouldn't have given sales a second thought.

How does the CPA credential help with sales and marketing?

You can build your personal brand on the CPA credential, which inspires trust. As you move up the organisation, you have to work on developing your image, and that requires you to develop your communication skills. In some business and other circles, the image of an accountant is an introvert who has trouble communicating. I led a communication workshop for government accountants, and one accountant stood out because he asked a lot of questions. After the workshop, I mentioned this to his supervisor, who said, 'Yeah, he's our resident extrovert.' Successful accountants have managed to overcome whatever reticence they may have and become effective communicators. They are not only good at listening and speaking, but at asking the right questions.

Why is it important for accountants to ask the right questions?

We are trained from grammar school that what is important is the right answer. We didn't get any credit for asking questions. But the right answer starts with the right question. As a CFO, you are expected to ask the questions that will give management new insights into solving a problem or capitalising on an opportunity, that helps to crystallise management thinking about issues, and that helps management with the decision-making process. This is what makes CFOs valuable to organisations.

What do young people who are starting their careers in accounting need to know about personal branding?

In my experience, some young accountants seem to think that once they graduate from college and pass the CPA exam that employers should be happy to hire them. In their cover letters, resumes and interviews, they talk about what they have accomplished. What an employer really wants to know is, what can you do for me? Young accountants—and accountants generally—have to be prepared to answer that question if they expect to get hired, change jobs or advance in organisations. So, instead of just saying they have done six major audits, for example, they should talk about how they can help a business to save $250,000 a year. Personal branding isn't just about you, it's about the value you bring to an organisation.

INTERVIEW 8: THOMAS D. FOARD, EXECUTIVE VICE PRESIDENT AND CFO OF PUBLISHERS FULFILLMENT, INC.

Thomas D. Foard, CPA, is executive vice president and CFO of Publishers Fulfillment Inc., Towson, Maryland. The company provides outsourced home delivery services for *The New York Times*, *The Wall Street Journal*, *USA Today* and a number of other newspapers.

Foard is a member of the AICPA board of directors and a past chair of the Maryland Association of CPAs.

What value do finance professionals bring to their communication with the leadership of companies?

It's a given that we have technical expertise. Where we can add value is in communicating effectively to management. We can present information in terms of how it affects the business and what actions management can take to meet business goals. The very best finance professionals excel at analysing, interpreting and integrating data and translating it into information that leaders use in decision-making.

So it's more about looking at the future than the past?

Computer automation has largely commoditised the historical function of our profession. It's not where we add value. We do that by interpreting the data and providing useful information.

What's an example?

We can look at leading indicators in the economy and the markets in which our companies operate, discern trends and identify risks. We can help managers to measure and evaluate the performance of their companies and make projections about future performance. This is somewhat analogous to sports broadcasting.

How?

The play-by-play commentator provides the data, which is what accountants do now. The colour commentator provides the analysis of the data, comments on the strategy of the teams, and talks about decisions they might face as the game progresses. This analysis and interpretation is what business leaders expect of their accountants.

How comfortable are finance professionals with this forward-looking approach to communication?

We need to develop the skills to communicate effectively. We must not only be comfortable but confident in our skills. If we aren't, the risk to our profession is that the CEO or COO will find people who are confident, and they may not be CPAs.

But is it realistic for accountants to think they can get better at communicating?

There is an argument that you either have communication skills or you don't, but these are skills that can be developed, improved and refined. If I play golf, I might be shooting, say, 95. With lessons, I might get that number down to 85. I won't shoot 68 and turn pro, but I'll be playing a lot better. This is what I am talking about with accountants. With better communication skills, you can become a valued member of a company's leadership team.

What are some of your suggestions for improving communication skills?

Read books and articles on the subject. A book I recommend is *The Exceptional Presenter*, by Timothy Koegel. Take professional development courses. Ask a mentor to help you. Practice by standing in front of a mirror and speaking and recording what you say. Practice before some friends and get their feedback. Evaluate your speaking style. Are you speaking too fast or too slow? Do you stay on message or get bogged down in details? Do you have the right inflection or speak in a monotone?

If you are preparing to present at a meeting, send a one-page summary of your talking points to your audience before the meeting. Keep your presentation simple—no more than three key points. State what you will cover, deliver your message and wrap up. Don't speak for more than 15 minutes. Otherwise, your audience will lose interest.

Final thoughts?

The accounting programmes in colleges and universities should help students develop not just technical expertise but so-called 'soft skills' like communication. As a profession, we should change the language around these soft skills. Call them success skills. Technical expertise means you get to play in the game. Success skills like communication will help you win.

INTERVIEW 9: ANDREW HARDING, MANAGING DIRECTOR OF CIMA

Andrew Harding, FCMA, CGMA, is managing director of the Chartered Institute of Management Accountants (CIMA) and is responsible for the operational performance of the Institute. In his role, Harding leads CIMA's corporate centre, which is based in the UK, along with all international markets, including Europe, North Asia, South East Asia and Australasia, Africa, the Middle East, South Asia, and North Africa.

He was previously executive director of CIMA Markets, and, in 2010, oversaw the Institute's largest ever growth in new students. Prior to joining CIMA, he was managing director of the Association of Chartered Certified Accountants (ACCA), where he drove success on a global scale.

Harding is a CGMA and holds an MBA from Henley Management College.

What is the role of today's CFO?

CFOs have gone from scorekeepers to positions of influence as company strategists and leaders. Yet, even in their strategic role, they must remain grounded in solid technical financial skills. Particularly important is their ability to assist companies to evaluate and guard against risks. CFOs deal in making sense of complex data and need to be skilled in presenting information so that the board can make the best decisions.

Why the focus on defending against risks?

Following the collapse of the global financial system a few years ago, boards came to realise that they didn't fully understand the risks that companies were taking on, especially in derivatives and other financial products. Now, they are turning to CFOs to advise on risk management. This means CFOs, as well as deeply understanding how the business works, must have the skills to communicate with board members and others who are not necessarily deep technical experts. CFOs must know how to explain risks and opportunities in understandable language.

How are companies training the next generation of management accountants to become strategists and leaders?

Companies expect management accountants to support management decision-making by making sense of complex data. Very often, this is a challenge for the management accountant, who is trained as an expert. The language of the expert doesn't always make for effective communication.

How are companies addressing this issue?

Companies are taking a very practical approach. They have management accountants working alongside line managers and learning how to support management's decision-making. The benefits of this collaboration are mutual. Management accountants are learning how to better communicate with managers, and managers are drawing on the financial and analytical expertise of accountants to make better-informed decisions.

Have companies established formal training programmes for management accountants to learn the business and advance in the organisations?

Larger companies have taken the lead in establishing training and development programmes for management accountants. Training is competence-based and includes the development and measurement of communication skills. These programmes are becoming more established in organisations, and the time is coming when best practices will emerge.

What can management accountants themselves do on their own initiative to improve their communication skills?

The first thing management accountants must understand and appreciate is that, outside of accounting, they are speaking to people who are not accounting experts. With this understanding, they can find quite simple skills programmes around effective writing and presentation. These programmes are available through schools, professional societies and other organisations, and they are based on demystifying language and building understanding.

How do management accountants build understanding?

Understanding begins with the audience. To communicate effectively, management accountants must know their audience and use language the audience understands. Accountants sometimes default to accounting jargon, using it as a shield to hide behind their expertise. Management accountants need to regularly review their communication style with colleagues and seek feedback so that the benefits of the support they give to boards and other key decision makers are maximised.

What does the broader role of management accountants in business mean for their careers?

Because of their expertise, management accountants are finding career opportunities across organisations. For example, some accountants are beginning to work in marketing. Over time, they will develop expertise in managing marketing, and some could advance to directors of marketing. We also see this working in other core business areas, such as HR, IT or operations. Beyond these, management accountants will see opportunities open up in other parts of the organisation.

How can management accountants worldwide learn how to work and do business globally?

The first thing is to have strong English language skills. With the exception of China, most international businesses use English. You can't rise to the top of the organisation without being fluent in English. You also must have the ability to build relationships across international boundaries. This requires an understanding and appreciation of other cultures, customs and ways of doing business, such as the need in Asian cultures to save face and whether 'yes' really means 'no.' Even in countries such as the UK, U.S. and Australia that share a common language, there are different cultural practices, behaviours and reactions, and different meanings given to words. To work globally, you must always be open to learning. It requires focus and hard work, and you will never stop learning.

How are colleges and universities helping accounting students to improve their communication skills?

The role of colleges and universities is changing. Schools no longer are simply teaching and testing knowledge. Using case studies and other resources, students are learning how communication is used in business, how to communicate technical information in easily understood language, and how to use communication in solving business problems. Communication is not simply about telling the story of money and finance but about all aspects of a business. We call it 'joining the dots.'

CIMA has commissioned extensive research and issued reports[3] on how businesses can incorporate sustainability into their business planning, practices and reporting. Why the focus on sustainability?

Some make the mistake of thinking that sustainability is about the environment, but it is much more than that. It is about businesses having robust business models and being successful in the long term. Accountants need to think about more than the numbers that affect the bottom line. It's about everything that can affect the bottom line.

What progress have companies made toward incorporating sustainability into their strategic planning and business models?

Companies are starting to develop sustainability strategies, but they have not realised the full value of sustainability. Management accountants can help them to tie sustainability to business performance and maximise value.

What are some examples of how management accountants can help?

Management accountants can assist companies to develop sustainable business practices that reduce costs by eliminating wastes and inefficiencies in business processes. They can help companies to manage risks by complying with safety regulations and preventing events that have social and environmental consequences and impact the bottom line. To support businesses, CIMA and the AICPA are working hard on developing 'integrated reporting,' which covers all aspects of business performance, not just the financials. By applying the same rigor to integrated reporting that they apply to financial reporting, management accountants can assist companies to implement and measure sustainable strategies that realise the full value of sustainability.

In March of 2011, the AICPA and CIMA announced a proposed joint venture to promote the Certified Global Management Accountant (CGMA) designation globally. The governing councils of both organisations subsequently approved the joint venture. Why create the CGMA designation at this point in time?

Today, businesses face a number of global issues and challenges. Increasingly, they are looking to management accountants for strategic guidance and insight in making decisions and managing risks. The CGMA designation is intended to promote the discipline of management accounting worldwide and provide a global designation that demonstrates proficiency and leadership in management accounting. CGMA is the first accounting designation to be used worldwide. It's a designation for the modern era, and it will help businesses meet their strategic goals.

INTERVIEW 10: CHRIS ROGERS, VICE PRESIDENT, FINANCE AND ADMINISTRATION, INFRAGISTICS, INC.

Chris Rogers is vice president, Finance and Administration, of Infragistics Inc., a global software company that publishes user interface (UI) development tools and components for a range of developer applications. The company is also a provider of developer support, testing tools, and UI and user experience (UX) training and consulting services. Prior to joining Infragistics in 2002, he served in senior financial positions from controller to CFO for various companies, such as Meridian Emerging Markets, Taratec (Patni Computer Systems), HealthAnswers, and Mobil Research & Development Corp.

What is your communication philosophy?

In a private company like Infragistics, where the CEO is an owner, my conversations with him are very open, very direct. He is as immersed in the numbers as I am. Our communication needs to be in lock step. I am more forthright in communicating with other senior executives than with employees. That is because employees may not have a need to know certain information, or if they did know, they might not understand it in the proper context.

What is your approach to communicating with minority investors?

I will give minority investors a crafted response to their questions, but I am not going to share everything because they won't understand the context. I can help them with the interpretation of the numbers, but I am not going to offer financial advice, such as whether they should exercise their stock options.

As far as communicating is concerned, what do you expect of people who report to you?

I want the whole truth, and nothing but. The accounting department cannot add value to the organisation without providing the information necessary for management to make decisions. I expect accountants to be forthright in their communication with senior management and not to sandbag the numbers. In any case, the CEO and I are going to take a very conservative approach in analysing and interpreting the numbers.

What are some of the challenges in communicating globally?

One challenge is the language barrier. Here's an example. On a visit to Japan, I was speaking with a junior accountant and an auditor. The accountant was a native Japanese who spoke little English. She did not have formal training in accounting but had some understanding of its concepts. The auditor was Chinese; she spoke Japanese as a second language. She understood Japanese GAAP but not U.S. GAAP. I do not speak Japanese. I had to explain the concept of accrual to the junior accountant and make sure that her understanding of the concept was the same as mine. Then, I had to impress upon her that she needed to explain the concept to the auditor exactly as I had explained it to her.

Another challenge with global communication is that the definition of things varies from country to country. In the U.S., if you negotiate a salary figure, it usually is a gross salary, before taxes. In certain other countries, if you were to negotiate a salary, it would be a net salary, after taxes. And the employer pays the employee's taxes. This can create a risk for an employer who signs a contract to pay a $50,000 gross salary and assumes it's a gross figure. But the employee counters that it's a net salary, and the employer is contractually bound by the laws of the country where the employee works to pay the employee's taxes. The cost of hiring the employee is much higher than the employer expected.

If you travel outside the U.S., and meet and work with people of other countries, you must be very sensitive to the differences in American culture and their culture. The worst thing you could do is to embarrass them, especially in front of their peers. You have to know how to present a business card in Japan or shake hands in India. You must know whether someone is nodding in agreement or simply to be polite. Above all, you must listen. It shows respect and a willingness to learn. And you will learn from listening and observing.

INTERVIEW 11: AMY WEINREICH, CPA, VICE PRESIDENT, FINANCE AND ADMINISTRATION, PUBLISHERS CIRCULATION FULFILLMENT, INC.

Amy Weinreich, CPA, is vice president, Finance and Administration, of Publishers Circulation Fulfillment Inc., Towson, Maryland. The company provides outsourced home delivery services for *The New York Times*, *The Wall Street Journal*, *USA Today* and a number of other newspapers. The company has about 1,300 employees and uses about 8,000 contractors nationally.

What are your responsibilities?

I'm responsible for all of the finance and accounting functions, as well as payroll benefits, employee data management, procurement and property administration.

How did you get interested in accounting as a career?

My parents owned a business in Baltimore, Maryland and also ran a farm. I learned about business from working with them. I went on to own some companies together with my husband. In the process, I learned about the accounting required to manage a business. I later decided to go into industry and started working for companies.

When did you earn your accounting degree?

After I graduated from high school, I attended college and, in 1990, I received my accounting degree. After that, I decided to wait to pursue further education. In 2007, I completed my master's degree with a specialisation in finance and, in 2009, I received my CPA. Originally, I did not think I needed to have my CPA because I never wanted to be an auditor. As I began to climb the corporate ladder, I realised the benefits of earning my master's degree and obtaining certification.

Where did you work?

I started with a small chemical company, moved to a learning centre for children, and then to an international company. Along the way, I advanced to higher positions in accounting and finance. About five years ago, I joined Publishers Circulation in my present position.

In your position, whom do you communicate with in the company?

I often speak with senior management and my direct reports. I'm available to others in the company to answer questions, give advice or help them work on various projects.

What sorts of questions do you get?

I get questions on all sorts of subjects. A project lead might ask for an analysis of the costs and benefits of a project or how to account for something, such as a capital versus an operating lease. A company lawyer might have a question.

How do you explain accounting to people in the company who are not accountants?

The key is not to go into a technical discussion but to explain the why behind a rule. For example, a capital lease hits the balance sheet and depreciation while an operating lease affects net income. Knowing the reason for a rule helps people in understanding it.

How has communication within the company changed since you started?

When I joined the company, a lot of written communication was in print. There were binders full of written rules, procedures, reports and the like. Now, much of our communication is electronic. It is less costly, faster and more efficient. Another important change is that our written communications are more concise. For example, if I prepare a report for our senior executives, I summarise everything on one page, with just enough detail that they can make a decision. If they need more details, I can provide them with specifics.

What's an example of a summary you might provide on one page?

If the company were considering an acquisition, for example, the summary would include why the seller has put its company up for sale, the asking price, the company's operating profit, our expected return on investment, why the acquisition makes sense, and possibly a few other details. This information would be summarised in bullet points.

Isn't there a risk with a one-page summary that you might miss a key piece of information?

It's a challenge to capture the essence of what you want to communicate. You can address this issue by knowing the people who will receive your summary report, knowing what is important to them, having a thorough knowledge of the topic and knowing how to provide the information to help drive a decision. If you work with the same people over time, you can get to the point where you anticipate some of the questions they might ask and address them in your report.

How are you training people under you to become better communicators?

In our company, people have to be comfortable talking with anybody in our organisation. That was my experience at a former employer. It wasn't unusual for the president of the company to talk directly with the person responsible for an area. In my current position, I am helping people to reach that comfort level. For example, a staff accountant who joined our company out of college, and who has good presentation skills, gave a presentation on what our accounting department does. It was given to a group of our human resource people, and it was well received.

As another example, I give a little class on proper use of e-mail. I ask everyone attending the class to bring examples of e-mails they have sent and received. We critique each one. For instance, don't put 'FYI' in a subject line. Instead, write a few words that succinctly state the purpose of the e-mail. Then, it's easy for the receiver to decide whether to read it. Also, if you attach a large file, such as a spreadsheet, write a brief summary of what's in the attachment. Then, the receiver of your e-mail can read the summary and decide whether to open the spreadsheet.

This is the same with reports. Unless there is a summary explaining a report, it is just a data dump. Recipients themselves have to do the work of analysing the report.

How would you summarise a report?

An old adage about speaking applies here. Tell the audience what you are going to tell them. This is the summary. Then tell them, 'these are the details.' Then, tell them what you told them. This is the conclusion.

Can you offer a suggestion as to how accountants can improve their communication skills?

Learn to listen. We are not trained to listen like we are trained to speak or write, but we can learn. For example, if you are asked to do something, make sure you really understand what's asked of you. If you're uncertain, ask questions to clarify what you must do. Sometimes a junior person may be reticent about asking because they are new or because they think they lack the knowledge. But unless they ask, they won't learn.

INTERVIEW 12: DAVID DUNCAN, PRESIDENT, DENIHAN HOSPITALITY GROUP

David Duncan is president of Denihan Hospitality Group, an independent owner and operator of boutique hotels in top U.S. urban markets. He was named president in January 2012 after serving as the company's CFO since 2003. His past experience includes tenures as a managing director at the Guggenheim Group, CFO of Winstar Communications and CFO of GE Capital's Real Estate Capital Markets Group. He started his career as a CPA with Kenneth Leventhal & Company in Los Angeles and Boston and then Ernst & Young, LLP.

What have you learned about communication from your experience as a CFO?

At GE Capital, I was in a very large, communication-intensive organisation, with layers of management. In working on complex transactions, I quickly learned to speak not only as an accountant but also as a businessperson. I understood the language of business from my experience with tax and accounting and technical issues while with Kenneth Leventhal and Company and Ernst and Young.

What is your communication philosophy?

Look at the big picture—start at the 60,000-foot level and drill down. Some people start with the details and soon get lost in complex technical discussions. Stay focused on the business strategy—people understand business issues. Keep communication simple.

In terms of communication, what do you expect of people who report to you?

When I talk to people in my company, I want early warnings. I don't want surprises. I want people to be passionate in making a recommendation. But they must understand all of the issues and marshal all of the facts in support of their argument. They should have their business reasons and analysis prepared, so they are ready not just for the first level but every level of questioning from management.

Can you give an example?

When I was at GE, a group recommended a transaction for several hundred million dollars, in a distant domicile that I would never have guessed would have been approved. But they had researched the facts to such a degree that there was no way to argue with them. They were so passionate and so well prepared that they succeeded in selling management on the transaction.

What's the most important communication skill?

The most important skill is to be able to talk candidly. As managers, we owe people we work with candour about things we like and don't like. People tend to shy away from difficult communication. You can talk in a way that is not personal. If someone is not doing a good job, you can make clear that you are criticising their job performance and not them personally.

Among other responsibilities, CFOs lead or participate in negotiations to acquire an asset or a company. What is your approach to negotiating?

If possible, you want a win for both sides. So you try to get everything on the table, and then do trade-offs. Price is important, of course, but it is not the only issue. In my experience, some people don't understand negotiating. They make it about one thing. That means one side would win and the other lose. Both sides have to come away with something.

How do you inculcate good communication in your company?

We teach employees across our company about good communication, and that begins with helping them to see our service from the perspective of our guests. If a problem comes up, our staff must show sincerity in assuring guests that it will be resolved expeditiously, and they must follow through by seeing that it is resolved. We have found that guests who have had a problem resolved to their satisfaction are among the most passionate advocates for our hotels.

What is your organisation's approach to communicating with the staff?

We expect our staff to show consideration to our guests, and our staff deserves the same consideration. Everyone should be treated equally whether they are the principals of our company or a bellman or a back office person. Our employees are more than workers. They are people. They are helping an aged parent or helping to put their children through college or volunteering in the community.

And your approach to hiring?

It's remarkably simple: hire pleasant, likeable people. We can teach them the technical side of the business. We have all sorts of training for new hires.

INTERVIEW 13: ANOOP N. MEHTA, VICE PRESIDENT AND CFO, SCIENCE SYSTEMS AND APPLICATIONS, INC.

Anoop N. Mehta, CPA, is vice president and CFO of Science Systems and Applications Inc., Latham, Maryland. The company applies science and technology to improve quality of life. Fields in which the company applies its expertise include space and earth science research and analysis, software development, data management, and instrument engineering. Mehta is the current chairman of the Maryland Association of CPAs.

At the Maryland association's Business and Industry roundtable and other venues, CFOs and other business executives say that skill in communicating is one of their top concerns. Why?

One reason for concern is that the communication skills of recent graduates are not the same as when I graduated 30 years ago. Technology has changed how we communicate. Young people today routinely use e-mails, text messaging, Facebook and other technology and social media tools that didn't exist when I started my career.

How has that changed communication?

Young people are very good with communicating with their peers, but compared with older generations, they do not communicate as well. For example, not many young people write letters today. E-mails and text messages have largely replaced letter writing. But letter writing disciplined you to organise your thoughts, consider the structure and content of the letter, use correct spelling and grammar and communicate clearly. By comparison, technology has made it easy to communicate through e-mails and other channels, and there is more of a tendency to dash something off, leading to miscommunications.

As far as communication is concerned, what are the expectations of young CPAs and others in joining and working for companies?

Young people want to receive information on their terms, not on a company's terms. They want to use social media, for example. Companies will have to adapt to their expectations if they expect to recruit and retain talented young people, which is why we are looking at the possible use of Facebook and other social media tools in our company.

How do young people feel about moving into leadership positions in their companies?

The first question is whether they *want* to become leaders. I see young people less interested in moving into leadership and management, and if they are interested, it has to be on their terms. They don't want to put in 50- or 60-hour work weeks. They want a balance between work and life. In fact, they are more disciplined about balancing work and life. That is not to say that they don't want to work. Just the opposite is true. They love to work, and they bring great energy and enthusiasm to their jobs. Again, meeting their expectations will be a challenge for companies such as ours, with our highly educated workforce and a need for talent in fields such as aerospace engineering.

How are you training the next generation of CPAs for leadership in their companies and in accounting?

We are looking at external training programmes, among other options, and we are utilising the resources of the Maryland association. Last year, the association held its first Leadership Academy, which was attended by young CPAs who aspire to become leaders. They wrote a white paper on their vision for the profession's future and how the profession can realise that vision.[4] One of my goals as the association's chair is to engage young CPAs and encourage them to become more active in the profession, for example, by attending our board meetings or retreats. They are our future leaders, and we want to do everything we can to support and encourage them.

Endnotes

1 For more on the Finance Academy, see 'Internal Cross-Training on a Budget,' Rhode Island Society of CPAs newsletter, 2012 www.what-counts.org/aicpa-national-topic/62-internal-cross-training-on-a-budget

2 Kaufman Rossin Fund Services (KRFS) is an independent full-service provider of specialised administration services to the investment community. KRFS was born out of Kaufman, Rossin & Co., a CPA firm headquartered in Miami. See www.krfs.com/history.php.

3 Examples:
1) Eva Collins, Stewart Lawrence, Juliet Roper and Jarrod Harr, 'Sustainability and the role of the management accountant,' Research executive summary series (vol. 7, issue 14), Waikato Management School, University of Waikato www.cimaglobal.com/Documents/Thought_leadership_docs/Sustainability%20and%20Climate%20Change/Management-control_NZICA.pdf
2) CIMA and Accenture, 'Sustainability performance management: How CFOS can unlock value' www.cimaglobal.com/Thought-leadership/Research-topics/Sustainability/Sustainability-performance-management-how-CFOs-can-unlock-value/

4 Adrienne Gonzalez, 'New MACPA White Paper Outlines Future CPA Leaders' Vision For the Industry,' *Going Concern*, Nov. 2011 http://goingconcern.com/2011/11/new-macpa-white-paper-outlines-future-cpa-leaders-vision-for-the-industry

Appendix B

CORPORATE ACCOUNTING CAREER PATHS

Chief Financial Officer	
Treasurer	Chief Accountant/Controller
Assistant Treasurer	Assistant Controller
Finance Manager	Manager
Supervising Financial Analyst	Accounting Supervisor
↖ ↗	
Senior Accountant	
↑	
Staff Accountant	

INITIAL YEARS IN CORPORATE ACCOUNTING

Numbers in parentheses are the minimum number of years usually required in a position before being eligible for promotion. The job descriptions and required years are intended only an overview. Every company has specific job requirements.

Staff accountant (1 year): Assists supervisors and managers with managing accounts payable, accounts receivable, payroll, general ledger, financial statements, account analysis and reconciliations, cash and cash balance sheet accounts, auditing cash and cash transactions, sales tax returns, and other work, as needed.

Senior Accountant (2–3 years): Supervises staff accountants and assists with reconciling various general ledger accounts, reviewing financial statements and trial balances for conformity to generally accepted accounting principles (GAAP), coordinating quarterly reviews and year-end audit, performing various account analyses and bank and other account reconciliations, and managing various projects as needed.

167

MANAGEMENT ACCOUNTING TRACK

Accounting supervisor (3–5 years):

- Supervises accounts payable; payroll and accounts receivable
- Monitors general ledger accounts to ensure accuracy and integrity
- Supervises monthly and year-end closing process
- Ensures accounting and closing routines are in compliance with corporate policies
- Oversees timely and accurate processing of information within general accounting
- Completes various projects as directed by management
- Supervises and trains staff to ensure adherence to company policies and procedures

Account manager (5–7 years): Manages general accounting staff.

Also responsible for

- general ledger, purchasing payroll, cash management, accounts payable, fixed assets, month-end close and expense reporting function
- enterprise resource planning production environment, including systems integration and enhancements that streamline processing
- budget reports and forecasts—develop projections and provide analysis with recommendations and conclusions
- providing U.S. GAAP or IFRS accounting guidance and support for management
- reviewing and updating legislation-mandated controls for responsible functions, support testing efforts and remediation as needed

Assistant controller (7–9 years):

- Assists controller with accounting, financial analysis and reporting
- Supervises accounting staff
- Coordinates internal and external reporting, ensuring compliance with regulatory requirements
- Prepares, controls, and verifies financial and operational management reporting
- Validates and controls inventories
- Prepares budgets, financial plans and forecasts
- Prepares a high level analysis of variances from financial plans, forecasts, budgets and other business related duties as assigned by the controller
- Supervises accounting research and new and updated corporate accounting and reporting policies

Controller (9–10 years):

- Designs, establishes, and maintains an organisational structure and staffing to effectively accomplish department of controller goals and objectives
- Establishes and implements financial best practices

- Recruits, trains, supervises and evaluates department staff
- Prepares financial reports required by banks and investors
- Prepares cash management reports and working capital analysis
- Prepares annual operating plans and forecasts
- Serves as interface with external auditors, bankers, insurance providers and so on
- Monitors and manages the company's line of credit
- Reviews financial data with senior management monthly
- Prepares financial analysis for contract negotiations
- Maintains customer and vendor relationships

Chief financial officer (CFO):

- Provides direction, management and leadership in the administrative, business planning, accounting, budgeting and automation efforts of the corporation
- Systematically and comprehensively assesses the financial opportunities, challenges and risks facing the company
- Drives development of a sound, comprehensive financial plan that promotes growth and financial stability
- Partners with leadership to ensure finance supports the organisation's performance and business strategy
- Oversees all aspects of financial management within the organisation
- Communicates to a variety of internal and external audiences about the company's financial performance, risks, opportunities and plans
- Directs the fiscal functions of the corporation in accordance with GAAP or IFRS
- Ensures the effectiveness of all regulatory compliance and legislation-mandated programmes
- Builds and maintains a responsive, high quality finance organisation within the company

FINANCIAL ACCOUNTING TRACK

Supervising financial analyst (3–5 years):

- Supervises senior and staff accountants
- Assists with short- and long-term planning, budgeting, and forecasting process
- Assists with monthly close process; supports project, service line or product line management
- Provides analytical decision support services or technical expertise for financial and operational issues
- Conducts project planning and product profitability analyses

Finance manager (5–7 years):

- Supervises assigned financial analysts
- Manages monthly accounting close cycle

- Prepares monthly financial statements and various detailed analyses

- Ensures all journal entries are properly recorded in accordance with GAAP or IFRS

- Ensures the accuracy of monthly reconciliation schedules

- Coordinates various audits

- Responsible for preparation and coordination of various ad hoc projects and reports

- Responsible for installing, modifying, documenting and coordinating the implementation of accounting system changes and accounting control procedures

- Assists in coordinating and preparing corporate budgets and forecasts

Assistant treasurer (7–9 years):

- Supervises assigned managers and staff

- Assists treasurer and the CFO in managing banking relationships

- Reviews documents pertaining to lines of credits and loans

- Assists with financial oversight of capital project spending

- Assesses foreign exchange risk and implements hedge programmes

- Oversees interest rate risk management

- Provides detailed consolidated cash flow projects

- Manages and facilitates general insurance policies

- Monitors adherence to corporate credit and cash management policies

- Manages the corporate accounts payable and accounts receivable functions

- Supports investor relations

- Ensures appropriate compliance with legislation-mandated requirements related to cash, debt and equity management

Treasurer:

- Responsible for assessment, systems design, implementation and maintenance of effective investment strategy, cash forecasting and debt management programmes

- Provides expert treasury management, analysis and advice to maximise growth and profit

- Provides analysis on optimal capital structure and financing strategies

- Participates in working capital financing decisions, including forms of financing

- Seeds debt financing efforts

- Builds and maintains relationship with banks

- Manages company insurance programmes

- Supports the activities of pension, investment and finance committees

- Manages investor relations

- Manages foreign exchange risk

- Assists with special projects as required

Appendix C

BUSINESS PROPOSALS

This appendix will address writing and presenting business proposals. The process is similar to reports and presentations, which were discussed in chapters 5–8. However, proposals have some unique considerations, which will be explained in this appendix.

If you are a management accountant working for a corporation, you could participate in writing proposals for external or internal audiences and, as you advance in the organisation, you could have more authority and responsibility for proposal writing. If you work for a small business, one of your responsibilities could be writing proposals. Conversely, you might assist with, or be responsible for, reviewing proposals submitted to your company by other organisations.

Let's look at proposals and where you can contribute.

BUSINESS PROPOSAL

A *business proposal* is an offer to sell something: a service, a product or perhaps an idea. For example, a company proposes to sell a service to another company. An entrepreneur tries to sell investors and lenders on the idea of investing in and providing financing for a start-up company. A small business proposes to enter into a contract to sell a product to a government agency.

Before a company invests the time, money and energy in writing a proposal, it should consider whether to write the proposal in the first place, based on the estimated cost, the resources required, the likelihood of its winning the proposal and other considerations.

Proposals can be external or internal.

An example of an *external proposal* could be an individual or organisation proposing to sell a service or product to another organisation. The seller could be a corporation, a small business, a professional services firm such as an accounting or law firm, a consultant, or other seller. The buyer could be a corporation, small business, not-for-profit organisation, government organisation or other buyer.

An example of an *internal proposal* could be someone in an organisation trying to sell to an idea. The CFO tries to sell the CEO on a proposal to sell an operating division. A business line manager tries to sell the CFO on the company's buying new equipment. A human resources manager tries to sell the CEO and CFO on a plan to give employees more flexibility about when and where they work.

Proposals can be solicited or unsolicited.

A *solicited proposal* is a company writing a proposal in response to a request. The request could come from a prospective customer or client, or it could come from within an organisation, such as the CFO asking the director of IT to submit a proposal to upgrade the company's information systems. The solicitation may be in the form of a request for proposal (RFP). By soliciting a proposal, a prospective customer or internal manager shows an interest in buying, although there is no guarantee that a transaction will be concluded.

An *unsolicited proposal* is submitted to a potential customer or client or internal manager without their having requested it and without any assurances that the proposal will be accepted. The seller may have seen that the customer has an unresolved business problem and demonstrates in its proposal how it could help the customer find a solution. The risk in making an unsolicited proposal is the greater uncertainty about whether it will be accepted.

WRITING THE PROPOSAL

If a company or individual decides to create and submit a proposal, it needs to consider the questions that are common to the writing of any document. These were covered in chapter 5, 'Write from the Start.' In addition to those considerations, a few more questions that apply specifically to proposals are as follows:

- *Why is the customer asking for a proposal?* Or, if the company is submitting an unsolicited proposal, what does it see as the customer's need? The customer may not have the expertise or the resources to achieve its goal on its own. It may want to draw on the experience and insights of the company that is submitting the proposal.

- *What is the customer's goal?* In other words, how can the proposal explain how it will meet the customer's needs? What is the customer's goal, and how would it benefit from the proposed product or service? The customer's goal might be to bring a product to market, and in asking for a proposal, it is seeking advice on how to expedite this process. If the product comes on the market sooner, the customer would benefit from gaining a competitive edge, increasing sales and generating higher profits—profits the customer could reinvest or use for other business purposes.

- *Who is the audience?* The audience is the customer—whether it is a corporation, small business, or other organisation. But within the customer's organisation are the people who will make the decision whether to accept the proposal: the CEO or CFO, other executives, a business line manager, or perhaps a committee. What does the company making the proposal need to know about the decision makers? For example, what are the background, profession and business experience of the decision makers? What are their positions in the customer's organisation? What is their management style? How receptive are they to a proposal? Did some people in the organisation favour requesting a proposal, whereas others were opposed or only lukewarm? The company can learn about the decision makers from reading an RFP, background research and speaking with them.

- *What does the audience want to know?* What does the customer want to know about the company making the proposal? The customer wants to know that the company has the knowledge, experience and competence to complete the project, that it is a financially sound organisation, and that it is trustworthy. The company will have to prove its experience, competence and trustworthiness, along with other attributes, to the customer. Most important, the company must demonstrate a clear understanding of the customer's organisation and its project requirements.

- *What is the process for completing the project?* If the company's proposal is accepted, what are the steps for it to deliver the service, provide the product, or suggest ideas? What is the timeline for completing the project?

- *What are the metrics for evaluating the company's performance?* How will its progress in completing the project be measured? How will its performance be evaluated? How will the customer determine that the results of the project are satisfactory?

- *What is the company's obligation once the project is completed?* The customer wants assurances that once the project is completed, the company will help to provide any advice or assistance or resolve any problems or issues concerning the project.

LEARNING FROM THE RFP

An organisation that wants to buy a product or service can write an RFP or a solicitation to prospective suppliers to submit proposals. Reading the RFP should be your first step when writing a proposal. The RFP includes information about the customer: its history, business goals, products and services, background of its senior executives, and other details, as well as specifics about the product or service requested. The RFP also requests information about a company submitting the proposal: company history, business goals, financial information, experience providing the product or service the customer wants, professional backgrounds, and its executives' experience and so on. Some RFPs may ask for only general information, leaving it to the company to provide details. Other RFPs may require a company to follow very specific requirements for writing and submitting a proposal, and a company must adhere exactly to those requirements, otherwise, it might be at risk of having its proposal rejected. If you are submitting an unsolicited proposal or do not have an RFP, try to find out the same information from another source.

WRITING THE PROPOSAL

Chapter 5, 'Write from the Start,' examined the process of creating a written document, and this process can be applied to writing a proposal. The proposal will include the following:

- *Executive summary.* States the theme, key messages, purpose, scope and context of a proposal, details of the product or service to be delivered, and the cost. Written for the decision makers in the customer's organisation who will decide whether to award a contract and who might read only the executive summary. Designed and written to entice others in the organisation—including those who would be involved in managing a project if a contract is awarded—to read the entire proposal.

- *Introduction.* Describes the customer's issue or problem and history of the problem. Elaborates on the purpose and goals of the proposal. Describes how the company submitting the proposal will solve the problem, and why it is best qualified to solve the problem. Demonstrates a clear understanding of the customer's needs. Transitions to the body of the proposal.

- *Body.* Amongst other information, the body describes
  - how the solution to the customer's problem can be achieved.
  - steps to achieve the solution.

- benefits of the solution.

- how to measure progress toward the solution.

- products or services to be provided.

- scope of the project.

- detailed descriptions and specifications of the product or service, including the costs.

- qualifications of the company making the proposal and its key executives.

- company's history and experience in its product or service line.

- timeline for completing the project.

- management: Who in the company is responsible for what aspects of the project? Who in the customer organisation is responsible for managing the project?

- the process for evaluating the outcome of the project and other information.

- case studies, testimonials, success stories and other supporting material.

- charts and graphs to capture key themes, summarise details and facilitate understanding of complex questions.

- *Summary*. This is a restatement of the theme and key messages of the proposal. The emphasis is on succinctly describing the client's problem or issue, how the company making the proposal can solve the problem, why it is best qualified for the project, and the benefits to the customer.

- *Call to action*. Finally, the proposal concludes with the company's request of the customer. It may ask that the customer hire the company to work on the project. It may request for a meeting to discuss the project in further detail before the customer decides whether to hire the company. Whatever the request, it is a call to action: The company wants the customer to make a decision.

PRESENTING THE PROPOSAL

In addition to submitting a written proposal to the customer, companies will often make a presentation of the proposal to the customer. The guidelines for planning, preparing and delivering a presentation were covered in chapters 7 and 8. Besides those general considerations, a few specific details to keep in mind for presentations of proposals are as follows:

- *Determine the purpose of the presentation*. The company's goal—its end game—is to win business from the customer. The presentation is a means to that end. How should the presentation be structured to help the company achieve that goal?

- *Know the audience for the presentation*. The decision makers in the customer's organisation who are managing the process of soliciting proposals would attend the presentation, but are there others in the organisation who might also attend? Is so, what influence will they have on the customer's decision-making process? If they are influential, how can the presentation be structured to persuade them, as well as others, in the audience to accept the proposal?

ROLE OF MANAGEMENT ACCOUNTANTS

As a management accountant, you could apply your financial, communication and other skills in helping your company to consider whether to submit a proposal, and, if it decides to go forward, to write and present a proposal. Conversely, you could assist your company in reviewing a proposal and deciding whether to purchase a product or service. Below are some specific areas of proposal-making where your expertise could be valuable:

The Money

At every step of the proposal process, there are money questions you could help your company address, including the following:

- What price should the company ask for the sale of a product or service?
- What would be the costs in labour, materials and other expenses in selling the product or delivering the service (the project)?
- What profit does the company want from the project? Can it meet its profit target?
- Is the company able to incur the costs of writing and presenting a proposal, and, if it wins a sale, carrying out a contract to complete a project?
- What is the budget for the project?
- How would the company track project expenses to ensure the project stays within budget?

The Customer

You could assist your company by

- researching the customer to determine whether it is a stable, financially sound organisation that the company wants to do business with.
- meeting with the customer to discuss the customer's reasons for wanting a proposal, what problem it wants to solve, how it expects to solve the problem, and how it will benefit.
- answering any of the customer's questions or addressing any of its concerns.

Researching and Writing the Proposal

You could help your company by

- analysing the risks of entering into a contract, for example, the company might underestimate the time to finish the project.
- mitigating the risks, for example, by building sufficient time for the project into the proposal and having a system for managing the risk to ensure it is completed on schedule.
- planning and writing a presentation, for example, by helping to prepare financial information about your company, participating on a team that writes the presentation, or helping to ensure that your company has met all the requirements in an RFP.

Evaluating a Proposal

You could also help your company evaluate a proposal from an organisation to sell a product or service to your company by

- researching the organisation's history, principals, markets, financial information, qualifications, experience in providing the product or service and other information.

- participating in meetings with the organisation's executives to discuss your company's reasons for asking for a proposal, the problem it wants to address, possible solutions and how the company can achieve them, and other topics.

- analysing the proposal, including whether the company has provided all the information required, whether it has demonstrated an understanding of your company's needs, whether it has shown that it can meet those needs, whether the price for the product or service is acceptable, and other information.

- making a recommendation about whether your company should accept the proposal and agree to buy the product or service.

If you are at an entry-level position in your company, you may not be directly involved in writing or reviewing proposals, but you could become more involved as you advance in the organisation and assume more responsibility. And if you advance to a senior executive position, such as CFO, or a managerial position, such as manager of a business unit, you could have a leadership role in planning and writing your organisation's proposals and presenting them to customers or in reviewing proposals made by other companies and helping your company decide whether to buy a product or service. So, if you have an opportunity to get involved in the proposal process in some capacity, you could start to develop skills in managing proposals.

Appendix D

CHECKLIST FOR WRITING REPORTS

This appendix is intended as a guide for writing reports based on the information found in chapters 5 and 6.

PLANNING

- What is the purpose of the communication?
- What is the subject?
- Who is the audience?
- What do you know about the audience?
- What does the audience know about you?
- How informed is the audience about the subject of your communication?
- How will the audience react to what you write?
- When is the right time to send the communication?

OUTLINE

Options

- Traditional
- Brainstorming
- Mind mapping
- Questioning

Research

- Why
- How
  - Inside the company
  - Outside the company
  - Interviews
  - Survey

REPORT

- Executive summary
- Introduction
- Theme
- Methods of development
  - Order-of-importance
  - Cause-and-effect
  - Chronological
  - Comparison
  - Contrast
  - General and specific
  - Spatial
  - Blending

CONCLUSION

RECOMMENDATIONS

Appendix E

CHECKLIST FOR PRESENTATIONS

This appendix is intended as a guide for writing and delivering presentations based on the information found in chapters 7 and 8.

PLANNING

- What is your purpose?
- What is your topic?
- Who is your audience?
- Why should your audience care what you have to say?
- How knowledgeable is your audience about the topic of your presentation?
- Who are the influencers in your audience?
- What are the circumstances of your presentation? (Number of people in audience, size of meeting room, time of presentation, seating, lighting and so on)

WRITING AND DESIGNING

- What is your theme?
- What type of introduction will you give?
- What are your key messages and support arguments?
- How will you conclude?

DESIGN

- What visuals will you use? (Flip chart, whiteboard, projector, decks, slides)
- What mix of text, pictures and charts will you use?
- How many slides will you have?
- What design elements will you use?

PREPARATION

- Review presentation
- Review visuals
- Practice
- Check equipment and venue

PRESENTATION

- Posture
- Eye contact
- Body language
- Voice
- Walking

FOLLOW UP

- Ask audience members for comments
- Review video of your presentation (if one is available)
- Send written summary to participants

Appendix F

RESOURCES

ASSOCIATIONS

American Institute of Certified Public Accountants (aicpa.org)

World's largest member association representing the accounting profession.

220 Leigh Farm Road
Durham, North Carolina 27707-8110
United States
P: +1.919.402.4500
F: +1.919.402.4505
Member e-mail: service@aicpa.org

AICPA Business, Industry & Government Group (www.aicpa.org/InterestAreas/ BusinessIndustryAndGovernment/Pages/BIGHome.aspx): Tools and resources for AICPA members who are financial managers and executives practicing in business, industry and government.

AICPA Insights (blog.aicpa.org): Official blog of the AICPA.

AICPA Links (www.aicpa.org/Research/ExternalLinks/Pages/ExternalLinks.aspx): AICPA gateway to other accounting related links on the Internet.

AICPA Social Media User Guides (www.aicpa.org/career/marketing/pages/socialmediamarketing.aspx): Available to AICPA members.

Other business communication publications and courses are available through the AICPA.

Examples:

> CPAs 'Four Rs' of Communicating: Talking, Listening, Writing, and Presenting
> Author/Moderator: Kelly Watkins, MBA
> Publisher: AICPA (www.cpa2biz.com/AST/Main/CPA2BIZ_Primary/ManagementAccounting/ Management/GeneralManagement/PRDOVR~PC-732812/PC-732812.jsp)

Best Practices in Accounting and Finance Writing: Being Clear and Accurate
Author/Moderator: Lin Kroeger (www.cpa2biz.com/AST/Main/CPA2BIZ_Primary/Accounting/
FinancialReporting/PRDOVR~PC-33554/PC-33554.jsp)

That's Not What I Said!—Effective Workplace Communication
Author/Moderator: Lisa C. Polack, MLHR and Michael S. Bruner, Ph.D.
Publisher: AICPA (www.cpa2biz.com/AST/Main/CPA2BIZ_Primary/ManagementAccounting/
Management/GeneralManagement/PRDOVR~PC-732950/PC-732950.jsp?cm_vc=PDPZ1)

Chartered Institute of Management Accountants (cimaglobal.com)

World's largest professional organisation of management accountants.

26 Chapter Street
London SW1P 4NP
United Kingdom
Tel: +44 (0)20 8849 2251
E-mail: cima.contact@cimaglobal.com

Chartered Global Management Accountant (cgma.org)

Professional designation for management accountants worldwide that was created through an agreement
of the AICPA and CIMA. You must be a member of either the AICPA or CIMA to qualify for the CGMA
designation. Contact your member organisation for more information on how to become a CGMA or visit the
CGMA website.

INSTITUTES

Business Learning Institute (bizlearning.net): Centre serving executives and managers in various
businesses. Its mission is to deliver competency-based curriculum, courses, content, and community to
enhance learning and grow intellectual capital for organisational and executive leadership. Enables business
leaders and managers to network, develop competencies, and share strategic knowledge to help their
businesses manage change. Affiliate of Maryland Association of CPAs.

LEARNING

TED (www.ted.com): Nonprofit devoted to 'ideas worth spreading.' Their website hosts videos of talks on a
variety of subjects. On the website, you can search for speakers on relevant topics using keywords like *business*,
entrepreneurs, *finance* and other professional topics.

PUBLICATIONS AND WEBSITES

Accountancy Age (accountancyage.com): Finance, business and accountancy news, features, advice, and resources for accountants and other UK finance professionals.

Accounting Today (accountingtoday.com): Provider of online business news for the tax and accounting community. News, opinion, special reports, practice resources, *Accounting Tomorrow* blog and more.

Bloomberg Business Week (businessweek.com): Business magazine that that covers business news and trends, stock markets, social media for business professionals, and more.

CFO (cfo.com): Monthly magazine for CFOs and other financial executives. Reports on news and trends, successes in facing complex problems, and analysis of critical economic issues specifically targeted to CFOs.

CFO Journal (http://professional.wsj.com/cfo): *The Wall Street Journal* service for CFOs and other senior financial executives. News, insight into trends, interviews with key newsmakers, as well as a financial data dashboard and morning briefing.

CFO World (cfoworld.com): Information resource for senior executives. Focuses on the intersection of finance and information technology.

CGMA Magazine (www.cgma.org/Magazine/Pages/MagazineHome.aspx): Web-based magazine that features global accounting news, articles, videos and research for management accounting professionals who guide strategic business decisions around the world.

CPA Journal (cpajournal.com): Publication of the New York Society of CPAs. Provides public practitioners, managers, educators and others with coverage of news, developments and trends in accounting.

CPA Letter Daily (www.smartbrief.com/cpa/index.jsp): Free AICPA e-newsletter with the day's top economic, business, accounting and other news.

CPA 2biz (cpa2biz.com): Exclusive marketing platform for AICPA products and services, including publications, webcasts, conferences, continuing professional education, and member benefits programs to CPAs and financial professionals.

CPA Trendlines (cpatrendlines.com): Online newsletter of news, analysis, commentary, insights reports, and research in accounting, tax and finance.

Economist (economist.com): Weekly publication focusing on international politics and business news and opinion.

Entrepreneur (entrepreneur.com): Magazine that provides entrepreneurs with 'how-to' information, practical resources and tools, and detailed instruction on how to effectively manage and grow their companies.

Fast Company (fastcompany.com): Magazine that focuses on innovation in technology, ethonomics (ethical economics), leadership and design.

Financial Times (ft.com): Newspaper that provides coverage of international business, finance, economic, and political news, commentary, and analysis.

Forbes (forbes.com): News magazine covering business, finance, industries, investing and marketing.

Fortune (fortune.com): Business magazine that reports on news and trends in finance, technology, industries and companies, management, and more.

Harvard Business Review (hbr.org): Research-based magazine that focuses primarily on management techniques and breakthrough ideas to improve the practice of management.

Inc. (inc.com): Magazine whose goal is to aid, inform and inspire entrepreneurs and small business owners to succeed and grow their business.

Journal of Accountancy (journalofaccountancy.com): Flagship publication of the AICPA. Covers subjects including accounting, financial reporting, auditing, taxation, personal financial planning, technology, business valuation, professional development, ethics, liability issues, consulting, practice management, education, and related domestic and international business issues.

Mashable (mashable.com): Online source of news and information on digital innovation. Focuses on social media but also covers mobile, video, technology, business and more.

Public Accounting Report (www.cchgroup.com/webapp/wcs/stores/servlet/product_Public-Accounting-Report_10151_-1_10053_26984000): Provider of competitive intelligence for public accounting firms and the profession.

The Wall Street Journal (wsj.com): International newspaper that covers general and breaking news worldwide. Emphasis on business, financial, management, and economic news, analysis, and features.

Printed in the United States
By Bookmasters